Yōko Tawada

AsiaWorld

Series Editor: Mark Selden

This series charts the frontiers of Asia in global perspective. Central to its concerns are Asian interactions—political, economic, social, cultural, and historical—that are transnational and global, that cross and redefine borders and networks, including those of nation, region, ethnicity, gender, technology, and demography. It looks to multiple methodologies to chart the dynamics of a region that has been the home to major civilizations and is central to global processes of war, peace, and development in the new millennium.

Titles in the Series

China's Unequal Treaties: Narrating National History, by Dong Wang
Precious Steppe: Mongolian Nomadic Pastoralists in Pursuit of the Market, by Ole Bruun
Managing God's Higher Learning: U.S.-China Cultural Encounter and Canton Christian College (Lingnan University), 1888–1952, by Dong Wang
Yōko Tawada: Voices from Everywhere, edited by Doug Slaymaker

Yōko Tawada

Voices from Everywhere

Doug Slaymaker

LEXINGTON BOOKS

A division of
ROWMAN & LITTLEFIELD PUBLISHERS, INC.
Lanham • Boulder • New York • Toronto • Plymouth, UK

LEXINGTON BOOKS

A division of Rowman & Littlefield Publishers, Inc.
A wholly owned subsidary of The Rowman & Littlefield Publishing Group, Inc.
4501 Forbes Boulevard, Suite 200
Lanham, MD 20706

Estover Road
Plymouth PL6 7PY
United Kingdom

British Library Cataloguing in Publication Information Available

Library of Congress Cataloging-in-Publication Data

Yoko Tawada : voices from everywhere / [edited by] Doug Slaymaker.
    p. cm. — (AsiaWorld series)
ISBN-13: 978-0-7391-2272-3 (cloth : alk. paper)
ISBN-10: 0-7391-2272-X (cloth : alk. paper)
ISBN-13: 978-0-7391-2273-0 (pbk. : alk. paper)
ISBN-10: 0-7391-2273-8 (pbk. : alk. paper)
1. Tawada, Yoko, 1960—Criticism and interpretation. I. Slaymaker, Douglas.
PL862.A85Z96 2007
895.6'35—dc22   2007023932

Printed in the United States of America

♾™ The paper used in this publication meets the minimum requirements of American
National Standard for Information Sciences—Permanence of Paper for Printed Library
Materials, ANSI/NISO Z39.48–1992.

Contents

Foreword

Marjorie Perloff

Yoko Tawada, the subject of *Voices from Everywhere*, was born in Tokyo in 1960 and studied literature at Waseda University. In 1979, she took a trip to Germany on the Trans-Siberian railroad (made famous by an earlier poet, Blaise Cendrars) and decided to stay on, continuing her literary studies at the University of Hamburg, the city where she settled in 1982. Since that time, Tawada has published dozens of books—poetry, fiction, drama, literary criticism, essays— both in Japanese and in her adopted language, German. She has lectured all over the world, held numerous residencies, and won many prizes, culminating in the Goethe Medal in 2005. She currently makes her home in Berlin.

In the English-speaking world, Tawada is now finally gaining the recognition she deserves. The short-story collection *Wo Europa anfängt* (1991) was published as *Where Europe Begins* by New Directions in 2002, and the same publisher is bringing out Tawada's new collection *Facing the Bridge* in 2007. In the decade to come—and here this distinguished collection of essays will surely be instrumental—Tawada's poetry, plays, and her remarkable essays on language and literature, especially her Tübingen lectures called *Verwandlungen* (Metamorphoses) are poised for wide dissemination in the English-speaking world. For Tawada is not just another accomplished "foreign" author; she is perhaps the leading practitioner today of what we might call, following the poet's own lead, *exophonic* writing—which is to say writing in a second language, a language always other from one's own. Tawada's German is not quite like that of any of her German peers, for she is aware—comically but also painfully—of its "foreignness," its distinction from her native Japanese, with its particular grammar, syntax, and way of forming vocabulary. In a recent piece called "Speech Police and Polyglot Play," for example—an essay written in commemoration of the great experimental Austrian poet Ernst Jandl—Tawada muses:

> Much about language is mysterious. Everything can be called into question, and yet there is no doubt that *elephant* is a noun. That is a riddle (*Rätsel*) with a long trunk (*Rüssel*). There are many adjectives that end with *ant*, for example:

significant, reluctant, elegant, or arrogant. Still, everyone knows that an elephant can never be an adjective.[1]

But exophonic writing is much more than an awareness of verbal or grammatical difference. If we believe that, as Wittgenstein put it, "the limits of my language are the limits of my world," then the poet/fiction writer is, as here, one who can delineate the clash of alternate worlds by studying syntax and etymology. In her own essay included here ("Tawada Yōko Does Not Exist") the author meditates on Creation myths, especially the story of Adam and Eve in Genesis—a story she cannot fully fathom because her native Japanese offers no parallel:

> We know the *Kojiki* was compiled by early leaders in order to clarify national origins and bolster their political aspirations. Nonetheless, there seems never to have been, in Japan, the thinking that a God produced humankind, meaning that for Japan the created thing known as humankind exists without any "creator." The god of a monotheistic religion is a man who creates sons with or without a wife; and it seems that the "creator" of literary works shares some of these qualities, at least in the West. . . .
>
> [In Japan, on the other hand], the informal word for author, *monogaki*, the "writer of things," is semantically connected to *mononoke*, a "changeling." Which means that this "writer of things" also describes a person in he clutches of changelings and shapeshifters, a person under the spell of the things.

It is also the case, as Keijirō Suga points out in the first essay in *Voices from Everywhere*, that exophonic writing like Tawada's inevitably involves *xenoglossia*, the use of foreign words and literal transposition in one's writing. "In translational poetics," writes Suga, "under the influence (or in-flux) of the original foreign texts, the translated text is charged with half-meanings, that offers itself to a variety of acceptations." In this sense, Tawada's poetry and fiction can be regarded as "Creolistic": they carry the sedimentation of other languages, whose particular locutions become part of the fabric of the poet's chosen German or Japanese.

Only a writer extraordinarily sensitive to the splendors and miseries of such exophonic writing could produce an oeuvre as distinctive as is Tawada's. Her familiarity with Greek and Roman myths (Ovid is a great favorite) as well as Japanese legend, and especially her knowledge of German literature from Kleist to Kafka as well as the French Surrealists, animates her work and gives it its extraordinary range and depth. German and Japanese, moreover, make a very special combination: for Anglophone readers, they are, after all, the twin languages of the enemy in World War II, even as their lexicon, grammar, and rules for "good" writing could hardly be more different. And in the U.S., where Japanese-American culture plays a central role, the triangulation produced when English is put into the mix creates an especially dense field of action.

But I do not mean to imply that Tawada's literary works are primarily language puzzles. She is a great story-teller—one who conveys, with great wit and precision, the strangeness of the ordinary. Her avowedly feminist fictions are at once "every-day" and fantastic. As the critics in this collection argue, this young poet-novelist-critic has an astonishingly rich imagination and a real gift for narrative and performativity. Indeed, the ten essays Doug Slaymaker has assembled here, prefaced by his own very helpful theoretical and scholarly Introduction as well as the poet's "Tawada Yōko Does Not Exist," which explores the role the media, especially the digital media, play today, will go a long way in helping Anglophone readers make sense of Tawada's oblique—and always challenging—writings. Not only is Slaymaker's collection, incorporating, as it does, German, Japanese, French, and American perspectives, valuable: it is a necessary collection of essays about a truly necessary writer.

Notes

1. Yoko Tawada, "Sprachpolizei und Spielpolyglotte," *Volltext: Zeitung für Literature*, 1 (2005): Sonderausgabe: Ernst Jandl, 14-16; trans. by Marjorie Perloff as "Speech Police and Polyglot Play," in *Lyric Poetry Review*, 9 (2006): 55-63.

Acknowledgments

The symposium that led to this volume, "Tawada Yōko: Voices From Everywhere," was organized by myself and Ted Fiedler, and held on the University of Kentucky campus, March 13, 2004, with funding from, at the University of Kentucky, the College of Arts and Sciences, the Japan Studies Program, The Asia Center, Germanic Studies, the Max Kade House and Cultural Center, the Office of Undergraduate Education, and the Graduate School. I am thankful to the effort and support of my colleagues. Generous support was also received from the German Academic Exchange Service and the Kentucky Humanities Council. Other conference presenters included Shigemi Nakagawa, Tomoya Nakamura, Miyako Otsuji, and Yuko Yamade. Unable to attend the symposium but represented here are Bernard Benoun, Suzuko Mousel Knott, Christina Kraenzle, and Margaret Mitsutani. I thank all the participants for their excitement and encouragement throughout this project.

This was one of the projects supported by a sabbatical leave in 2004 and I thank the College of Arts and sciences for its provisions. I am grateful to the support of the John W. Kluge Center at the Library of Congress for fellowship support, and the Library of Congress support staff who proved themselves invaluable. I also thank the librarians at the University of Kentucky for unflagging help.

Special thanks to Erika for hours spent copyediting this manuscript. Thanks to Reina for her energy and spirit.

And thanks to Karen, again, for many things.

Chapter One
Introduction
Yōko Tawada: Voices from Everywhere
Doug Slaymaker

This volume grew from an event that encapsulates the range of Yōko Tawada's work. I had invited Tawada to give a reading at the Kentucky Foreign Language Conference.[1] This presentation and its overlapping languages—its polyphony, exophony, omniphony, and symphony—mirrored the qualities of surprise, absurdity, laughter, and profundity consistent in Tawada's work and the reactions of her readers. The surprise came (to me at least) from the audience that this reading drew: I anticipated that readers of Japanese literature, like myself, would attend; to my surprise, the audience was evenly divided between German and Japanese scholars and readers. I knew, of course, that Tawada was a German writer, but naively assumed that the language I knew her in, the language of her birth, was the one with the widest readership. A further surprise came in the profoundly differing responses from the two audiences. Even ostensibly parallel texts, when presented in the different languages, elicited divergent responses. It was quickly apparent that Tawada is not *simply* a writer with a mirror existence in two different languages, but a writer very different in Japanese than in German.

There are precious few chances for writers and readers comfortable in differing language traditions—German, Japanese, English, in this case—to convene around so diverse a group of texts linked to the same author. Tawada's texts confound traditional comparative approaches because the lines of organization are too unbalanced, pulling in (at least) three directions. Multiple identities, spectral nations, leaky boundaries, porous bodies, polyphonic languages, and fragmented spaces: these are among the most persistent of issues in Tawada's oeuvre, and are amply reflected in the essays collected here.

This volume opens with an essay—"Tawada Yōko Does Not Exist"—that Tawada delivered in San Diego early in 2004 and is followed by ten essays explicating different aspects of Tawada's writing. We find here, starting with Tawada's title, artistic features common to Tawada's work: parody and tongue-in-cheek joking, non sequiturs that hide surreal punches, winks at myths and folktales, and persistent toying with national identities and linguistic traditions.

She develops four modalities in this essay that reoccur in her work and that are reiterated by the essayists. They are: 1) the constitution of subjectivity, 2) the relationship of individual identity to national identity, 3) the nature of the body, and 4) the shape of space and place. Within the first, and most complexly, she posits her own nonexistence, which suggests the tenuous nature of both being and the category of author. Closely related to this doubt about authorial presence are questions concerning subjectivity. What is an individual? How does a person exist? What occurs when one speaks? What enables the author/narrator to speak? These lead to the concerns of the second cluster, as we ask if, and how, the subject's language connects to a nation-state and a national identity (configured in this essay as German to Germany? Japanese to Japan? Spanish to the United States?). Tawada's writings reflect her concern for language and her awareness and experience of moving across linguistic terrains. She weaves contested relationships among languages and nationalities into her writings, and those complexities are further teased out in the subsequent essays. A third concern is the concrete physical body of the enunciating subject: What is the body that speaks? Of what is it comprised? How is it imagined? The physical body of the speaker is insistent in her writings, and words and languages exist with a physicality that matches that of the speakers. A fourth concern has to do with the space between languages and identities. Location, space, place, and geography are the topics of many of the essays that follow; these build from an expanding collection of writing that is tipsy from the euphoria and exhaustion of travel.

Tawada's fiction takes place in the watershed historical moment of increasingly globalized experience, of the mass movements and speed that seem to delineate the contemporary era and its different relationships to the world and our experiences of it. She may be the only author who approaches these questions through German and Japanese, and with such searing imaginative force, but she is not the only writer giving voice to these questions. Arjun Appadurai (the Bombay-born University of Chicago professor[2]) has identified and explored the context, the break, where national and individual identities are subdued; the context, that is, of Tawada's works: "The world in which we now live—in which modernity is decisively at large, irregularly self-conscious, and unevenly experienced—surely does involve a general break with all sorts of pasts."[3] In Tawada's work (and Appadurai's and others, many referenced throughout this volume), borders marking individuals, like those marking nations, seem not so much ruptured as insubstantial; in Tawada's writing the immaterial and insubstantial loom large, people are ghosts, languages flow through them like mists, and travelers move across space, across time, back into memories, and out again into the future. Such ruptures suggest leaky borders, vainly patched up by passports and government officials. Edges regularly dissolve into haze.

This oblique relationship to national identities, that is, the situation wherein such identities are ostensibly as insignificant as the question is insistent, evokes Terry Eagleton's suggestion of "nationalism as irony." One is haunted by national identities and passports even as we argue that stable national identities do not exist.[4] This seems to be one impetus to travel, and to wander, in Tawada's work: the character/self is driven by the need to show that national identity has no iron hold, that the passport in the bag ties one to no particular place (indeed, in *The Fugitive's Night-Time Railway* passports are misplaced, stolen, and reappear with someone else's picture inside the front flap). But the attempt to demonstrate such freedom only highlights the strength of bindings and boundaries, as indeterminate ethnic/national/linguistic identities are consistently brought up short by borders intended to fix those characteristics. The nationality of these characters cannot be determined by any of the traditional markers of passports, dress, physical features (for example), nor is it of any import to their internal stories; nonetheless, there is no escaping the fact that somehow, somewhere, much rests on firm determinations of these questions. The internal stories are marked, molded, and guided by external demands to fix these parameters.

To further place this in historical context, Azade Seyhan invokes adjectives such as exilic, ethnic, migrant, and diasporic in her discussion of writers working in this trans-national space;[5] Seyhan's description of the impetus behind such writing illuminates much of the movement of Tawada's work. But these terms point to the experience of travel in earlier centuries, and need updating. I follow Seyhan's lead and wish to think of them as "signifiers of texts conceived in and operative between two or more languages and cultural heritages"[6] because Tawada does not write of immigrants or migrants, of the abject desperation of refugees and runaways.[7] She does write, however, of a contemporary malaise, of living in more than one language, with identities in more than one cultural tradition, of subjectivities defined by overlapping and often contradictory linguistic webs. This writing marks a new moment in the experience of exile.[8] Indeed, the sense of living in more than one language is central in her work. For example, "I do not wish to cross the boundary that separates languages and countries, rather, I want to reside on that border [*kyōkai*]."[9] Such borders are imaginary in every sense of the word; Tawada's characters' experience of migration and movement exists and shapes them even as it takes them to places not marked in bureaucratic imaginations or on government maps. (At the same time, there is the tug of a contradiction here: Tawada, in essays such as the one quoted from, identifies a bounded place to reside—a border, a ravine—even as the fiction portrays a terrain of amorphous and unstable boundaries.) Salman Rushdie explains a congruent sensibility when he writes:

> the effect of mass migrations has been the creation of radically new types of human beings: people who root themselves in ideas rather than places, in memories as much as material things; people who have been obliged to define themselves—because they are so defined by others—by their otherness; people in whose deepest selves strange fusions occur, unprecedented unions between what they were and where they find themselves. The migrant suspects reality: having experienced several ways of being, he understands their illusory nature. To see things plainly, you have to cross a frontier.[10]

These "new types of human beings," these migrants squatting in an in-between place that has no existence according to laws governing passage at those borders, are the characters we find in Tawada's tales, and they embody the imagination at work in her writing. (This idea of the in-between place will also be considered by Kraenzle and Yildiz.) "Crossing frontiers" is a powerful, organizing metaphor in Tawada's work.

Perhaps Rushdie's sense of the need to cross borders, to see things through different lenses, to hear through different languages, is only the most recent permutation of art as defamiliarization, but the actual travel to locations neither clearly defined beforehand nor ever arrived at (as in the logic of *The Fugitive's Night-Time Railway*) also points to schizophrenic, rhizoid relationships with those places, with performativity in the world, and porousness with geography. This may point to a postmodern existence. At the same time, as Seyhan cogently points out,

> Although the contemporary tales of migration, exile, and displacement are often seen as mirroring the fragmented consciousness of postmodern culture itself and certainly participate in many of the aesthetic and literary legacies of the latter, they part company with it in terms of certain historical and geographical boundaries. For if the postmodern is to be defined either as a sociohistorical epoch or a philosophic or aesthetic school of the late-twentieth-century Western world, then it would be impossible to contain the culturally and temporally diverse articulations of diasporic experience in the postmodern syntax.[11]

If "postmodernism" in this context refers to its sensibility, however, these writings fit right in. Further, if one supposes that modernism (as Appadurai's placement of postmodernist sensibility vis-à-vis Modernism suggests) contained within it the seeds of watershed moments to follow, we will not be surprised to find that the wanderings of the aimless, rootless urban individual which characterize modernism's flâneur, having traveled from farther shores, will be more in evidence in subsequent ages. Postcolonial theory might also articulate exilic experience, as Emily Apter suggests[12] and Seyhan discusses.[13] The essays will essays included here filter these concerns through thinkers such as Fredric Jameson and Benedict Anderson. "Postmodern" is a term to be turned and refracted throughout these essays and through Tawada's writings.

Hélène Cixous, speaking more as creative writer than as critic, suggests similarly that "the author writes as if she were in a foreign country, as if he or she were a foreigner in his or her own family. . . . We write, we paint, throughout our entire lives as if we were going to a foreign country."[14] Cixous' sentence resonates with the term *Exophony*, which is the title of Tawada's 2002 collection of essays; a further clue to her meaning echoes in the subtitle of that volume, "traveling outside the mother tongue." As Tawada writes, "Moving outside the circle of one's mother tongue is akin to giving oneself over to a strange music. Exophony is turning one's ears to a new symphony."[15] Or, as she expresses it later,

> If one lives in unquestioning belief in the "naturalness" of one's native language [*bogo*], no true interaction with that language can develop; [without such

questioning] there would be no contemporary literature. Thus, moving outside one's native language is not, for literature, some special situation, it is simply the extreme of the usual situation.[16]

If this is so, if everywhere is outside, and outside is the only place from which we can write, then where do we go, where do we reside, where do we locate ourselves and our voices? This acute awareness of residing in a foreign country lies behind Seyhan's assertion that writers need "an alternate space, a third geography. This is the space of memory, language, or translation."[17] The breaks fostered by the changed flow of media and migration have made it necessary to forge such a space.[18] This compulsion marks our contemporary situation and highlights another stage in this history. Tawada is not the first to explore such linguistic displacements—essayists invoke many of the predecessors: Paul Celan, Thomas Mann, Nelly Sachs, or Hilde Domin, in one tradition, and Natsume Soseki, Nishiwaki Junzaburō, Mizumura Minae, and Ian Hideo Levy in another, with Conrad, Nabokov, Ionesco, Cannetti, Pascoli among the many illuminating the backdrop.

Our lives in bureaucracies and our travels through nation-states compel us to assert identifications with one place or another; polarization (in the form of binaries and either-or choices) is more insistent at the moment when multiplicity of identity is exceedingly common. As with Tawada's characters, demands of identity are made regardless of (an individual's lack of) national identity, origin, or most-comfortable language. Her imagery suggests that our inevitable occupancy is in the crevasse (*sama, kyōkoku*) that extends between two borders, is on the border, or on buses, trains, and planes, traveling from place to place: a place with no representation on any map. This is, in short, a third space, a place stubbornly between the polarized choices offered. Tawada continues,

So, the fact is, I do not have all that much interest in the study of many languages. More than any particular language, it is the gap [*sama*] formed between two languages that seems important. I don't desire to become a writer of language A or language B. I would rather find the poetic ravine [*kyōkoku*] separating language A and language B and descend into its depths.[19]

To turn away from this history and back to the first of the modalities I have identified, many of Tawada's works ask, "How much authority or autonomy does an author, or any individual, have?" In her introductory essay Tawada suggests that the "author" in the Christian European tradition is akin to a creator, with a lineage traceable to God. She establishes this (in a fairly unproblematized lineage and binary between East and West) in order to highlight differing assumptions embedded in the language traditions she writes in. In contrast, she suggests that the writer in the Japanese tradition is, if anything, a craftsperson, an amanuensis, or a scribbler, perhaps nothing more than a medium for some ghostly spirit that possesses one. Does the writer create and control the story, or is the story in charge and, by possessing the author, get itself written? The most truly living thing in this scenario seems to be the language that imposes linguis-

tic structure on a nearly helpless writer/narrator, a trope insistent in Tawada's
work, as words within a linguistic system take on concrete physicality, and language wraps itself around speakers with tensile fishnet strength. The author (or
reader, or character) is denied the illusion of control. As many essayists will
note, language threatens one with captivity and suffocation, but words also provide the keys to loosen such constraints.

Agency, constraint, and identity are central questions in Tawada's work,
and they are manifested in and through bodies. The narrator/writer is sometimes
a medium, sometimes a conduit, sometimes the pavement trampled in the onrush
of language and speakers. The narrator of Tawada's essay is but one of many
possessed by words and driven to the edge of madness. Tawada describes her
own experience as an author taken over by and changed by words, at times en-
tranced by the ghost in the computer. The ghostly wraith haunting the speaker
appears in many of her texts. But her characters are also bridges between places,
languages, persons, or cities. Much violence, or threats of violence, accompanies
these bridgings, which often require the blasting of rock in order to establish a
span connecting two outcroppings, or the burrowing of a rail tunnel through
mountains, the traversing of tongues to cross oceans and other chasms. The
euphoria of traveling across and to turns to fear and dismemberment. (The consistent questioning of agency and unity is a theme I take up in my essay.)

Violence—the breaching of body borders—is suggested in the essays by
Mousel, Brandt, and others. Tawada is a writer between languages, literally and
figuratively; her characters also span ravines. Thus, translating and translation is
a central concern in her writings, and one expanded on by many of the essayists.
Translators are, as Margaret Mitsutani writes, "creators and destroyers," as are
any who would construct bridges. Translation seems, deceptively, to be a trans-
parent exercise in moving meaning from one set of words to another; the act is
fraught with dangers and layered meanings (as Walter Benjamin noted in the
1920s, and as many of the essays reference). Margaret Mitsutani explicates a
tale, *Wounds in the Alphabet*, with translation as its central theme. As she writes,
Tawada places "herself in the space between [languages] in order to explore and
exploit the strangeness of both." And strange they do become, in this tale and in
many others. Suzuko Mousel Knott also explores the meaning of travel across
borders of terrain and language, and invokes the German concept of *Migrantenliteratur* to complicate the relationship of a person, their language, and a place.

Keijirō Suga's essay on translation ties to these ideas at another level (while
also drawing from this story, which becomes, in his translation, *Transplanting
Letters*) when he writes that "translation without an original is creation." He
brings the discussion back full circle by showing how Tawada never reconciles
the differences between creativity and translation, between *ex nihilo* production
and a mirroring reflection, between individual agency and a more passive reaction, between a possessed craftsman and a possessing god. Bodies and meanings
are shuttled from one place to another. The body of the author/character often
forms the bridge and transports meaning between two spaces, yet Tawada suggests that the space vertiginously stretching out below the bridging body forms

the most compelling places to reside (as I explore in my essay), as are the spaces that open between persons and identities. Bernard Banoun's essay also explores the tug and pull of these languages across spaces.

It is just as likely that subjectivity is created out of that chasm because texts and their spaces make subjectivities possible. Yasmin Yildiz also explicates the ways that language and its defamiliarization/deconstruction prove to dismantle many received ideas of subjectivity; conversely, the imagination of language in Tawada's writings may, Yildiz suggests, provide the mental maps that we need to navigate the terrain of our beings. At times these spaces are bordered by rock face that cannot be scaled from below but are only approachable from above, via the access provided by bridges; at other times they are as porous and liquid as water, nets, and sponges.

Hiltrud Arens approaches these issues of translation from another vantage point, by a close reading of Tawada's explications of the poetry of Paul Celan. Tawada's explication of Celan's "pluralizing German" (as Suga phrases it) is a tour de force, and is one reason so many of us reference it. In this approach to Celan, we find that the vistas stretching out before us are liberating: think of the possibilities of a poetry that is being written for a translator and a language that is as yet unknown to the writer (as in the future translation, into Japanese, of Celan's German poetry). Who/what is in charge of the production in this scenario? Is it the author? More likely the poetry/language is breathing itself into existence in more languages than any of us know. Tawada's analysis of Celan gives us an idea of what she herself is trying to attain: the pluralizing of language. "Omniphone" is Suga's contribution to the critical lexicon we now have to work with when reading such writers (a concept that he goes on to situate in a history, itself a sort of archeology of the future). Writing in a single language is impossible; Suga allows us, via Tawada's writing, to imagine writing in all languages at once.

"Omniphone" is Suga's contribution; "exophony" is Tawada's. As the subtitle of her 2003 volume of that title suggests ("traveling outside the mother tongue"), one may move to territories not represented by the "mother tongue," yet fragrances from that new, unknown, territory may still waft through it. What is one getting beyond? The stranglehold of essentialist identities. Celan did it within one language (German) whereas Thomas Mann could not do it from within the same language, as Tawada pointedly reminds us. Omniphony may be a goal, but her oeuvre leads us to suspect that even as none of us can master all the languages potentially at our disposal, neither are "monolinguals" truly fluent in all the idiolects identified with their mother tongue. Tawada calls our attention to the space between those idiolects, in part because they reflect the experience of modernity and contemporary globalized society. Even as the space between languages and cultures collapses, this body of work suggests that spaces persist and, bridges or no, we tend to fall into them.

The awareness of space and place raises the question of boundaries: What is delineated by the borders? Tawada raises this question in the introductory essay; it is reiterated by many of the essayists. Her writing is often located, literally, in the spaces between, often as the specters of national borders and boundaries, sometimes as solid cliffs and massifs (to borrow imagery from Tawada's *Exophony* volume, as well as the Gotthard mountain that must be burrowed through, as Mousel, in particular, notes). The essentialist association of language to national identity is one that haunts these writings, for the place in which a character lives rarely accords with the language by which that terrain is navigated. Tawada vigorously resists an equivalence of language to national identity (to remind us of the second modality), yet the worlds we experience, the environments that her characters travel through, and the places that we, the essayists, teach and breathe in, constantly remind us of the insistence with which these ideas structure the world, shaping the ways that our words are heard.

As I elaborate in my essay, the specter of borders is, literally, one of the energizing aspects of Tawada's novel, *The Fugitive's Night-Time Railway*. The referencing of national tales, myths, and folklore is another way that Tawada (and her characters) wrestle with national identities. Other essayists (e.g., Arens, Yildiz) note how the parodic invocation of mythic tales and canonical figures suggests subversive intent. Indeed, Yildiz has suggested that Tawada's imagination, especially in the German writings, provides tools to think beyond entities that are usually themselves cordoned off (language, subjectivity, history). Mousel gets at this in her explication of *Partnertexts*, seemingly parallel works that split off in different directions to be mapped in different languages. Many of these myths and images are turned upside down, most notably in the tales collected in the English-language volume entitled *The Bridegroom was a Dog*, where bridegroom stories are given an aura of historical predecessors in ways that destabilize both the telling of tales and the accumulated national and individual history subsumed in such folktales. Mousel's explication of "The Gotthard Railway" points out how the burrowing through and eating up of mountains, bodies, and rivers is an iconoclastic sparring with landscapes that carries strong nationalistic identity markings. The parodic thrust of Tawada's introductory essay also take us in this direction, as her quixotic researcher is nearly undone by his assumption about the solidity of language fenced off by political borders.

In those moves, the bodies of languages and the bodies of narrators are the recipients of a fair degree of violence. The very act of writing begins the violence: the scratching of a stylus in wax that Tawada connects to the act of writing, the filling in or scraping out of hollows formed by *o*'s in a text (told of, after all, in a text itself named *Wounds in the Alphabet*). Language is closely knit to a physical body. She establishes this in another way when she tells us that the style of writing forms its body, and develops the point with examples of conflations between that body and her own physical body. I have already pointed to the body-borings suggested in the "Gotthard" stories; in the German collections that seem to be about language, *Überseezungen* (i.e., *Overseas Tongues*) and *Talisman* (with the torso imprinted on the book's cover), physical bodies are central. *Überseezungen* may mean "overseas tongues," but Tawada certainly wants us to form pictures of those tongues, in how many mouths, which have been transported across oceans in boats and planes. And *Überseezungen* may also mean "tongues across the water": perhaps the physical tongue forms the bridge that allows us to cross chasms, bodies of water, and link places and people. Tongues grow to represent subjectivity. The tongues we speak (with) stand in for identity cards: "To declare one's linguistic ties is thus akin to producing identity papers," writes Kraenzle. Tongues take on the characteristics of a parent—the mother (tongue). The possibilities and layerings that attend the imagery of the mother tongue all tie to the essentialist assumptions that Tawada so clearly chafes at in her essay included here, in *Exophony*, and in the imagery that accompanies her numerous writings on dreams and dream-language. (The dissonance of dreaming in Afrikaans, for example, occurs, insistently and significantly, in both the German and Japanese works. The cross-references available among languages, and beyond languages, is a thematic explored by both Suga and Yildiz.)

As Arens points out, Tawada "goes beyond the body of language [*Sprachkörper*] to incorporate the language of body [*Körpersprache*]." Some of these impulses take us to cannibalism, to literally ingest the body in order to own or control unruly language, as in "The Gotthard Railway," and other tales. Yildiz's discussion of Tawada's oft-employed practice of experimenting with the grammatical gender of German and casting it in terms of human gender or sex is another example. Bodies and body parts provide more than metaphor and imagery when talking about language; language is comprised of and concretizes our bodies. Brandt explores the concrete forms of language and reveals the surrealist impulse that organizes much of Tawada's writing. "Surrealist" is a descriptor that often comes to mind while reading Tawada's texts; Brandt explains in just what way surrealist aesthetics provide an important key to allowing access to these works.

Such physicality is manifest at various points, as Bernard Banoun explicates. Banoun speaks from a linguistic (and geographical) place unique in this collection: He is the translator of Tawada's German writings into French. He brings to his reading of Tawada the French literary tradition, and develops the implications for speaking from a third space. In this context he connects the destruction of language identity to national identity, achieved in many ways, as it is in Tawada's work, by a radical concretization of language. Words become hard red bricks that deconstruct, rather than fortify, borders of nation, identity, and gender. Ideograms and letters go on to reinforce this concretization. Here, we find, the strongest material objects, by being obstacles, help us over different hurdles. And yet this physical place is also a *Heimat*, a homeland, the final place where the writer/individual exists.

Many essays reference the importance of movement and space in Tawada's work—the space between, the modern sense of place that doesn't exist but in movement, the body in the space of travel. In this fourth modality, Tawada's characters are consistently to be found in places where they are not comfortable, on the way to someplace else, rarely on the way "home," but in and out of languages, back and forth across borders. Tawada's work is a meditation on travel and communication, on mobility and language, and on the relation these have to the constitution of identities. Many essayists make a point of the centrality that Celan's poetry holds for Tawada's own creative output; Arens explores how Celan's work can be seen as a translation of space. The space of this writing also suggests the third space of possibility suggested in Azade Seyhan's writing, as invoked in my essay and Arens'. A place is needed for reference, to work from, but one finds it impossible to arrive there, or to fully inhabit it. The third place for writing becomes the temporary space of travel, perhaps a way-station while travelling to another place, but that "temporary" space of train compartments and stations often proves to be as much stability as we will find.

Writers of the world, of Tawada's generation and most of the essayists represented here, find in that space the landscape of writing, the terrain of the present (the site of a future archeology) the place to serve as home. That home is no *Heimat*, no *furusato*, no entity bounded by language and passports. We are now "in a world where the only sense of home is to be found in a state of constant flux," as Charles Taylor recently phrased it.[20] A space that is no place, the perpetual place of the traveler, of shifting signs and sands, may be the only place from which we can speak and write in the contemporary world. That is our world, and that is the world that Tawada imagines and describes.

Notes

1. This conference is hosted annually at the University of Kentucky. This first reading was entitled "Japanese Studies 1: Special Session With Yōko Tawada" and presented on April 25, 2003.

2. For Appadurai's self-characterization, see *Modernity at Large: Cultural Dimensions of Globalization* (Minneapolis: University of Minnesota Press, 1996), 1-2.

3. *Modernity at Large*, 3. I have been tempted to speak of a more particular historical "break" in which Tawada and her sensibility are placed on "this side" of a moment. This is to suggest a modernist linearity and valorize Tawada as "cutting-edge," "new," or perhaps "avant-garde." The temptation is strongest given the alignment of historical moments in both the Japanese and German traditions in which she works: 1989 which saw both fall of the Berlin Wall and the death of the Shōwa emperor.

4. Homi Bhabha's seminal work introduced many of these questions.

5. Azade Seyhan, *Writing Outside the Nation* (Princeton, N.J.: Princeton University Press, 2001), 9.

6. Seyhan, *Writing*, 9.

7. At the same time, I take seriously Ian Buruma's reminder that while "exile is in fashion," the "exile" of rootless wanderings of middle-class intellectuals in first-world societies is nothing like the terror and desperation of the forced exile, "the poor, shivering Tamil, sleeping on a cold plastic bench at the Frankfurt railway station; or the Iraqi, fleeing from Saddam's butchers, afraid of walking the streets of Dover, lest he be attacked by British skinheads; or the young woman from Eritrea, standing along a minor road to Milan, picking up truck drivers so that she can feed her baby" (33). A similar point is made by Ackbar Abbas, especially in his critique of Edward Said, 130.

8. The intellectual as exile has a long heritage as well, and establishes lineages slightly different from what I find in work like Tawada's. This lineage introduces hierar-

chies and elites at odds with the articulations I am thinking of here. Emily Apter writes cogently on this history; see "Comparative Exile: Competing Margins in the History of Comparative Literature," in *Comparative Literature in the Age of Multiculturalism*, ed. Charles Bernheimer (Baltimore: Johns Hopkins University Press, 1995), 86-96.

9. Yōko Tawada, *Ekusophonii: bōgo no soto e deru tabi* (Tokyo: Iwanami Shōten, 2003), 35.

10.Salman Rushdie. *Imaginary Homelands: Essays and Criticism, 1981-1991* (London: Granta Books, 1991), 124-125.

11. Seyhan, *Writing*, 4.

12. "Comparative Exile."

13. Seyhan, *Writing*, 5.

14. Hélène Cixous, *Three Steps on the Ladder of Writing*. Trans. Sarah Cornell and Susan Sellers (New York: Columbia University Press, 1993), 20-21.

15. Tawada, *Ekusophonii*, 77.

16. Tawada, *Ekusophonii*, 114-115.

17. Seyhan, *Writing*, 15.

18. Appadurai, *Modernity*, 3.

19. Tawada, *Ekusophonii*, 31-32.

20. Quoted in A.O. Scott, "What is a Foreign Movie Now?" *The New York Times Magazine*. November 14, 2004: 79-86.

Bibliography

Appadurai, Arjun. *Modernity at Large: Cultural Dimensions of Globalization*. Minneapolis: University of Minnesota Press, 1996.

Apter, Emily. "Comparative Exile: Competing Margins in the History of Comparative Literature." In Charles Bernheimer, ed. *Comparative Literature in the Age of Multiculturalism*. Baltimore: Johns Hopkins University Press, 1995, 86-96.

Cixous, Hélène. *Three Steps on the Ladder of Writing*. Translated by Sarah Cornell and Susan Sellers. New York: Columbia University Press, 1993.

Eagleton, Terry, Fredric Jameson, and Edward W. Said. *Nationalism, Colonialism, and Literature*. Minneapolis: University of Minnesota Press, 1990.

Rushdie, Salman. *Imaginary Homelands: Essays and Criticism, 1981-1991*. London: Granta Books, 1991.

Seyhan, Azade. *Writing Outside the Nation*. Princeton, N.J.: Princeton University Press, 2001.

Tawada, Yōko. *The Bridegroom Was a Dog*. New York: Kodansha International, 2003.

———. *Ekusophonii: bōgo no soto e deru tabi*. Tokyo: Iwanami Shoten, 2003.

Chapter Two
Tawada Yōko Does Not Exist
Yōko Tawada
Translated by Doug Slaymaker

I intend, today,[1] to present an academic paper on the nonexistence of the writer Tawada Yōko. So, I should probably take myself off to the aquarium and erase myself from view. "Nonexistence" is, of course, the usual state of the writer being discussed at a literary conference, nonetheless, this writer has made special arrangements to come here and talk about the writer's nonexistence.

This is not my first visit to San Diego. Some years ago I went to Sea World and, for the first time in my life, had the chance to stroke the head of a porpoise. When our eyes met, I felt enveloped by the strangest sense of elation. In Japan, there is a child's song about porpoises that asks, "Are you there, porpoise, are you porpoise, or not?"[2] It seems that porpoises, more than any other creature, swim like otherworldly messengers between existence and non-existence.

There is an old tale still told in one part of Okinawa: long long ago, the people of the earth did not know how to make children. Some of those ancient people chanced to see porpoises mating in the sea. They mimicked the activity of the porpoises and learned how to make children. These would be an Okinawa-style Adam and Eve, a story with much more appeal than the tale we have in the ancient Japanese *Kojiki*.[3] There we read that Izanami and Izanagi were circling a pillar. They peer at each other the way one would inspect a machine. One of them says, "Here is a protrusion, there is a depression; let us fit them together and see what comes of it." They end up with children, but it seems to take place in exceedingly barren terrain, a place not only without animals, but with no trees, no grasses or plants, no flowers, nothing whatever. And that is not all, for the area seems swept clean like the grounds of a Shintō shrine, silent and shut in by the tall cedar trees, just the sort of place I cannot abide.

Go to any European art museum and you will find paintings of Adam and Eve next to a tree with a snake coiled around its trunk, but I have never seen a painting that represents the meeting of Izanami and Izanagi. There is a song about Urashima Tarō[4] that claims the dragon castle under the sea to which he went was "too beautiful to be painted in a picture," but the place where Izanami and Izanagi produced children seems simply too desolate for any picture. (It is after the trip to Yomi-no-kuni that this story gets interesting, however.[5])

Be that as it may, we know the *Kojiki* was compiled by early leaders in order to clarify national origins and bolster their political aspirations. Nonetheless, there seems never to have been, in Japan, the thinking that a God produced humankind, meaning that for Japan the created thing known as humankind exists without any "creator." The God of a monotheistic religion is a man who creates sons with or without a wife; and it seems that the "creator" of literary works shares some of these qualities, at least in the West. So I wonder sometimes if contemporary scientists are not also looking to be this sort of "creator" of life as they move things around with genetic engineering.

"God is dead," claimed Nietzsche, and that was long before Roland Barthes proclaimed the death of the author, which suggests there might have been a period of time when the author still lived even though God had died. During those years the writers remained the last of the gods, but what with exiles and murders, it seems to me to have been a rough time for them.

Now, authors go by a variety of names in Japan. We call the ones who write *sakusha*, *sakka*, *chosha*, or *shōsetsuka*.[6] My personal favorite is the decidedly informal *monogaki*, as in "writer of things." Further, in Japanese *kaku*, the word used for writing with a fountain pen or computer arose from the same source as *kaku*, the word used for digging trenches, when scratching and scraping ditches. Then we remember that the "thing" of *monogaki*, the "writer of things," is semantically connected to *mononoke*, a "changeling." Which means that this "writer of things" also describes a person in the clutches of changelings and shapeshifters, a person under the spell of the things. The writer takes what the things have said and carves them into shapes by scratching out lines, making the wounds and scars on paper that we call texts. But when these writers begin writing they have no clear idea what sort of tale it will turn into because even as they write, the "ling" underlying these changes takes charge and decides how the tale will progress. I think that even people who are not professional writers have had this experience; we all experience joy when our plans take off on their own and form into something grander than expected, but it doesn't always turn out that way.

I often get mail from students writing papers. They want to know, "What were you trying to say in this novel?" I always tell them that the reader—and the creator as well—should give little thought to what was trying to be said through it, but rather be thinking how to approach this fictional tale, these scratches and scars, on their own.

Whenever I think of the English word "author," it associates to the grand-sounding "authority," and it sounds so majestic. In Japan, however, the *monogaki*, the "writer of things," is the changeling's secretary, and that seems pretty far from majesty. In the Meiji period, perhaps because literature became one of the cornerstones of Japanese modernization and nation building, people started calling the writers by the imposing name of *sensei*, a term of address with all the ring of "authority." One still hears writers addressed as "sensei."

With my generation of writers things have changed somewhat. We are now invited to overseas literature festivals, and that style of public readings with their question-and-answer sessions has become commonplace. Speaking merely from my own experience, I have the sense that more and more people, young people included, wish to pose questions directly to the writer. Authors made presentations twenty years ago as well, of course, but those seemed to be one-way lectures, with the "sensei" standing behind a lectern and delivering a speech to the quiet listeners in the audience. Now, it seems that speakers and writers both want to have a conversation, addressing each other at the same level.

One of the major changes to occur in the last thirty years is the ease with which anyone at all can take any text, make copies, and increase its numbers. In the 1970s, when I was still in school, photocopies were rare, hardly anyone had a computer, and, in the case of Japanese, there were no typewriters either. So, we used a metal stylus and wrote our characters out on a wax tablet—here again dragging and carving. We would then make stencil copies from this sort of engraving. This was the way to make multiple copies of our own coterie-magazines, for circulation among the friends who had contributed to it. But now, almost anyone can burn a CD-Rom.

So, here we are in an age where anything can be easily copied and distributed widely; there is no fixed number of copies. As a result, the individual body of the creator, which we cannot so easily reproduce copies of, gains added value for its particularity. And given that there are probably not all that many clones in existence, an individual can be in no more than one place at any given time. Written materials can be printed and can exist in numerous places at the same time, but the author's body can be located in only one place at any given time.

In this age when cell phones and electronic text messages have become central to our communication, books have come to take on a special aura precisely because they do not immediately disappear. The person who writes them actually exists, with ears and nose, having pulled shoes onto his or her own feet; the experience of talking to such particular individuals seems all the odder in our contemporary world. While there is really nothing the least bit unusual in all this, book culture has nevertheless come to be enveloped in a special aura of physicality.

Even so, when a person appears in front of the reader and claims "I am the one who has written this book," can the reader believe it? Is there not in fact something a bit odd about this? While reading a book, one usually imagines what the writer looks like. The imagined writer rarely conforms to the actual one, but that is not sufficient reason to proclaim that the imagined one is an error. The authorial image produced from the work is the true author, and the living person who exists as the author may be, in relation to the text, a complete stranger.

For example, I have had people look at me and say, "I expected someone of about seventy, but you are somewhat younger than that, aren't you?" I think this comes from my writing style, which, in Japanese at least, seems rather archaic. The style—the form of the sentences—of a book is its body. Thus, one tries to deduce the form of the author's body from the form of the words and sentences in the books. In Germany, my writings are very different from *anime* and J-pop, and often include references to old tales, Noh drama, and the *Kojiki*, so it seems that even more people there think I am quite old. The author's body is constructed from the style of the book.

Some books carry a picture of the author. People say to me: "You look like the person in the photograph." This seems to me another example of how disconcerting it is to have the author appear before one, and the reader feels the need, like at passport control, to compare the photograph of the author with the actual author.

In the past, the trace of a brush on paper formed one face of the author, but we no longer see manuscripts written by hand. With a handwritten manuscript there can be but one single original (which can later be copied, of course), whereas in the case of a computer, there is no original at all, in the strictest sense. One writes on the computer, gets tired of it and stops halfway, and turns off the computer. On the following day one boots up the computer and what was written yesterday appears anew. That is, what I wrote yesterday re-*appears* in the same form and the electric currents allow me to see it again. But there it ends: the body of the text, the style in the form of scars and traces etched like ditches onto the paper, is gone. Not even the traces of ink exist in any place any longer.

The computer is, however, host to changelings that make shapeshifters of the letters on the page. Given the steps that a computer uses to change Japanese sounds to the corresponding written character, any character can be "possessed" by the computer and changed to another form entirely. Characters written by brush are also shapeshifters when exposed to the rain, for example, but in that case one immediately recognizes the changes. When characters are possessed by the computer, however, the change is more thorough. In the case of Japanese, one types in the sounds of words which are transformed to the hiragana syllabary, and then a further keystroke transforms these into Chinese characters (*kanji*). Since there are so many homophones in Japanese, the word one entered as sound often transforms into an entirely different word. Even so, I can't help but think that these variant readings and homophones are not simply flukes but expose something at work at an unconscious level, like those Freudian slips where a mistaken phrase carries more "truth" than the intended sentence. I think of a friend of mine who was secretly contemplating a divorce. Every time she typed the word for "interwoven"—*orikonda*—the screen would display its eerie homophone—*o rikon da*—or, "your divorce." I remember that in my own case I was writing about a "literary prize"—*bungakushō*—only to find on my screen *bun ga kushō*—"the text wryly smiles."

There are even more complicated examples of this. I was once writing about the theatrical troupe that has often staged my work, the "Lasenkan" they are called. Well, in the essay I called them "stage animals" (*karera wa butai dōbutsu*). For the life of me, I can no longer recall where this phrase came from. I can only attribute it to some typographical error, some arbitrary possession of the text by the computer, but no matter how many times I consider it, I cannot reconfigure any sequence of steps that could have changed my intended phrase to this one. I think it just as likely that while I was writing those words I was possessed by one of the changelings and lost consciousness. Later, when this essay was in preparation for a volume from the Iwanami Press, one of the editors who was reviewing the changes asked me if referring to the actors and actresses as "animals" did not seem insulting? Yet all the members of the Lasenkan troupe were very much taken with the phrase "stage animals," and they went so far as to make it the title of a new play. Sometime later I remembered Walter Benjamin's explanation of the way that buried memories are associated in Kafka's work with animals. Thinking along those lines, I realized that the place where animals frolic resembles the theatrical stage, and I felt better: "stage animals" works just fine.

To return to the subject of manuscripts written before the age of computers, in them the letters and characters penned by the author remain as the author left them. One can even see the editorial changes made to the manuscript. But computers do not preserve the traces of such editorial changes. And then, especially for writings that were never published, when researchers open the files after one hundred or more years have passed, they will no doubt find only computer symbols in a now unreadable form. The characters were changed to an unreadable format, and no one can any longer reconstruct how they got there.

The manuscript begins its changeling process even before the author dies. For example, I had a message from a student somewhere working on my writings for a Master's thesis, who noted that "there are many writings by 'Tawada Yōko' on the internet." However, I know that I have only published one piece on-line. So, if numerous pieces are available on-line under my name, then clearly someone other than me has taken my work and reworked it for on-line publication. One also finds pieces that have been changed from the form in which I wrote them. For example, it seems that in a university seminar somewhere my work was taken as the starting point and the students were admonished to write their own endings; the resulting essays were published on-line. No explanation accompanied these pieces, however, so the reader could not know that portions of these essays were not mine. There is another example of this process. Someone took a taped interview and reinscribed it as a first-person essay and then published it on-line under my name. It appeared to be an essay I wrote. By and large the content is consistent with the sorts of things I would say, but because there are stylistic forms and word choices that I would not use, I don't want readers to think that I wrote it.

Given all that, think what might happen when another 1,000 years have passed. The nonexistence of the writer will be even more pronounced. The meaning of the author's nonexistence will itself have changed. Maybe by that point in time the official language of the United States of America will be Spanish. Fortunately, a single volume of a Spanish-language book with my name noted as the author exists in the San Diego public library. The book doesn't contain any biographical information about the author, but it does say that it was translated from Italian, and given that the author's name, "Yoko," ends with an "o," most readers have assumed that it was written by an Italian man. Given that to specify an author's birth year or country was now considered discriminatory, such information had been forbidden long before, meaning nothing other than the name is known of the author. Now, suppose that a student known as D is studying at San Diego University. This student picks up this lone volume, a long-ignored work called *El Baño*, reads it and becomes engrossed. He then decides to do some research on the writer. On a summer holiday trip to Italy he visits the library at Salerno University near Naples. There is indeed a volume there written by this same author, in Italian, with the title *Il Bagno*. After consulting one of the librarians who is proficient in Spanish, he finds that this has the same meaning as the Spanish *El Baño*. However, on the title page of this Italian version he reads that it is a translation from German. This D is in a quandary. But, Germany being so close, on the following day he makes the trip to Munich University and finds there many works by this author. Further, with the help provided by a librarian who knows Spanish, he discovers a German volume with the title *Das Bad*, a title with the same meaning as these others. Yet this novel proves to be a translation, from Japanese, by a professor of Japanese at Munich University who had worked there 1,000 years before. But Japanese is no longer taught at Munich University and it seems there is no longer anyone at the university who knows Japanese. Nor does the library any longer have any Japanese-language holdings, so he is unable to find the original text at this library. With that, D decides he will travel to Japan on his next holiday. At this point, D gives himself the name "Don Quixote," for in an age when there are no longer any people who think that a thing called a manuscript still exists, he travels, alone, from country to country in search of one.

Well, the following year he travels to Japan and makes his way to the National Diet Library and finds numerous volumes by this author. None of them, however, carries a Japanese title anything like these other volumes, such as "Ofuro," "Showering," or "Entering the Bath." Nothing even close. He again consults a copy of the German version. The author of both works was born the same year in Tokyo, but the photos of the author seems slightly different. All the names are the same, but because it is impossible to determine with which Japanese characters the name would have been written, the Japanese translator helping him says there is no way to know with 100 percent certainty if these were all the same people.

At this point Don Quixote makes another trip back to the U.S., and begins to study Japanese. It proves very difficult to find anyone who can still teach Japanese, but someone does tell him about a researcher at the aquarium who is studying the Japanese blowfish, and who is quite proficient at the language. D goes off to meet this person, who is simultaneously developing ways to use the blowfish's poison for military uses and developing a way that the poison could be used in the treatment of cancer. But Japanese proves to be very difficult and D makes little progress.

One day he has a revelation. There has clearly been a blind spot in his wandering and research: he has overlooked the role of English. English had once been the common language of the United States, and in San Francisco there is a library with more than 10 million English-language volumes in its collection. He is reminded of the Japanese saying: "It is dark at the base of a lamp." Even though he has been living in California all this time he has spent all his time searching far-flung and distant places. He goes to the San Francisco library to consult the catalogs. He finds there two English language volumes by this author. One of them is a translation from Japanese called *The Bridegroom was a Dog*; he had seen the Japanese original for this work in Japan. The other volume, *Where Europe Begins*, contains a short piece called "The Bath." This is, without mistake, the piece he has been searching for. *Where Europe Begins* contains work translated from both German and Japanese, yet it remains unclear from which language the piece called "The Bath" has been translated. This piece is not included in the list of copyrights. From all appearances, no one held the copyright to this work. Perhaps there was no original manuscript for this piece. If that is possible, then perhaps there was no author of this piece either.

And then, in the midst of this, he makes an even more surprising discovery. One of D's friends who has been studying theatrical history brings him an old pamphlet on an International Spanish Theater Festival held in Miami in 2003. The name of the author that D has been searching for was noted there. The name of the theatrical piece is "Sancho Panza," and was this not Don Quixote's sidekick? D decides, then and there, to give up this research topic before it drives him mad. He cannot help but think that the spirit of a long-dead author, some changeling in the text, is tormenting him with dead ends and nonexistent texts.

Notes

1. Unless noted otherwise, all notes are supplied by the translator. Tawada presented this essay at the annual conference of the Association for Asian Studies, 6 March 2004, in San Diego, California as part of a panel entitled "Tawada Yōko Does not Exist." Other presenters included Margaret Mitsutani and Doug Slaymaker.

2. "Iruka, inaika, inaika, iruka." This word play succeeds because the word for porpoise—*iruka*—is a homophone for "are you there/ do you exist?" Thus, "are you there or not there" is equally "porpoise, or not?"

3. Translated as *The Kojiki: Records of Ancient Matters* by Basil Hall Chamberlain (Rutland, Vt: Tuttle, 1982). See also *Kojiki*, trans. Donald L. Philippi (Tokyo: University of Tokyo Press, 1968).

4. Urashima Tarō is the main character in an old tale about a fisherman who rescues a turtle and is rewarded with a visit to the Dragon Palace at the bottom of the sea.

5. Yomi-no-kuni: "The Japanese Hades or Sheol, a subterranean land of the dead which Izanagi visits in his search for his deceased wife Izanami." *Kojiki*, 642.

6. A similar list in English might include creator, artist, writer, or novelist.

Chapter Three
Translation, Exophony, Omniphony
Keijirō Suga

A language is not fully alive when translated into another. Half-dead, it gives a new life to the host language. Its original meaning becomes distorted and somewhat obscure, but at the same time the translated form is charged with an aura of discovery and excitement in a new environment. Transformation of a language through the process of translation offers the framework for Yōko Tawada's writings. In her works, seemingly two different operations, translation and creation, merge into a continuous effort of a writer. Considering that Tawada writes constantly in two languages, Japanese and German, this comes as no surprise. Still, there must be some irreducible differences, or unsolvable conflicts, between the two processes. In this paper I will take up Tawada's fascinating novella *Moji ishoku* (*Transplanting Letters*)[1] to discuss how translation intervenes in the imaginary of a writer to eventually have repercussions on the language in which she writes. Then I will expand the horizon toward the general problematics of exophony and omniphony, to concepts that are rapidly becoming salient in today's world literatures.

Section I

"Translational poetics" is a phrase I have been using for years, without really giving thought to its full potential. What does translation have to do with literary creation? Translation as an operation requires at least two different systems of signs. I cannot go far back in time to the origin of human language and I am in no place to talk about its long process of differentiation. Neither have I an idea if human language was, at the very beginning, monogenetic or polygenetic. Let me just assume that there have always been different languages, already spreading over a vast geographical horizon. Given the current post-Babelic plurality, each language is an accumulative result of translations—interactions and exchanges with other languages.

A language is like an island, constantly changing its shape, whose coastline is being washed by the incessantly approaching and breaking waves from many other languages. To imagine how translation intervenes in the obscure matrix of literary creation, we may first consider some cases of bilingualism. Consider, for example, somebody like the Italian poet Giovanni Pascoli (1855-1912). A major figure in Italian literary history, Pascoli was a teacher of Classics and later the chair of literature at the University of Bologna. A poet and a Dante scholar, he also wrote poetry in Latin, knowing very well that this was a dead language.[2] Pascoli's choice of language is intriguing, as a turn-of-the century Italian poet writing in Latin seems somewhat like Natsume Sōseki (1867-1916), the greatest Japanese modern novelist and an exact contemporary to Pascoli, writing *kanshi*, poetry composed in Japan in Classical Chinese. This is the kind of culture that was lost forever after Sōseki's generation.[3]

Giorgio Agamben wrote an interesting essay on Pascoli's onomatopoeia, and I was especially attracted to the following passage:

> Polemicizing against the proposal to abolish the instruction of Greek in schools, Pascoli writes, "the language of poets is always a dead language," and immediately adds, "a curious thing—a dead language used to give greater life to thought."[4]

A dead language's ability to empower comes from its distance from the currently circulating language. In this sense, we may say that "the past is a foreign country," and project this chronological distance onto the synchronic plane of the present to tentatively conclude by modifying Pascoli's formulation: a foreign language can give greater life to thought.

But then, this transposition may only be a truism, because in one case or the other what is taking place in a writer's mind is simply a similar process of translation. Classic or modern languages, it matters little. In the case of Pascoli, I can only imagine how his Latin intervenes and gives strength to his composition in Italian. In the case of Natsume Sōseki the situation is somewhat visible to me, as his writings are obviously imbued with an erudition in the classics that has since become foreign to Japanese readers. What about the other writers, our contemporaries, who find their sources of inspiration not particularly in classic cultures but in more or less contemporary, foreign cultures? It is not difficult to name bilingual or trilingual poets from any country, from Rainer Maria Rilke to Paul Celan, from Fernando Pessoa and Ivan Goll to Nishiwaki Junzaburō and Joseph Brodsky. Again, I can only imagine what's going on in their inner creative process in one language or the other, but I think, essentially, that what takes place in the linguistic exchange is the same; foreign languages that empower their writings are, in a sense, already dead languages—precisely because of the importation into the foreign body of their texts, such foreign languages lose their original life.

All modern writers are inspired in one way or the other by foreign strains of national literatures that have their own respective phylogenies. The whole institution of modern literature is founded upon translations between national languages, the fact that gives legitimacy to the discipline of comparative literature in its incipient, influentialist aspect. Sometimes the influence can be identified as motifs, structures, themes; at other times the influence is literally "in-flux," the direct use of words or transposed locutions from a foreign body of work. In such a case, if a foreign word (or expression) were completely meaningless to the reader, it wouldn't have any poetic power. The kind of foreign words that are dynamically meaningful within a new context remain foreign but are already translated — to the degree of being half-comprehensible and half-opaque.

This may turn out to be the general logic of "xenoglossia," which I'd like to define as the use of foreign words and literal transpositions in one's writing. In translational poetics, under the influence (or in-flux) of the original foreign texts, the translated text is charged with half-meanings that offers itself to a variety of acceptations. Like a stranger's utterly incomprehensible glossolalia, half-translated foreign words and expressions can become seeds for a heightened verbal sensitivity. Theodore Adorno once defended the use of foreign words against those who advocate the pureness of German and communicative transparency. I take sides not with transparency but with opacity. Poetry is the kind of language that aspires to present itself as a foreign force in the current state of language, as something to attain the estrangement effect from the re-configuration of speeches. Poetry doesn't need communicative transparency, but an unexpected opacity to attract the reader's attention. Of course, seen from the poet's side, such opacity needs to be just the right amount to sustain the reader's interest. Foreignness is like an ambivalent poison that can serve for a good result, but only when used in appropriate doses.

In the practice of translation, there have always been opposing positions within the community of translators: literalness and naturalness. You have to decide how much you naturalize or how much you leave the foreignness untouched. Of course, all translators place themselves somewhere between these two extremes. But most of the interest in a translated text comes, at least to me, from the translation's literalist aspect. Within certain limits, what makes literary (or poetic) language interesting is its aberrancy within syntagmatically possible choices of words. Translation abundantly offers such possibilities and becomes a ready source for radically new poiesis.

Section II

Let me continue to discuss a little more about translation per se. Without any knowledge of Greek and Latin, I only recently learned that the words "translation" (from the Latin word *translatio*) and "metaphor" (from the Greek-to-Latin word *metaphora*) were used synonymously from the Classical ages until the Renaissance period. Both of them seem to mean transfer, transport, transpose, and other such words that implicate physical movement. And the two words, translation and metaphor, were used interchangeably.

This is understandable. When you look at an English dictionary, Shakespeare's phrase "The world is a stage" is often quoted as an example of metaphor. This sounds already so trite, as we all have heard this phrase any number of times, but when you take a close look at it, it is marked with an undeniable, underlying truth: that the world is never equivalent to a stage. It is precisely this commonly held consciousness of non-equivalency, or non-identity, that gives rise to the metaphoric, shocking effect. By juxtaposing the two within a metaphorical phrase, each time we enunciate the phrase we reconfirm and reinforce the non-identity of the two terms. To look at the world's reality as if it was played within a fictive frame of the stage, or to see in the performed theater a fundamental mechanism that also is working behind our so-called reality—we empirically know that there are such experiences. And the lift of feeling we get from such experiences of intuition is guaranteed solely by the absolute non-equivalence of the world and the theater. The world is never a stage, hence the strength of the metaphoric equation: "the world is a stage."

Now, isn't this consciousness of non-equivalence that we see in the metaphoric use of language also shared by the act of translation? The more closely we look at the whole process of translation, the more abnormal and unnatural it becomes. There is no resemblance in characters or sounds between the original and its translated version. By matter-of-factly transcending this non-identity, we say: "Here, this is the finished product, the translation of the original, take it or leave it," and the translation is offered to the reader. Isn't the translated text at this moment but a half-made metaphor of the original's role in the original sphere of reception, the original's position in its native habitat?

This structure may send us back to the fundamentals of our understanding of the world. None of us understand what surrounds us as a whole, in its entirety. We pick up only a part of what comes into our perception, make choices according to hidden reasons of the mind, reorganize the information into retrievable units that can be retold or represented to a certain extent when necessity occurs. In other words, "reality" in this sense is always already translated, metaphorized, put into parentheses. Seen from this standpoint, Shakespeare's "The world is a stage" is not just an example of metaphor, nor a sort of ritual to reconfirm the non-equivalency of the two terms, but something that designates the inevitable schema that we can never talk about the world as a whole unless we first translate and metaphorize it into its infinitely simplified miniature.

Now, as a practitioner of literary translation, sometimes I wonder if translating such and such work has any meaning at all. Of course the work of translation offers moments of joy—joy of discovery and enlightenment, of surrogate creation, of the feeling of fulfillment when the work is finished and put into print. I can be content with these. But what about its socio-historical and linguistic scope? Is a translator's satisfaction sufficient for a translation to be produced? What actually happens when a translation is finished, materialized and circulated in search of its readers? We translators know that the translated versions do not resemble the original at all. This feeling of inadequacy may lure us to believe—could it be out of guilt?—that there is something that survives translation. What survives is the work's "soul," we are tempted to say. Our faithfulness in translation is meaningless without an inexistent contract with such "soul" of the work. It's all the better for a translator to remain silent about what he has done.

One thing is certain, though. As I have said earlier, we empirically know that any language is constantly washed over by other languages. Given this consciousness, my minimalist answer for the question "What is translation for?" is that it serves to transform the body of a language, to let the language speak something that it has never spoken before, to inscribe the matters or emotions that have never been formulated on the visible surface of the language. If I, as a Japanese translator, can say "this has never before been said in Japanese, nobody's seen a sentence like this in Japanese," then there should be no reason to doubt the translation's validity. But once you begin discussing in this manner, there would be no more distinction between "translation from an original" and "translation without the original," because this is simply creation. A translator may aim at bringing about a local transformation of his language through the act of translation. A poet aims at the same through the act of writing, which in fact is never a creation ex nihilo. The boundary between the two is blurred. Literary creation is a revolution within an accepted boundary of language. Translation is a part of such creation but it flies with borrowed wings. The wings are borrowed from the original text that inhabits another language. By transposing and transplanting the kind of expressions that originates in another language's words and phrases, a translation, while being nothing more than a metaphor for the original text, transforms the landscape on this side of the linguistic border.

Section III

Let's take a look at Tawada's *Transplanting Letters*. The narrator is a woman who stays on one of the Canary islands to translate a short story about St. George, the princess, and the dragon. The translation doesn't go well and the translator wonders why throughout. She's also waiting for her friend Georg to arrive but he never comes. Nothing is clearly stated. The whole story proceeds with an atmosphere of ambiguity and absurdity that is often associated, rightly or wrongly, with Kafka. Apart from the slowly developing story line, the novella is full of insights about the difference between so-called creative writing and translation, as well as the difference between the perception of letters in the European alphabetic languages and the Japanese. It seems that the Japanese, who are accustomed to so-called *kanji kana majiri*, a mixed-character writing of Chinese ideograms and two series of phonetic transcriptions invented more than a thousand years ago in Japan, tend to notice in the Roman alphabets some peculiarities in their shapes, such as that of the letter *O*. When scattered around a page, these *O*'s look like so many holes that you cannot see through and give you the impression of being so many impasses. Threatened by an ineffable anxiety, the translator/narrator fills in the letter *O*'s openings.

There are places where the narrator expresses her opinion about translation. Her editor, when talking over the telephone, is told that the story the narrator is translating is about St. George, the princess, and the dragon. The editor responds by saying that it's got to be rewritten to today's taste incorporating, for example, some ideas of feminism. Then the translator says: "I don't like to solve the problem easily by rewriting like that. That's why I chose translation as my profession instead of rewriting." The editor doesn't like the reply and asks further what then is so interesting about the work of translation. The translator responds, as if by a reflex, in an unnecessarily passionate tone: "Something abruptly comes out."[5]

At another point her novelist friend tells her to write her own novel instead of just translating. According to the novelist friend a translator is never counted as an artist. To this the reaction in the translator's mind is that she doesn't want to write a novel or anything, that she wants to translate and she doesn't translate because she couldn't be a novelist.[6] Then comes this dialogue with the post-office clerk of the island, who asks her a series of questions.

"Is there a book that's never translated into another language?"
"Well, most of the books in this world are."
"Is there a book of which only the translation is left, I mean a book from old days?"
"Yes. There are books of which only translations survive and the originals are lost."
"If only the translations are left, how do you know that these themselves are not the originals?"
"Oh, that's easy to tell. Translation is, like, itself a language. You can tell because you feel as if some pebbles were falling down on you."
"You'd better not go to the sea."[7]

I feel here that the narrator/translator is quite rightly pointing out the secret of her craft. Translation leaves you with such a physical, material sensation. In the process of translation, something abruptly comes out. Some pebbles from an unknown sky will threateningly fall on you. These are the moments when language's unexpected apparition surprises you and disturbs the order of your established repertoire of available words and phrases. It is the moment of transformation of the language in which the work is being written. This may be taking place anywhere that a poet is at work. But in translation, its moment of transformation becomes crudely locatable. To me the beauty of this novella *Transplanting Letters* resides in this disclosure of truth, and seldom have I encountered a literary work that acutely sheds light on this aspect of translation's mechanism.

Section IV

Tawada's 2003 book of essays is called *Exusophonī: bōgo no soto e deru tabi* (*Exophony: Traveling Outward from One's Mother Tongue*). By exophony she means the use of a foreign language as a medium of both daily interaction and artistic creation. Seen from this perspective, an important part of contemporary literature in any major languages is literally exophone literature, written not in one's first language. Is this a new phenomenon? Probably not. The implicit command to write a literary work in one's own mother tongue, or the language of one's national belonging, is itself a rather modern attitude. In the earlier part of the twentieth century, the literature of high modernism world-wide dictated that this impulse of writing in a language other than one's own be put into practice. In other words, the very ownership of the language and the membership within a monolingual community were questioned by a group of eccentric (or centrifugal) minds from Conrad and Joyce to Nabokov and Beckett.

In the context of the global economic and political migration of the late twentieth century, this attitude has now generalized itself. Many writers world-wide have taken up the newly self-assigned task of writing in a language outside of their mother tongue. In Tawada we have a very fine example of such an adventurous mind for whom exophony is the basis of creative inspiration. Exophone writing, imaginably, involves a constant process of self-translation. One's mind is kept alert by constantly going through the available phonetic and semantic resources in (at least) two languages, and this agitation within the writing gives one's style an extraordinary agility. It is this agility born out of her own inherent translational poetics that gives her work a joyfully thrilling, magical touch.

Exophony is another book of translational poetics put into practice. Exophony, as I already mentioned, designates the state of being outside of one's mother tongue. But come to think of it, isn't all literary creation an attempt to step out of the very language that the work is being written? Gilles Deleuze talked about Proust's stuttering within his mother tongue. Tawada, here as an acute critic, talks about the case of Paul Celan's pluralizing German (a discussion that many of my fellow essayists will continue). Considering these examples, exophony is not something special for literature; it is rather a basic condition of an innovative literary language that is always trying to implode and break its own vessel from within. Only through self-destruction can a language attain a new life. And each one of us can freely participate in such destruction not out of obligation but as one's own right.

There are many memorable statements in the book *Exophony*, but I will only take up the following passage where she talks about the accents one acquires by consciously meandering through the world. (What follows is my tentative translation).

To write literature is at the opposite end from repeating and recombining arbitrarily the words that you hear on a daily basis. It is an attempt to face and confront the possibility of the language in which you write. By consciously doing so, the traces of your memory are highly activated and your mother tongue, your older linguistic stratum, intervenes to transform the actual language you use for creation.

When I write and read aloud sentences in German by searching the correct rhythm, my sentences come out differently from the usual, natural sounding German. People say my sentences in German are very clear and easy to hear, but still they are "not ordinary" and deviant in some ways. No wonder, because they are the results of the sound that I as an individual body have absorbed and accumulated by living through this multilingual world. It is of no use if I tried to delete my accents or remove my habits in utterance. Today a human subject is a place where different languages coexist by mutually transforming each other and it is meaningless to cancel their cohabitation and suppress the resulting distortion. Rather, to pursue one's accents and what they bring about may begin to matter for one's literary creation.[8]

Now, to pursue one's own accents means to retain all the memories of linguistic collision that one has gone through. This I take to be our common destiny in today's translational poetics. Let me proceed to elaborate on what I mean by the phrase "omniphone exilography."

Section V

Several years ago I was asked in Japan to write the entry "Creole literature" for a little thematic encyclopedia on Latin America.[9] There I made distinction between "Creolophone literature" per se and "Creolistic literature." The former refers to works of literature written in Creole languages, be they French-lexicon-based or English-lexicon-based. We can easily think of the cases of the great Haitian writer Franketienne or the Martinican Raphaël Confiant, who write in Haitian Creole and Martinican Creole, respectively, with their own French translations following. On the other hand I defined "Creolistic literature" as a group of literary work written on the conflicting interface between cultures with traces of cultural collision consciously inscribed. Many works of what since the 1980s have been called "Third-World literature" or "emergent literatures" fit into this category. I went so far as to give this "Creolistic literature" another concise definition: that "Creolistic literature, even when written within a single language, is omniphone exilography."

What do I mean by this? Omniphone means a state of language in which many other languages of the world resonate. As long as all the languages of the world are shaped through constant process of translation and mutual transformation, this is an undeniable, material fact. Only there are minds that refuse to see omniphone nature in any given language and believe in a very abstract notion of "purity" and stability of a national language. I do not stand by them. I use the word exilography to designate a group of writings, be it fiction, non-fiction, poetry or drama, that inscribe one's own experience of stepping outside of one's native culture. In my own career as a translator I have come to focus on writings by Chicanos, Native Americans, Asian Americans, Francophone Caribbean, or Latin American exiles. All of them live and write from their own borderlands, in-between spaces, or as Tawada calls it "Zwischenraum." If not for the collective efforts of their trans-linguistic and trans-cultural rewriting of this world that was initially worlded by the expounding force of European-lead modernity, world literature today would offer a very impoverished landscape.

From my perspective of translational poetics, the Martinican Edouard Glissant's relational poetics and relationist world view becomes an anchoring point. Glissant's own neologism *echos-monde* or "world echoes" comes in very handy. By this he seems to mean something like the core of crystallization of a local expression in a spatio-temporal continuum of the forces at work that are end-lessly shaping and reshaping the world. As a matter of fact, almost everything we see around us can be considered an *echo-monde* if we pay enough attention to see through its texture and hear its resonance. Glissant uses the word "poetics" in its original sense; not just a series of rules and techniques for composing poetry but a generalized logic of poiesis (or creation) across different genres. He enumerates examples of *echos-monde* in the following manner:

> William Faulkner's work, Bob Marley's song, the theories of Benoit Mandelbrot, are all echos-monde. Wifredo Lam's painting (flowing together) or that of Roberto Matta (tearing apart); the architecture of Chicago and just as easily the shantytowns of Rio or Caracas; Ezra Pound's *Cantos* but also the marching of schoolchildren in Soweto are *echos-monde*.
>
> *Finnegans Wake* was an *echo-monde* that was prophetic and consequently absolute (without admission into the real).
>
> Antonin Artaud's words constitute an *echo-monde* outside of the world.[10]

One may begin to see that what Glissant means by *echo-monde* is something that underlies an expression and alludes to its planetary resonance and connotation. Still, mind you, it has nothing to do with an abstract mantra of universality! It is something that remains local, individual, singular, incomparable, not fixable, and vibrant like an invisible animal. An *echo-monde* itself is value-free; it can be good or bad, beautiful or ugly. In itself, it is beyond aesthetic or moral judgment. Still, at any moment it points to a set of relations, making one conscious of the vast, ever-transfiguring textuality of the world.

There is little wonder that such an acute consciousness about the relations of the world should arise from the Caribbean. Because of its historical background, the Caribbean basin is a remarkably multilingual area. The languages of colonizing Europe—Spanish, Dutch, English, and French—along with several Creole languages, Creole English, French-based Patois, Haitian Kreyol, and Papiamento of the Dutch islands, are spoken, written, and printed. Living in the Caribbean one is very aware that other languages that could have been theirs by a turn of luck are spoken in one's proximity. Even if one doesn't understand languages other than one's own, one accepts their opacity and accepts that they form together a linguistic archipelago. Glissant reports what the Cuban novelist Alejo Carpentier once told him: "although we of the Caribbean write in four or five different 'langues' (languages), we share a common *langage* (linguistic attitude)." What is being shared is an omniphone consciousness.

It is Patrick Chamoiseau, another Martinican writer, who introduced the term omniphone in the following fashion, in the spirit of Glissant's *echo-monde*.

> L'imaginaire omniphone est en présence des langues. Aucune qui soit pauvre, petite ou inutile. Chaque Écrire s'accrochera ainsi aux saveurs de la sienne et l'informera des fragrances entrelacées des autres. Rabelais, Dante, Joyce, Faulkner, Mallarmé, Céline, Franketienne, Glissant . . . Tous omniphones par un langage ameutée dans une langue.[11]

Again I give my own rough translation:

> Omniphone imaginary is in the presence of languages. No language is poor, little, or useless. Each Writing is thus attached to the taste of its own language and gives it fragrances mixed with those of other languages. Rabelais, Dante, Joyce, Faulkner, Mallarmé, Céline, Franketienne, Glissant . . . They are all omniphone by sharing the linguistic attitude gathered within a single language.

This then is at the basis of their collective poetics of relations. Omniphone does not simply mean plurality of languages. It is an attitude that hears in any language echoes of a multitude of others. It is itself at the same time practice and a product of relational and translational poetics. Many contemporary writers of exilography, regardless of their language of expression, are trying to make themselves instances of *echos-monde* through their omniphone writing.

Section VI

Let me quote once again a passage from Tawada's *Exophony* that is quite relevant to the significance of omniphone literary practice.

> Literatures written in small languages are not accessible to most people and so they get translated into major languages that may provide a larger audience. Then, by translation, the small language's endangered vocabulary, its rhythm of thinking, diction and narration, images and myths take refuge in a major language and bring about displacement, distortion, hesitation, fluctuation, etc. Nothing is more stimulating than this for literature. Literature in translation plays a role of transforming a major language.
>
> When a writer whose mother tongue is a minor language begins to create in a major language such as English, a certain change occurs in the target language. The change is not limited solely to the linguistic level. A particular take on history, or a new sensorium to grasp the magical, come into literary language. One who belongs to a small linguistic community is less likely to run the risk of looking at history from the victorious side. Moreover, because of the community's small size, there arise in the industrial process temporal and qualitative differences that serve to cause the magical world to surface unexpectedly in their language.[12]

I remember Gayatri Spivak talking somewhere about her critical view of so-called "world literature" taught in English translation within the American academia. Spivak seems to think that world literature, translated into English and taught monolingually by way of the products of American publishing industry, gives a very inadequately represented image of other worlds. As a comparatist myself, I firmly believe in the virtue of pluri-lingualism in literary study. But at the same time I want to be more optimistic than Spivak about translation's power to actually rewrite English and the attendant worldview from within. A constant flow of translation, or verbal immigration, creates an omniphone space within a given language. And it is this self-generating space that serves as a matrix not only of an individual artistic creation but also of a certain future civility, a protocol of loose belonging, for a planetary community to come.

Section VII

Besides Yōko Tawada, who migrated to Germany and its language as a designated space for creation, are there other such cases in contemporary Japanese literature? Certainly there are many others, among whom I will take up the very interesting case of Hideo Levy, a very strong prose writer by any standard.

He is a Jewish-American, the son of a Chinese language specialist for the U.S. Department of State, and grew up in Taiwan, Hong Kong, U.S., and then Japan, where, at seventeen, he finds a place to escape from his father's house and into the excitement of Shinjuku, Tokyo's liveliest downtown district. The period was 1967 and 1968, so we can imagine the color of the time. After pursuing a brilliant career as a scholar of ancient Japanese poetry, at the age of thirty-nine, in 1990, he resigned from his tenured professorship at Stanford to become a full-time novelist based in Tokyo writing in Japanese. He thus became the first full-blooded Westerner (I'm not sure if the phrase "full-blooded" is appropriate or not, but I don't know how else to put it) to choose Japanese as his language of expression. This is another case of extreme self-exile of a committed exophone writer.

To him Japanese is a third language. It is not the first language learned from his mother, nor the second language of his childhood, Mandarin, that filled his still amorphous, tender ears. Japanese is the third language encountered in his unstable teenage years, and it surfaced as a means of rewriting and redirecting his life. Discussing the abnormality of Japanese writing of the past thousand and several hundred years, that freely mixes parallel systems of kanji and kana characters, he calls Japanese "an ultimate mish-mash language," and "the language with the most powerful creativity among my three languages from three ages."[13] His numerous essays on the themes of border crossings and cultural differences, not only between Japan and the U.S. but also between Japan and China, are all illuminating. According to Levy, "Japanese as a spoken language is nothing special or unique. It is only one language among thousands in the world. If there really was uniqueness in Japanese, it resides in the written language, in other words, letters."[14]

Japanese, needless to say, is a language of the oceanic archipelago at the margin of the Chinese world fashioned under the influence of and in resistance to Chinese, the language of the powerful empire. Linguistically, the two languages belong to totally different groups. The central destiny of the Japanese writing is *kanji kana majiri*, as I noted above. The combination of these different systems of writing leads to a certain productivity that may be utterly unique in the world's writing culture. It is to this characteristic that Levy refers. One of his essays talks about his decision to write in Japanese, and there is a memorable and extraordinary passage about an old, humble, small Japanese-style room that he rented in the heart of Tokyo. Now his life as a Japanese-language writer is based at this small, eight-mat room, from where he occasionally departs over-seas to America and China, the lands of his mother tongue and the land of his childhood's language. Levy writes:

I go on trips to two continental countries that declare themselves to be "multi-ethnic," the countries to which I have always maintained enough relations on the level of the speech, only to return again to this island country that declares itself to be "mono-ethnic," the country of which I am not an original member, and write about "there" by the language of "here." I go on trips to two continental countries that firmly believe in the "universality" of their cultures, only to return to this room in this island country that very consciously claims its "uniqueness," and in my turn become very conscious about the modern written language of "here" that the writers of the past hundred years have collectively shaped while disputing the "universality" of "there," I write in Japanese about those continents.

To write in Japanese has meant for me writing within such a movement. Once securing a "room to write Japanese in" and by beginning such back-and-forth movements, I feel that I began to see a characteristic of the language of "here" that is absent from the languages of the continents and that I didn't notice while I reflected upon Japanese from afar. Simply put, it is the discovery that the written languages of the continents that declare themselves to be "multi-ethnic"—English that is written all in alphabets and Chinese that is written all in simplified Chinese characters—look "mono," and on the contrary the language of this island country that has been believed by the natives and the foreigners alike to be only understandable by the members of the "mono-ethnic" group inherently has a very complex richness far from any "monotony."[15]

This is no place for going into a detailed analysis of any of his stimulating fictions, that are often written in the language of para-autobiographical realism, with a backdrop of Japan and continental China. But his struggle as someone who lives always on the move and by constantly translating his emotions into an adopted language of creation, offers an ex-centric example in today's world writing. Yōko Tawada and Hideo Levy writing in their own idiolect of om-niphone Japanese are to me two fine examples in literary praxis individually attempted of what Glissant called *echo-monde*.

Notes

1. Yōko Tawada, *Moji ishoku* (Tokyo: Kawade Shobō Shinsha, 1999). Originally published as *Arufabetto no kizuguchi* (*Gaping Wounds of Alphabets*), 1993.
    2. Those who are familiar with Ferdinand de Saussure's life may remember Pascoli as the person to whom Saussure wrote about his putative great discovery of anagrams in Latin poets. Pascoli never answered.
    3. I can only think of the novelist Ishikawa Jun (1899-1987) as a younger-generation literatus who could actually compose *kanshi*, abiding by its rules of composition. The culture of *kanshibun* (Classical Chinese poetry and letters) has been a staple of Japanese culture for well over a thousand years; Classical Chinese as a written language (and never

as an orally spoken language) prevailed among the cultured milieu. Even during the Meiji era, it was considered that four subjects, English, mathematics, national language (Japanese), and *kanbun* (Chinese letters), were essential in the secondary education curriculum, and this continued until the end of WW II (1945). The situation is probably comparable to the role played by Latin in Christian Europe.

4. Giorgio Agamben, *The End of the Poem: Studies in Poetics* (Stanford, Calif.: Stanford University Press, 1999), 62.

5. Tawada, *Moji*, 41.

6. Tawada, *Moji*, 68.

7. Tawada, *Moji*, 82-83.

8. Yōko Tawada, *Ekusophonii: bogo no soto e deru tabi* (Tokyo: Iwanami Shoten, 2003), 78.

9. Yoshio Onuki, *Raten America o shiru jiten* (Tokyo: Heibonsha, 2000).

10. Edouard Glissant, *Poetics of Relation*, trans. Betsy Wing (Ann Arbor: University of Michigan Press, 1995), 93-94.

11. Patrick Chamoiseau, *Ecrire en Pays domine*, (Paris: Gallimard, 1997), 266.

12. Tawada, *Ekusophonii*, 89, my trans.

13. Hideo Levy, *Aidentitizu* (Tokyo: Kodansha, 1997), 79.

14. Ian Hideo Levy, *Nihongo o kaku heya* (Tokyo: Iwanami Shoten, 2001), 163.

15. Levy, *Nihongo*, 34-35, my trans.

Bibliography

Agamben, Giorgio. *The End of the Poem: Studies in Poetics*. Stanford, Calif.: Stanford University Press, 1999.

Chamoiseau, Patrick. *Ecrire en Pays domine*. Paris: Gallimard, 1997.

Glissant, Edouard. *Poetics of Relation*. Translated by Betsy Wing. Ann Arbor: University of Michigan Press, 1995.

Levy, Hideo. *Aidentitizu*. Tokyo: Kodansha, 1997.

Levy, Ian Hideo. *Nihongo o kaku heya*. Tokyo: Iwanami Shoten, 2001.

Onuki, Yoshio. *Raten America o shiru jiten*. Tokyo: Heibonsha, 2000.

Tawada, Yōko. *Ekusophonii: bogo no soto e deru tabi*. Tokyo: Iwanami Shoten, 2003.

Tawada, Yōko. *Moji ishoku*. Tokyo: Kawade Shobō Shinsa, 1999.

Chapter Four
Missing Heels, Missing Texts,
Wounds in the Alphabet
Margaret Mitsutani

Part One: Benjamin's Fragments

My point of view is not so much that of a scholar as one of Tawada Yōko's translators. (Tawada has suggested in the preceding essay that she herself does not exist, which probably means that I don't either, but I won't let that stop me.) Tawada's stance as a writer who writes in two languages, placing herself in the space between them in order to explore and exploit the strangeness of both, is akin to the position of the translator. Although translation is often thought of as a process of going back and forth between two languages, translators also tend to occupy the space between, where they are constantly discovering the strangeness of both languages, particularly that of the so-called "target language," which is frequently their native tongue.

The text that will be the focus of this paper, entitled *The Wound in the Alphabet*, is both a meditation on, and an experiment in translation. This title is my translation of Tawada's title *Arufabetto no Kizuguchi* which in turn is a translation of "Der Wunde Punkt im Alphabet," the title of a story by a German writer named Anne Duden who, like Tawada Yōko, may or may not exist. The narrator of Tawada's story is a Japanese woman who has come to the Canary Islands to translate. Since Tawada states in an endnote that the text the narrator is translating is Anne Duden's story "Der Wunde Punkt im Alphabet," it is tempting to think of this German work as "the original." But as many translation theorists have pointed out in recent years, "the original" can't really be said to exist. In a *taidan* with the writer Ikezawa Natsuki,[1] Tawada herself observed that, while language itself is already a translation of our amorphous, pre-linguistic thoughts, whether or not those unformed thoughts can then be called "the original" is a moot point. She then went on to suggest that perhaps it is the very act of translating our thoughts into language that makes it possible for us to conceive of an amorphous "original" that we are translating from.

But there's another reason why we can't call Duden's story "the original." "Der Wunde Punkt im Alphabet" is actually only one of a very long series of

35

translations of the legend of St. George the Dragon-Slayer. As we shall see, Duden's version differs from those of her predecessors in that the dragon, rather than St. George or the Princess he rescues, is the protagonist.

The narrator's translation of Duden's story unfolds passage by passage as a text-within-the-text. The translation, however, is a very different text from the one in which it is embedded. It is, in fact, a sort of translation I myself have always been tempted to try, but would never have the courage to hand over to an editor. The first passage, which is also the opening passage of *The Wound in the Alphabet*, reads as follows:

> in, approximately, ninety percent, of the victims, almost all, always, on the ground, lying, shown as, desperately raising, heads, on display, are, attack-weapons, or, the points of, in their throats, stuck, or²

This is clearly not a reader-friendly translation. Although the narrator has been repeatedly advised by her friend Ei, once a professional translator who is now writing novels, to "reread the whole manuscript several times from the reader's point of view," she finds this advice impossible to follow. "I could never step into anyone else's shoes," she protests. Throughout *The Wound in the Alphabet*, Ei, the successful translator who blithely observes that "Translators don't count as artists," serves as a foil for the narrator, who doggedly persists in her task despite never having received either praise or money in return. We can assume that for Ei, who translates for the market, translation is a matter of transmitting information. The following quotation from Walter Benjamin's famous essay "The Task of the Translator," however, leaves the impression that he would have much preferred the narrator's attitude to Ei's:

> any translation which intends to perform a transmitting function cannot transmit anything but information—hence, something inessential. This is the hallmark of bad translations.³

Benjamin goes on to observe (again in Harry Zohn's translation) that "A literal rendering of the syntax completely demolishes the theory of reproduction of meaning and is a direct threat to comprehensibility."⁴ Although he is actually referring to Hölderlin's translations of Sophocles, which "the nineteenth century considered . . . as monstrous examples of such literalness,"⁵ he could just as easily have had the narrator's translation in mind. She indeed literally renders the German syntax, breaking Duden's sentences, which are the repositories of meaning, into fragments which readers are left to reassemble on their own. We might even say that the narrator's aim as a translator is to free individual words and phrases from the restrictions of the sentence, to give them a life of their own.

"Fragments," of course, is a key word in Benjamin's essay. "The Task of the Translator," he tells us, is to make "both the original and the translation recognizable as fragments of a greater language, just as fragments are part of a vessel."⁶ The image of words as fragments of a broken vessel to be lovingly fitted together is surely one of the most beautiful ever to be associated with translation. Yet for translators like myself, Benjamin is a constant source of both wonder and frustration. How, exactly, does one go about "making both the original and the translation recognizable as fragments of a greater language, just as fragments are part of a vessel"? Tawada's narrator seems to be trying to do just that, and her radical experiment is nothing short of inspiring. Taking her lead, I will now present to the readers of this essay two translations from the main text of *The Wound in the Alphabet*. The first I would be willing to show to an interested editor, while the second is the same passage translated in the manner of the narrator:

> Dark cacti protruded sporadically from the sandy slope stretching out before me for a distance that might have been long or short, I couldn't tell which, before being swallowed up by ominous waves of banana trees with the sea beyond although there was no visible boundary to show where water turned into sky. The sea doesn't ascend and gradually become sky nor are sea and sky like two countries that meet at the border; in fact, they exist entirely independently of one another so it's strange to regard them as two colors side by side, like in a landscape painting.

Now for the one I will probably never show to any editor:

> Darkened, cacti, rising, sticking out, sand-colored, slope, to what degree, even if asked, cannot answer, near-like, far-like, that sort of, distance, about, continues, presently, banana grove's, ominous, waves, inside, is absorbed, that, beyond, ocean, is seen, but, that ocean, from where, sky, becomes, boundary-like, thing, at all, cannot be seen, sea, rise up, little by little, sky, into, transform, the case, is not, sea, and, sky, two, countries, as if, country border, come into contact, the case, is not, sea, and sky, mutually, not at all, touching, without existing, so, both, one, landscape painting, within, neighboring, two, areas of color, to see, is strange.

In the first of these two passages, we see the narrator taking in the strangeness of the scene before her, deconstructing the conventional way of looking at scenery that centuries of landscape painting have taught us. Or we might say that, true to her calling, she is translating the scene into words. In Tawada's Japanese, these two sentences contain no punctuation, so the reader is forced to absorb them in a single breath, so to speak. When these long flowing sentences are broken into fragments, however, the syntax that kept the words in order disappears, and they are free to do their own dance. With linear significance gone, the reader is left with sound—the alliteration of "sticking out, sand-colored, slope" in the first line, for instance, and repetitions such as "near-like, far-like" and "the case, is not," which give the passage its own peculiar rhythm. Are these unfettered words the "pure language" that Benjamin says must be liberated in translation? To tell the truth, I don't really know. They do, however, seem to be trying to go back to being poetry, in which sound and rhythm take precedence over linear significance. In his book *The Art of Translating Prose*, Burton Raffel states that "Every human culture of which we have any record, whether it be living or dead, has developed poetry. . . . Not all human cultures, however, develop prose."[7] If what Raffel says is true—that poetry, with its strong link to oral expression, always precedes prose, which comes into being only after a culture has developed a system for writing its language—then it would seem that once they are released from the prison of prose, words seek to return to their original poetic state.

Part Two: Translating the Dragon

Let us return to the narrator's translation. The "victims" that appear in the passage I quoted earlier (the narrator later changes this word to "sacrifices") are the dragons slain by St. George. The word for them in the German text is "Opfer," and the *O*'s scattered over the page she is translating are a source of anxiety for the narrator, for they seem to be holes backed by a white wall (the white page), which she cannot break through. Only when she has blackened the insides of all the *O*'s with her fountain pen does she feel "a slight sense of relief."

These troublesome *O*'s can be interpreted in a number of ways. One possibility is that in blackening the insides of the *O*'s with her fountain pen, the narrator has turned the holes backed with a white wall into tunnels. Speaking of tunnels, Tawada's story "The Gotthard Railway" contains a memorable scene in which the narrator, after emerging from the Gotthard Tunnel, becomes very excited when she discovers the tunnel's twin exits inscribed in the surrounding place names, each of which has two *O*'s—Lavorgo, Bodio, Como, and Locarno. "The exit wanted to turn into an entrance,"[8] says the narrator of "The Gotthard Railway." In *The Wound in the Alphabet*, the holes-turned-into-tunnels provide an entrance into a foreign language. Through it, the narrator can pass each word over to "the other side." And since *Übersetzen*, the German word for "translation," contains the meaning "to pass something over to the other side," this also means that the tunnels have made translation possible. We should note once again here that the narrator's method of translation is to forget about sentences, or the text as a whole, and concentrate on carefully passing each word over to "the other side."

Yet these *O*'s might also be "wounds in the alphabet" that the narrator has literally dug out with the tip of her fountain pen. We should remember here that *kizu*, the Japanese word for "wound," can also be written with a character that means "creation." In other words, in Japanese, "wounds" and "creation" are connected through the common pronunciation of the word *kizu*. If writing can be said to begin with "creating wounds" in language, then translation is the process of inscribing those wounds in a foreign language. When the German *wunde* is translated into the Japanese *kizu*, the character for "creation" appears alongside the one for "wound," thus giving the word an additional layer of meaning that was absent from the original. In this way, translation can indeed create new possibilities.

But then again the *O*'s can perhaps also be the wide-open mouths of dragons, howling in pain. Looking back and forth between the detail from the painting St. George and the Dragon by Paolo Uccello, which is used as an illustration to Duden's text,[9] and the page of German text covered with *O*'s, one gets the impression that the *O*'s are actually the mouths of the dragons sacrificed to St. George, inscribed in the German text. When freed from its role as the first letter of the German word "Opfer," the letter *O* can transform itself into a part of the creature that word refers to.

But of course there is more to the dragon than a wide-open mouth. In fact, the fragmented style of the narrator's translation is well suited to the subject of the story, for the dragon himself is a collection of fragments. (Since there are also female dragons, there may be some question as to the appropriateness of the pronoun "he." This is a problem I will return to later.) This is what the translation has to say about the dragon:

> he, for example, has, the claws of a wild cat, the fur of a bear, the skull of a crocodile, the tongue of a snake, the skin of a lizard, the tail of an American alligator, he, has, huge, bat wings, movable, armor of an armadillo, and, sometimes, also, three eyelids, a nictitating membrane, exactly, like a dog's

Although his body is a catalogue of characteristics from a wide variety of animal species, the dragon himself belongs to none of them. He is everywhere—in the air, on the earth, in the sea—and yet belongs nowhere. To human beings, who have sought to bring order to the natural world by classifying animals and plants into orders and species, the dragon is a most unnatural trespasser, an eternal outsider. But this is not his worst crime. He has violated another taboo that is sacred to humanity:

> not at all, attempting to hide, his anus, above all, testicles, overripe, between his hind legs, sticking out, at the same time, possessing, on the same body, occasionally, in addition, breasts, or, several, pointed, protruding, or, wantonly, hanging down, nipples, never before heard of scandal, is, this leviathan

As an occasional hermaphrodite, the dragon has broken the gender taboo, and for this humanity will never forgive him. It is here that the narrator is faced with an obstacle to "translating the dragon": namely, what pronoun does one use to refer to a creature of undetermined gender? "He" is certainly not appropriate for a creature with breasts. The narrator goes through her manuscript, crossing out *kare*, the Japanese word for "he." But when memories of an older and more versatile *kare* come back to her, she decides that perhaps it was the right choice after all: "I seemed to remember that the Chinese character for 'he' doesn't only refer to a man but can also mean 'the other side.' The other side as a living thing called 'he.'"

As violator of all our most sacred taboos, the dragon is in eternal opposition to human society, and in this sense, he is truly a creature of "the other side." The Japanese pronoun *kare*, in its narrow, modern sense, is not sufficient to express his radical, alien qualities. But the word *kare* could originally refer to both things and people, and until early in the twentieth century was used to refer to both men and women. The character used to write it is also found in words like *kanata*, a loosely defined, far away place, and *higan*, "the other side." Sometime during the nineteenth century, it was assigned the role of acting as an equivalent to the Western masculine pronoun. We might say that this role was forced on it like an ill-fitting suit of clothes, for as the translation scholar Yanabu Akira points out, the word *kare* still does not function in exactly the same way as the English pronoun "he." When a Japanese girl talks about her *kare*, for instance, she means her boyfriend. (Monica Lewinski once referred to Bill Clinton as "the big He," but this can hardly be called conventional English usage.) A Japanese colleague once told me that when she started studying English as a junior high school student during the mid-1950s, she felt uncomfortable—embarrassed even—when her teacher forced her to translate the English pronoun "he" as *kare* every time it appeared in her English text book. Now that the fact that *kare* is a relatively new word, created as a translation of "he," has receded into the oblivion of memory, however, many Japanese probably continue to feel uncomfortable about this usage of the word without really understanding why. And when we lose our awareness of words, they are, in a sense, dead. By pointing to a premodern usage of the character for *kare* in words like *kanata* or *higan*—the other side—Tawada has brought the modern pronoun back to life, transforming it into a word that is far more suitable to express the alien character of the dragon.

My problem in translating this passage into English is that, as far as I can see, I have no alternative but to translate *kare* back into "he." I can tell English readers that the Chinese character for "he" can also mean "the other side" (wincing as I remember what Benjamin said about translations that transmit information). But I cannot give them that "shock of recognition" that Japanese readers must have when that awkward, moribund pronoun *kare* takes on new life as "the other side."

Part Three: The Dragon Comes Back to Life

In museums and in public squares all over Europe, the dragon continues to be slain by St. George, over and over again. Perhaps his greatest tragedy is that his destruction has blended so perfectly into the European landscape that people no longer see it:

> wherever, people go, wherever, arrive, sacrifices, always, already, there, it is,
> so natural-seeming, there to be, like a monument, like a well, like a sidewalk or
> traffic light, therefore, in the same way, naturally, overlooked, passed over

One of the purposes of Anne Duden's story "Der wunde Punkt im Alphabet" is to make the dragon visible once again by making him the protagonist of the legend of St. George.

As we have seen, the dragon must be slain because he is a threat to the natural order established by human beings—in short, because he is so very "unnatural." Yet one of the reasons for establishing a "natural order" is so that human beings can exploit nature, using it to their own advantage. Once the dragon is safely dead, his body lies waiting to be harvested like the rest of the natural world:

this, monster from, even, things to be harvested, must have been, for example,
to shear, like sheep, to milk, colorful, feathers, one by one, to pluck out, a hide,
to tear off, over the ears, in one piece, and then, eggs, to take, to fry, to boil, to
freeze, to use, to make aphrodisiac

When we begin to see the dragon, he in turn shows us the contradictions in humanity's view of nature. Slain so that the natural order will be preserved, he then
becomes a part of the natural world that human beings seek to exploit.

Like the dead dragon, stripped of his hide, his feathers, his milk, his eggs—
everything that human beings can use—the land of the Canary Islands where the
narrator is translating his story lies barren and desiccated. Because all the mois-
ture has been pumped from underground to water the banana grove, rivers no
longer flow and the air is extremely dry. But bananas are the island's only ex-
port, and therefore its sole source of foreign currency, most of which is used to
buy pesticides for the banana grove. The sole beneficiaries of this strange "trade
balance" are the developed countries that buy bananas from the islanders and
sell them pesticides in return. Yet the islanders, who have been seduced into
believing that they depend on the banana grove for their livelihood, fail to see
the absurdity of their situation. They insist that it is not the banana grove that has
desiccated their land, but a mysterious weather phenomenon they call the
"dragon wind." The narrator learns from a shop attendant on the island that the
"dragon wind" is "like an electric hair drier blowing on you all day. Just awful.
Your hair starts to fall out and your face gets so dry the skin peels off in flakes."

The "dragon wind" can perhaps be seen as an incarnation of the legendary
dragon, murdered countless times by St. George, now come back to life to tor-
ment the islanders. Or perhaps this new dragon is nature itself, taking vengeance
on the islanders for having sacrificed their natural environment to the banana
grove, in order to support a global trade balance that benefits them not at all.
This possibility never occurs to the islanders, who view the trade balance as a
new kind of "natural order" on which their lives depend, and which therefore
must be defended at all costs. Blind to the fact that their troubles are rooted in
their reliance on the developed countries, they intend to rely on them once again.
The local fishmonger admonishes the narrator: "That's nonsense, saying it's
because of the banana grove. . . . It's the dragon wind dries things out," before
informing her that engineers from "up north" will soon build a huge seawall to
protect them from it.

If, as I have suggested, the ominous "dragon wind" is the dragon of the legend, come back to life in the Canary Islands, then surely St. George cannot be
far behind. In the next section, let us watch as the text the narrator is translating
invades her life.

Part Four: The Translator's Choices: St. George, the
Princess, and the Unfinished Text

From the very beginning of *The Wound in the Alphabet*, the narrator is dreading
the immanent appearance of someone named George, whom we later find out is

indeed the legendary dragon-slayer. With his arrival, the tenuous boundary between the narrator's life and the text she is translating collapses. Before the text completely invades the narrator's life, however, let us see what it has to say about the two remaining characters, St. George and the Princess he rescues from the dragon.

Unlike the hermaphrodite dragon, St. George is generally viewed as a figure of purely masculine power, the proverbial "knight in shining armor." But no one has ever seen what's behind the armor. The narrator's translation offers a portrait that is very different from the legendary hero:

> the attacker, eternally, will live, the attacker, how, commonplace, flavorless, is, only, he himself, still, does not know, that, merely a plume, metallic, only the outer covering, under that armor, just like type cases, drawers, many, are hidden, perhaps, and the helmet, the cheek guard, behind, probably, a pale weak face, is

Supported by god and the angels, who always assure him of victory, St. George is actually a cowardly man, hiding behind a protective layer of metal. And what of the Princess?

> the Princess, somewhere, safe, at a distance, the Soldier of God, in back of, the battle, shyly, with admiration, is watching, not qualified to speak, politely, with downcast eyes, only, can wait, and, to everything, devoutly, hoping, for her, the armor-clad man, on him, in attendance, for her, the savior, to her protector, to the master of her sex, does not forget her gratitude, so that, the monster, will go to hell, can only hope, that

Immediately after translating this passage, the narrator confesses that she has never found young women very attractive: their pale, washed-out faces are so full of distress that they look like "sacrifices." The narrator is clearly associating the young women she sees around her with the figure of the Princess she has just translated. But we should take special note here of the word "sacrifices," for this is also the word that the narrator finally settled on as a translation for the German word "Opfer," which refers to the dragon. Thus the word "sacrifice" forms a link between the Princess and the dragon, preparing us for the passage which follows in the translation:

> inside, shut away, Virginal, Princess, of life, from one stage, another, stage to, shrinks, but, almost, hidden, and, in a trance, seemingly, at all costs, she, to something, fast, wants to hold on, seems to, and, to the dragon, namely, is holding, little by little, to his own death advances, the dragon, groaning, stocking, or, belt, is, of that cord, one end, of the dragon, neck, is wrapped around, the other, end, is holding, she, with both hands, both hands, to the same cord, are holding on, by that cord, she, the dragon, or, the dragon, her, to the city, will take, will be taken, in the city, with one stroke, will lose his head, and, she, will be baptized

According to legend, St. George tied the Princess's garter around the dragon's neck, whereupon the monster followed her to the city as meekly as a lamb. But by juxtaposing the active and passive forms of the verb "take," the fragmented style of narrator's translation makes it difficult to tell who is leading whom. The Princess will not lose her head, but the translation leaves us with the impression that baptism is a similar fate, a necessary preparation for the Princess's final sacrifice to St. George.

Fortunately, the narrator herself is not sacrificed to St. George. When she is on her way to the post office with the manuscript of her finished translation, she meets not one but four St. Georges, and manages to escape from all of them. While running away from the last St. George, however, she loses her manuscript and picks up a piece of old carpet instead—an exchange that perhaps mirrors the absurdity of trading bananas for pesticide. The loss of a seemingly essential text is a motif that can also be found, for instance, in the story "Missing Heels," but here it would seem that once the translator has entered the world of the text she has translated, the text itself is no longer necessary. Having lost the completed translation, however, the narrator finds herself trapped in a story to which there can be no real conclusion. As a translator, however, this narrator always had a certain horror of completion. In her own words (mine, actually), she is "afraid of reaching the point of no return, of being forced into making unjust decisions." On a purely practical level, this is a fear that most translators can sympathize with. The fact that the Japanese word for "perfect" also means "complete" has interesting implications for translation—since a translation can never be perfect it is impossible, perhaps, to complete it in any true sense.

On a different level, however, this comment refers to the translator's inevitable participation in the story she is translating. No matter how strenuously she may claim to be "only the translator," the narrator cannot avoid joining the long line of the dragon's creator and destroyers, for it is her words that will retell his story.

By losing the manuscript of her translation and entering the world of the text, the narrator escapes the horror of completion. In doing so, we might say that she herself is enacting the open-ended, on-going process of translation. The story ends as she runs toward the sea, wondering—as she did in the opening scene—whether it is far or near. And where will she go? Probably into another text, another translation, for it is within the text that writers and translators truly exist.

Notes

1. This *taidan*, or public conversation, was held to commemorate Tawada's having been awarded the Deux Magots Literary Prize, sponsored by the Deux Magots Café in Shibuya, Tokyo. It was published in the June, 2003 issue of the magazine *Subaru*, pp. 146-155.

2. All quotations from *The Wound in the Alphabet* are from my own unpublished translation.

3. Walter Benjamin, "The Task of the Translator," in *Illuminations*, trans. Harry Zohn, (New York: Shocken Books, 1969), 69.
4. Benjamin, "The Task of the Translator," 78.
5. Benjamin, "The Task of the Translator," 78.
6. Benjamin, "The Task of the Translator," 78.
7. Burton Raffel, *The Art of Translating Prose* (University Park, Penn.: The Pennsylvania University Press, 1994), 7.
8. Yōko Tawada, "The Gotthard Railway," in *The Bridegroom Was a Dog*, trans. Margaret Mitsutani (Tokyo, London, New York: Kodansha International, 1998), 154.
9. See Anne Duden, *Der wunde Punkt im Alphabet* (Hamburg: Rotbuch Verlag, 1995). A detail from Paolo Uccello's "St. Georg und der Drache" and Friedrich Herlin's "Der heilige Georg als Drachentöter" appear as illustrations to the title story.

Bibliography

Benjamin, Walter. "The Task of the Translator." In *Illuminations*, trans. Harry Zohn. New York: Shocken Books, 1969.
Raffel, Burton. *The Art of Translating Prose*. University Park, Penn.: The Pennsylvania University Press, 1994.
Tawada, Yoko. "The Gotthard Railway," In *The Bridegroom Was a Dog*, trans. Margaret Mitsutani. New York: Kodansha International, 1998.
———. *Arufabetto no kizuguchi*. Tokyo: Kawade Shobo Shinsa, 1993.
Tawada, Yōko, with Ikezawa Natsuki. "Taidan: Sakka no shisen, kotoba no omowaku." *Subaru* (June 2003): 146-155.

Chapter Five
Writing in the Ravine of Language
Doug Slaymaker

> Only in one's mother tongue can one express one's own truth;
> in a foreign language the poet lies.
> —Paul Celan[1]

Japan wafts through Tawada Yōko's writing like a memory, and "Japanese-ness"[2] haunts at the edges of her tales. "Japan" (both as nation and cultural imaginary) hovers dream-like at the margins of her work, but Japan is more than an apparition; it forms an important reference point in the peripheral vision of the characters, a touchstone, a landmark, for navigating their travels. A tenuous relationship with a country of origin, subtle acts of sparring with cultural traditions, and the choosing exhibited in Tawada's writings align with increasingly common experiences in an age of migrations and in a time of remembered and chosen traditions. This essay is an exploration of those negotiations and migrations via interactions with history, language, and memory.

Tawada writes in Japanese and German. Much of her fiction represents travel and the space between cultures; many of her essays articulate experience in the space between those two languages (and by extension, cultures). Tawada's tales are organized by migrations and traveling, by language and loss, cultural practice and memory; the resultant gaps, gullies, and the self-serving misrememberings give her work their landscape, a terrain that extends beyond national boundaries in the face of globalizing cultures. Foregrounded in that exploration are the nature of language, the constitution of subjectivity, and the markers of identity; they all play out on the unstable terrain across which the characters travel. These themes are particularly prominent in her 2002 novel *The Fugitive's Night-Time Railway*, which will be my focus here.

The interplay between remembered pasts and lived presents locates one of the more striking thematic nodes of her work; by invoking ancient tales of co-habitation with animals in *The Bridegroom was a Dog*,[3] for example, she presents a version of a postmodern, globalized, modernity (in the senses used by Arjun Appadurai and Salman Rushdie). One of the many attractions of a work like *The Bridegroom was a Dog* is the masterful interplay between the recounted traditional tales and their placement in contemporary settings. These tales have

45

the ring and the timbre of actual folktales and come complete with variants recounted with an anthropologist's cataloguing completeness. Yet they are as spu-
rious, self-serving and, likely, as false and misremembered as anything spouted
off by Salman Rushdie's Saleem Sinai, for example.[4] Culture and memory, with
myth and imagination, form the glue binding the novel's elements. Interplay
between past and present is represented through migration and travel; the characters straddle various worlds, with one foot in a particular cultural tradition (a
remembered past) and the other foot in the (also mediated) present. The narrators in many of Tawada's stories are, apparently, from the region traditionally
referred to as "Japan," yet they exist in a contemporary "place" without concrete
referent; it could be any of a number of cities, or perhaps none. Either way, the
place is mediated, remembered, and imagined.

For example, the novel-length *The Fugitive's Night-Time Railway* is organized into chapters named after cities visited by an unnamed narrator (for example, "To Beijing," "To Paris," and the last chapter, "To a town that is nowhere"
[*dokodemonai machi*]), but these places rarely figure as more than a nondescript
street or train station. The named place does not host the activity narrated there.
Likewise, in the novella "Persona" Michiko's experience of navigating a single
German city (Hamburg) takes her to numerous ethnic enclaves within that city.
The walk develops into a journey through different countries and cultures; she
travels on foot through Hamburg but the cacophony resembles a round-the-
world flight with embarkations at cities across the globe. These movements are
an organizing principle in the fiction and I will focus on the moving between,
across, over, and through, by also looking closely at the choosings, remember-
ings, and reconstructings that accompany these trips.

Maps, passports, and bureaucracies demand fixity and are troubled by mobility. In Tawada's writing language becomes a place, a geography, the web that
envelops one. The codes of verbal representation that contain us form our
homes; these places, not on any map, supply the contours and borders that matter. Our languages contain us, not us them. As Tawada writes:

> We refer to a "single language" but no language is single. I feel this more
> strongly all the time. I have no special interest in writers who do nothing more
> than write in multiple languages. One does not have to leave the mother lan-
> guage because multiple languages can be constructed within the mother lan-
> guage. "Within" and "outside" become gradually less meaningful.[5]

Paul Celan's poetry is an especially powerful component in Tawada's thinking
about these places and it informs her understanding of how it is that "inside" and
"outside" lose their meaning. Celan's experience gives shape to her conceptualization of a new geography.

By way of example, her short-term residence at an artist's colony in California in 1997 led Tawada to ruminate on Thomas Mann's residence at the same
place half a century earlier; she has to wonder why there is no mention of California in his writing. How could he have lived in this place, looked out this same
window, heard this language, and not left a trace of it in his writing? she asks.

Celan, in contrast, who (like Mann) wrote solely in German, lived his last years in Paris. Even so, according to Tawada, Celan's "single language for writing" is shot through with elements from other languages. Celan insisted that he could write poetry in but one language, and chose to do so in his native language, his mother tongue, a language with which he had a very complicated relationship: German was the language of his parents and those parents perished in German work camps; he chose to write "in a mother tongue that had suddenly turned into his mother's murderers' tongue."[6] Having been born a Romanian citizen, and later becoming a naturalized French one, "Celan scarcely ever inhabited a country whose official language was German."[7] He was gifted with languages but focused on one; even so, these various languages existed simultaneously in his imagination and their traces are evident in his writing. Tawada finds in this an example of how to live in the ravine that separates language: "For in his German is contained French and Russian. They are not contained there as foreign language elements, but form a base of poetic insights, where all these languages are intertwined into a web."[8] Indeed, he incorporates these other languages not only as words and phrases, but draws visual and aural elements from them into his poetry. She goes on to note that this conception of poetry that brings various strands of language into a single item resonates with Benjamin's conception of the work of translation. The point being that although Celan insisted on working in a single language, German, that language had, in his experience as a foreign-born Jew, been subjected to harsh crossings and amorphous arbitrary borders; further, that single language web included and evidenced many others. Thus, the Exophony that Tawada articulates is not, as noted above, as simple as mastering one or another language, nor as facile as writing in more than one language. Celan and Mann provide two contrasting examples: the webby net containing German is porous, she suggests, as it was for Celan, not impervious as it was for Mann (whose experience of American English has no apparent influence in his writing).[9]

Language as an enveloping web, full of holes, containing and constricting, is a powerful image in Tawada's writing. It may appear diaphanous, but its pull is steely when one pushes against it. Languages recur as magical wizard's webs, as witchy nets (*mahō no ami*), whose sometimes suffocating constriction can only be loosened with other words that have magical power to break the grip of the threads.[10] Thus, for example, Kazuko, of "In Front of Trang Tien Bridge,"[11] has descended into the Cu Chi tunnels of Saigon and feels the walls of those narrow tunnels moving in on her:

A dampness that was neither the tunnel wall nor her own skin clung to her like a fishnet and she could no longer move. It was cold and numbness, a sense of loathing about to explode; it was her mistrust of everything around her. This clammy web she was caught in could not be real; if she chanted some magic spell surely it would disappear. But nothing came to mind. Not even "dark." She was not trapped, she would eventually get out, she could go back as well as forward, she was not going to suffocate, she could not possibly die here. None of these reassurances had any effect. And then, by a route as yet unknown to Kazuko came two words: "all right." ALL RIGHT. They were suddenly on her

tongue then reached out to envelop her shoulders and belly until her whole
body was covered and the fishnet melted and disappeared.

Language encloses one like a fishnet, but its spell is broken by the right word in
the right language. In wafts the Japanese word *daijōbu*: "everything is alright, all
is in good order," no need to fear. A powerful word destroys the spell, it loosens
the bindings.

Language also has the totemic power to establish one's place in the world,
to root one's experience. A sentence and its (apparent) translation anchor an
important moment of self-knowledge in *The Fugitive's Night-Time Railway*, for
example. Near the conclusion of this tale, the narrator is in a cheap Bombay
hotel. Averting her eyes from what appears to be insects on the wall, she sees
ball-pen scribbling beside the bed. In English was written "This hotel is great."
Directly below it, in what would appear to be a translation, but conveying a
message entirely different, were Japanese phrases: "The owner of this hotel will
come asking if you wouldn't like to buy a good camera for cheap; you should
not buy it."[12] This is no small discrepancy in apparently parallel passages. "On
that day, you laughed for the first time," the narrative continues. The gap, the
ravine, that opens between two linguistic passages elicits laughter from the heretofore stoic main character. The absurdity of such gaps in languages have
plagued her throughout the work, but she can no longer contain them and the
reaction rumbles forth in a guffaw. It seems that those who can navigate such
linguistic and cultural shoals come upon the "truth" of the situation; surely the
Japanese phrasing carries more "reality" than the English phrasing: all is not to
be trusted in this place. The foreign language that marks the weak outside status
of the traveler becomes here the conduit for knowledge and agency. The world
is distressing, parallel lines do not align, but laughter erupts in this space between imaginary geographies.

Can one live in the fissures between languages without absurd laughter,
without positing an alliance with one side or the other? There are many pressures to posit an alliance, these are the pressures that are routinely resisted in
Tawada's work. "I am often asked," Tawada writes in *Exophony*,

> what language do you dream in? It is a question that gets to me every time. The
> question suggests to me an implicit assumption: "If a person speaks more than
> one language then their true nature cannot be known. One may be the truth, but
> the other must then be false." [13]

Her frustration and anger is directed towards the implicit assumptions that there
is a "true" and "basic" subjectivity, that the individual is one, and that one can
only truly inhabit a single language. "Is Tawada Yōko a Japanese or a German
writer?" is a question posed with almost equal frequency. The concern about
language and a perceived tie to a stable, nation-based, language-rooted identity
is reflected in these questions. While the series of questions that Tawada raises
here tie directly to myriad, related assumptions about moorings for the subconscious, and about dreaming and the non-rational, un-willed mind, Tawada is, in
this passage, looking hardest at the desire to tie rootedness to language. Stated

another way, an important component of my argument is not only to note the mistake in insisting that Tawada is a Japanese (or German) author, but to underscore how misdirected (precisely because so "commonsensical") are such desires.

Tawada chafes at the assumption that there must be a unity between a language—Japanese or German—and identity. Questioners seem to want to align the internal language—the language of dreams, of creativity, the subconscious/unconscious—with an actual stable identity, to align the internal processes with the external manifestation in language. She suggests that her Japanese interlocutors want to be assured that although she speaks and writes in German, in her soul, in "truth," she is (still, nonetheless) Japanese. Tawada asserts that if such a thing as an "actual self" (*hontō no jibun*) exists, then that is the self that speaks/thinks/dreams in multiple languages. It could not be otherwise, for one person does not equal one language, one person speaks/knows/feels multiple languages, although that capacity is usually driven underground. To state this point another way, the insistence on a single, stable identity denies the messy complexity that constitutes the individual subject who is not, in the end, comprised of pure categories, but of multiple minds and positions. All the pejoratives such as cacophony, babble (and Babel, the Tower of), both sides of the mouth, etc., miss the point entirely. The assumption that one has a single language in identity is misguided, she suggests, for the true self (again, should such a thing exist) speaks in many voices. Tawada's fiction and her essays underscore this basic point: no such thing as a stable individual/subject exists. Think of dreams, she suggests.

She takes much from Freud's suggestion that dreams are a translation without an original.[14] This trope is reflected in the essay included in this volume, where she puts her name and work into a scenario that imagines the implications of this. Not only does this tale suggest that Tawada the author may not exist, but the "proof" of that contention is that an author by that name has been assigned to writings in numerous languages, for which no original can be found. She reminds us with wit and tenacity that the existence of a writer named Tawada Yōko is a fiction in ways parallel to dreams—stubborn and insistent in the material manifestations, entirely "real" even if one cannot point to the reality, the concreteness, of their source: a "translation without an original," to borrow from Freud.

The characters in her fiction consistently resist markers of identity such as language. Are her characters Japanese? The Japanese stories are written in Japanese, for example, which suggests its place in that lineage. Many of the characters in her fiction seem Japanese in that they are not denying or fleeing their national identity, even though such identity introduces conundrums and confusions. Characters seem comfortable reading Japanese, or thinking in Japanese, for example, which is a very powerful marker of nationality in Japanese reading practice. (The incident in the Bombay hotel, for example, in *The Fugitive's Night-Time Railway*, of which I have more to say below, suggests such an identity.) Yet national origins often become confused: the character identified as "American" in "At the Foot of Trang Tien Bridge" speaks Japanese, for example, and anxieties about "Japaneseness" plague the main character, Minamiyama Kazuko, throughout her travels to Vietnam. Kazuko has received an alluring letter from Vietnam inviting her to visit. Kazuko, a Japanese woman in Berlin, flies to Vietnam, but this perpetual traveler is haunted by the condition of travel: being a tourist is one of Kazuko's great anxieties, and her peripatetic nature is immediately tied to anxieties about homelands and ethnic, national identities. "I'm a member of the tourist race," she says to herself, and then finds herself at the visa office explaining her need for a visa:

> She had to get to Vietnam. When she asked, "Can you get me a visa?" the travel agent adjusted his glasses and inquired cautiously "Do you need one?" He's mistaken me for a Vietnamese going home for a visit, Kazuko thought, but couldn't quite bring herself to say, "Yes, because I'm Japanese." How could she claim to be Japanese when she wasn't wearing a single piece of jewelry or even carrying a brand-name handbag she asked herself, and nearly burst out laughing.

What marks the native or non-native? Can she be "Japanese" if she doesn't look like one? Kazuko is often mistaken for a Vietnamese, or, at least, she is consistently anxious about being mistaken for one. And, as suggested here, these markers of identity are not as simple as language and body type, but also the practices of conspicuous consumption and the relationship to a robust national economy. Not until a visit to the Cu Chi tunnels, however, does she feel the conclusive physical reasons for that difference: "The reason why the passageways are so narrow in places," explains the guide, "was so the Americans, whose bodies are shaped differently from ours, wouldn't be able to crawl through." But Kazuko, while "also" Asian, does not fit into the tunnels either. She is seized with a claustrophobic sense that her body was dissolving while in the tunnel, enveloped in a mesh, as I have noted. This crisis of body in space convinces her of her difference, for if her body is not appropriate for these tunnels she cannot, thereby, "be Vietnamese": "Comparing the flesh on her belly and hips to the soldier's sinewy body, Kazuko realized it had become impossible to claim that she looked Vietnamese."[15]

Hers is not the only body that does not accord with physical and linguistic markers. Kazuko meets up with an American, James, who speaks Japanese, and begins to travel with him:

> "How come you speak Japanese?" The words were out before she could stop them. She had more interesting questions in mind for him, but out of fear or just plain laziness, this is the one she ended up asking. "Because I'm Japanese," he answered gravely. "And how did that happen?" she countered, a bit put out, but James, sipping his shellfish soup, calmly threw the query back at her. "What about you? How did you become Japanese?"

The question is left at that, unresolved, for the marker of nationality is as indeterminate at the end of the tale as at the beginning. And these identities gradually dissolve until it is no longer possible to determine who is real and who is not, for James is a shade, and Kazuko finds herself on the bus, in Vietnam, and all the passengers look like her:

> "So now I've finally come home," Kazuko announced in a voice loud enough for all to hear. The woman in front of her turned around and scolded, "You're Japanese and you know it. So just keep quiet." Kazuko was about to fire back, "And what are you, then?" when she gasped in surprise, for she was looking into her own face.

Perhaps, the imagery suggests, if there is no grouping of characteristics by which we can determine who is Vietnamese, who Japanese, who American, then it may be equally likely that we all look the same.[16]

To the end, it remains unclear where the source of identity lies, or even why it is such an obsessive concern. These spirits and ghosts arise out of the mist of history, where cultures and languages meet and join, where tales of origin and purpose are constructed, where national narratives of war and retribution play large, as myth. Appadurai suggests, referencing the magical realism of the writer Julio Cortázar, that "like the myths of small-scale society as rendered in the anthropological classics of the past, contemporary literary fantasies tell us something about displacement, disorientation, and agency in the contemporary world."[17] Such contemporary fantasies, Tawada's among them, are sort-of-real, almost-conceivable tales that ring true to contemporary experience the way that older myths—those catalogued in *The Bridegroom was a Dog* for example—seemed, in an earlier age, factual in their explanations of the world. In short, these tales of displacement work as contemporary myths. Many of Tawada's tales, for example the re-working of tales from the *Kojiki* and from Ovid, limn the contours of myth. These tales contribute to the group of stories that help us make sense of the world. They do so at multiple levels. They describe the experience of living between cultures, distilling the disorientation that accompanies travel and migration, forced and voluntary, familial and single, across languages, borders, time, and space, as discussed by Appadurai and Seyhan. They also ring true to the experience that accompanies the first-time acclimation to a new language and culture, a surreal off-kilter flanerie, seemingly without heels and with only half an ear (to borrow imagery from Tawada's "Missing Heels"[18]). As Appadurai suggests, this sort of "imagination" is the "constitutive feature of modern subjectivity"[19] where the speed of imagery gives us, every day, the sensory overload that was once (perhaps) solely the province of cross-cultural encounters. This marks one level where these stories assert their imaginative power as myths, proving to be as much about the swells and shoals of living in another language as about the reality of "modern subjects" in a stimulus-saturated present.

Imagination and memory are central in this because the artifacts that the exile and immigrant carry to new places gain substance as memory. And this leads to a corollary, for articulations and expressions of those memories also constitute culture. Memories are insubstantial and the places remembered are insubstantial, another no-place, sometimes of the imagination, sometimes in reality, often outside bureaucratic categories. This activity of memory is central to nostalgic longing for places of the past; the characters in Tawada's stories come to embody, as they move through, the no-place of nostalgia and memory. The articulation of memory is, literally, what binds together *The Fugitive's Night-Time Railway*; the entire tale of traveling is a work of memory; we quickly find while reading it that the places being traveled to may or may not exist.

The existence or non-existence of the places does not impinge on the story. The act of travel, however (in contrast to places traveled to or arrived at), is central to the structure of the story that follows a traveler who meets travelers traveling. Ostensibly, location and identity are important: each chapter references a place and people of particular places—particular cultures, that is—each chapter, or story, bears the name of the place where one assumes the character is "off to," but no destination is ever reached. The chapters are, then, narratives of occurrences on the way to the city of the title, not about the city once the narrator has arrived; they are about the traveling, the people met, and the narratives spun in transit. Those cultures and identities are built on memories, the filling in of loss, of places and times not known. This particular narrative chronicles the reconstruction of an identity and an experience. That the entire work then turns on a disappearing passport is but a further instance of this logic. The non-linearity of this novel is consistent with Tawada's entire oeuvre and, should it need pointing out, with much postmodern fiction.

In *The Fugitive's Night-Time Railway*, travel is often exasperating, increasing the main character's confusion as simple trips are endlessly deferred, trains are cancelled, and signs changed; station attendants and conductors respond to questions inconclusively or with blank stares. Is this the experience of the foreigner, where everyone but me knows how to get where they need to go? Where only my questions garner insolence and unhelpful responses? Where the words sound right to my ears but the information received does not accord with that desired? Is this culture-shock, the on-rush of imagery and sensory overload? At one level, it is certainly these things, but the ramifications are much wider, as they tie to the increasing normalcy of exile and transience.

Place is not the only issue, for the characters may not exist either. They may be "actual" ghosts or fictional constructs. The phantasmagoric disconnect is heightened throughout *The Fugitive's Night-Time Railway* by the use of "Anata," the pronoun meaning "you," where one expects a character's name or a different pronoun such as "he" or "she" (*kare; kanojo*). By way of example, I translate a few lines from early in the book-length text:

> After a little time has passed, comforted by the rocking of the train, Anata/You fall(s) into sleep. On the other side of sleep, the sound of metal screeching on metal continues. A sleep shallow yet deep, somehow. Thus, when suddenly awoken by the conductor, I/You [an explicit pronoun is not in the Japanese] drop the bag of memories on the floor, and at that moment I/You [*jibun*] don't even know where I am/You are.[20]

Now, who is the Anata of this tale? Even as I argue that this fiction intentionally disrupts this sort of ontological certainty, I imagine I am not the only reader who finds (found) myself making this query while reading. "*Anata wa shibaraku suru to,*" the passage begins. "Anata" is the active character. So we must ask ourselves as we take our bearings at this introductory stage of the tale: Is "Anata" the name of the character? Are we, the readers, being addressed as though this tale is happening to us? Or are we, the readers, listening in as a narrator recounts the story to an unnamed protagonist? That is: Did Anata fall asleep here? Are we, the reader, being told that we fell asleep? Or are we listening in on someone else having their life recounted to them, that is, "Then you fell asleep"?

Like this sleep, a "sleep shallow yet deep, somehow"—*asai yō na, fukai yō na* "seemingly shallow, seemingly deep"—so are we, as readers, seeming to understand, seeming not to understand—*wakaruyō na, wakaranaiyō na.* There is some resolution of this problem at the end of the novel, but the sense for the reader is of another landscape in which we are without heels, unbalanced, unable to determine where the firm ground lies. The "terrain" of the text is unstable throughout.

Things change abruptly in the penultimate chapter, "To Bombay," which begins "anata wa oboete iru ka, inai ka?": "Anata, do you remember, or perhaps not." But the construction of the query includes the ambiguity and double entendre we encounter with the story of a porpoise in Tawada's essay included in the same volume: *iruka, inaika; inaika iruka*—"Are you there porpoise, or not? Are you a porpoise, or not?" Thus, this question could be a simple "do you remember, or not," yet could be, equally plausibly: "Do you remember this part of the story; are you even there?" The intended activity of the agent is in doubt, as is, indeed, the existence of that agent. This question, and the change of voice it represents, reorients everything in the narrative while its singsong phrases resonate across essays and stories (and time and memory, with this connection between childhood rhymes and adult experiences). With this query, lines are disentangled as we now envision a questioner and a queried.

Central to this final installment and the overlapping identities is the crisis of confused passports. The traveler, Anata, stays at a cheap hotel in Bombay (a hotel, you will remember, with graffiti and insects, on the wall). The hotel manager says he needs to hold her passport (gender identifications are also clarified here, but more of that in a moment) while she leaves for a day trip; Anata complies with this request. The passport is then returned at the end of the day's sightseeing. Because Anata keeps her passport in a flower-patterned cover, there is no concern when a similarly-patterned passport is received. It is only on the long train ride that night that Anata discovers that the picture inside the passport is of someone else. Another quandary: continue on to the distant destination of Bombay and the plane which will take Anata away from this tortured travel, or make the now time-consuming return to the hotel and try to retrieve the original passport that is surely gone by now. These quandaries and confusions are consistent with the instability of existence and identity on which the narratives revolve. Given the degree to which this work and this oeuvre are obsessed with border crossings, language, place, and identity, the fact that this crisis is balanced on passports—the identity documents that tie a person to a place and, usually, a language—focuses many important elements in this work. (Indeed, the initial paragraphs of this chapter re-align the novel in such foundational ways that I resist explicating them. I do not want to threaten the delicious instability of the novel. Readers of Japanese are requested to read this novel before proceeding past this point of this essay. And yes, I write this with irony.)

For one, there is a shift in narrative focus as the narrator identifies himself; this takes the reader back to the ambiguity of the first sentence. We discover that the chapter must begin "do you remember, or not," because the speaker continues, "Do you remember that train and the first meeting between you and me [watashi to]?" The introduction of this first person pronoun, "I" (watashi), reorganizes all the relationships established thus far, between each of the characters and also between the reader and those written. We learn here that the "I" is a particular being: Vishnu. This stable narrating point—a slight stability though it may be, given that the narrator is a Hindu god who appears and disappears like another vaporous apparition—is nonetheless significant in a palette of characters as chimerical as this one. ("Hall of mirrors" is an image that has come to mind more than once.)

But also, in the course of this passage, we learn how "I" (watashi) can no longer use this pronoun in reference to herself, and can only be "You" (Anata). Vishnu had appeared to Anata as she stood in line in Patna, Northern India, to buy a train ticket for Bombay. Anata holds a plane ticket from Bombay to Singapore which, at this point in the story, promises a flight to release her from her ceaseless wandering. The snake-like line at the ticket window never seems to shorten and Anata fears that even if she arrives at the window, she will not have sufficient money to purchase the train ticket to Bombay. Resolution of this cursed travel continues to be deferred.

The ticket is eventually purchased and Anata boards the extremely crowded train. A bearded man beside her watches her, this non-Indian, purchase a samosa and chai, then suggests she be careful with the drinking cup lest it be used to put a spell on her. He asks her,

> "Where are you from?"
> Without a second thought you answered "from Japan." At that time you were not troubled by any doubts as to your identity as female (josei) and as Japanese.[21]

Which suggests, of course, that such categories are now very much doubted within Anata's consciousness, as they have been for readers, up to this point. At a single stroke, genders, names, narration and narrator, are clarified.

However, it is the way that identities are so often tied in this oeuvre to travel documents—passports, in this case—that marks a rich node of understanding, because passports tie an individual to a political entity, and from there to an ethnic and language identity. The crisis with the passport initiates the series of crises that make the entire narrative, and with it all the travel, possible and inescapable; in the process, it seems to force a reconsideration and a clarification of all sorts of identities, not just the one of citizenship, but of national, gender, and cultural identity. This is an anxiety that goes much deeper than the practical difficulties of boarding trans-national airplanes, for the disconnect that arises between the picture in the passport photo and the face in the mirror leads Anata to fear that everything previously assumed to be true—experiences, names, physical features—is in doubt, including the stability of language and national identity. And this is why the complications of language and experience in Tawada Yōko's writings go much deeper than an articulation of cultural discombobulation, of humorous misunderstandings, and push on to the heart of the matter, the way that we conceive of ourselves, the possibilities of our own nonexistence. Travel documents tie the characters to one imaginative terrain—nation-state and bureaucracies—and force reconsiderations of another imaginative terrain—that of identities. Existence in the gap between those two terrains—the ravine—catches many of us where we live, negotiating multiple languages and identities. The multiplicities and possibilities of that gap align with increasingly rich expressions of exile, travel, and porousness.

Notes

1. Paul Celan. Quoted in Chalfen, Israel. *Paul Celan: A Biography of His Youth.* Translated by Maximilian Bleyleben (New York: Persea Books, 1991), 184.

2. I am thinking of "Japaneseness" as an individual identification with that nation and language. Such identification is often strong in these works, but not necessarily essentialist.

3. "Inu mukoiri" was first published in *Gunzō* in 1992, and was later awarded the Akutagawa Prize.

4. The novel in which Saleem Sinai figures is *Midnight's Children.* Rushdie writes about this "unreliable narrator" in *Imaginary Homelands,* p. 22 ff.

5. Yōko Tawada, *Ekusophonii: bogo no soto e deru tabi* (Tokyo: Iwanami Shoten, 2003), 38.

6. Paul Felstiner, preface to *Selected Poems and Prose of Paul Celan* (New York: W.W. Norton, 2001), xxi.

7. Michael André Bernstein, *Five Portraits: Modernity and Imagination in Twentieth-Century German Writing* (Evanston, Ill.: Northwestern University Press, 2000), 101.

8. Tawada, *Ekusophonii,* 36. For a concrete elucidation of this, see Bernstein, especially page 113.

9. This difference has chilling ramifications if one filters it through the experience of Shoah, as did Jean Améry, and thereby "feared that 'no bridge led from death in Auschwitz to *Death in Venice.*'" Quoted in Bernstein, 115.

10. Tawada employs this phrase, "witchy webs," to discuss the linguistic structure of Celan's poetry, which contained the filaments of languages Celan did know (e.g., Russian and French) but also of Japanese, which he did not. Tawada has written brilliantly of Celan's poetry, suggesting a poetic space where Celan's writing was articulated in Japanese. "Hon'yakusha no mon: Shelan ga nihongo wo yomu toki" is the Japanese essay; see Hiltrud Arens's essay, in this volume, for a fuller discussion of the German language essays on this topic.

11. Unless noted otherwise, all translations for this story are from Margaret Mitsu-tani, "In Front of Trang Tien Bridge," In *Facing the Bridge* (New York: New Directions, 2007).

12. Yoko Tawada, *Yōgisha no yakō ressha* [The Fugitive's Night-Time Railway] (Tokyo: Seidosha, 2002), 145.

13. Tawada, *Ekusophonii*, 39.

14. Private conversation, March 2004. Cf. *Ekusophonii*, 37.

15. Translation modified.

16. It seems entirely plausible to me that the "key" to these works lies with these narrating characters: the stories could be easily explicated as the delusional constructs of a singular character. In this case, Kazuko may be "imagining" these people and conversations, of buses filled with look-alikes, of the Japanese-speaking American wraith named James, whom no one else seems to see. The same reading could be applied to the various encounters described in "Persona," and to the people who appear in *The Fugitive's Night-Time Railway*. I find here another layer of richness informing these stories.

17. Arjun Appadurai, *Modernity at Large: Cultural Dimensions of Globalization* (Minneapolis: University of Minnesota Press, 1996), 58.

18. "Missing Heels" is collected in *The Bridegroom was a Dog*.

19. Appadurai, *Modernity*, 3.

20. Tawada, *Yogisha*, 9.

21. Tawada, *Yogisha*, 149.

Bibliography

Abbas, Ackbar. "Building Hong Kong: From Migrancy to Disappearance." In Stephen Cairns, ed. *Drift—Migrancy and Architecture*. New York: Routledge, 2004, 129-141.

Appadurai, Arjun. *Modernity at Large: Cultural Dimensions of Globalization*. Minneapolis: University of Minnesota Press, 1996.

Apter, Emily. "Comparative Exile: Competing Margins in the History of Comparative Literature." In Charles Bernheimer, ed. *Comparative Literature in the Age of Multiculturalism*. Baltimore: Johns Hopkins University Press, 1995, 86-96.

Bernstein, Michael André. *Five Portraits: Modernity and Imagination in Twentieth-Century German Writing*. Evanston, Ill.: Northwestern University Press, 2000.

Bhabha, Homi K. *The Location of Culture*. London: Routledge, 1994.

Buruma, Ian. "The Romance of Exile." *New Republic* 224 (7): 33-38.

Chalfen, Israel. *Paul Celan: A Biography of His Youth*. Translated by Maximilian Bley-leben. New York: Persea Books, 1991.

Cixous, Hélène. *Three Steps on the Ladder of Writing*. Translated by Sarah Cornell and Susan Sellers. New York: Columbia University Press, 1993.

Felstiner, Paul. Preface to *Selected Poems and Prose of Paul Celan*. New York: W.W. Norton, 2001, xvii-xxxvi.

Heidegger, Martin. "Who is Nietzsche's Zarathustra?" In David B. Allison, ed. *The New Nietzsche: Contemporary Styles of Interpretation*. Cambridge, Mass.: MIT Press, 1985.

Massey, Doreen. *Space, Place, And Gender*. Minneapolis: University of Minnesota Press, 1994.

Rushdie, Salman. *Imaginary Homelands: Essays and Criticism, 1981-1991*. London: Granta Books, 1991.

——. *Midnight's Children*. New York: Knopf, 1981.

Seyhan, Azade. *Writing Outside the Nation*. Princeton, N.J.: Princeton University Press, 2001.

Tawada, Yōko. *The Bridegroom was a Dog*. New York: Kodansha International, 2003.

———. "Chantienbashi no temae de" [In Front of Trang Tien Bridge], *Hikari to zerachin no raipuchihhi*. Tokyo: Kodansha, 2000. Translated by Margaret Mitsutani. In *Facing the Bridge*. New York: New Directions, 2007.

———. *Ekusophonii: bogo no soto e deru tabi*. Tokyo: Iwanami Shoten, 2003.

———. "Hon'yakusha no mon: Shelan ga nihongo wo yomu toki." In *Katakoto no uwagoto*. Tokyo: Seidosha, 1999.

———. "Persona." In *Inu mukoiri*. Tokyo: Kodansha, 1998.

———. *Yōgisha no yakō ressha* [The Fugitive's Night-Time Railway]. Tokyo: Seidosha, 2002.

Chapter Six
Das kurze Leuchten unter dem Tor oder auf dem Weg zur geträumten Sprache: Poetological Reflections in Works by Yoko Tawada

Hiltrud Arens

This essay is an exploration of some of Yoko Tawada's central poetological concepts articulated in a selection of her works in German and a discussion of how her own aesthetic understanding is reflected in her prose. I will highlight the connections among her earlier novel *Ein Gast* (1993), the theoretical reflections as discussed in her essays "Das Tor des Übersetzers oder Paul Celan liest Japanisch" (The Gate of the Translator or Celan Reads Japanese) and "Erzähler ohne Seelen" (Storytellers without Souls) published in the collection of literary essays *Talisman* (1996), and her poetic-lecture series delivered in 1998 at the University of Tübingen published under the title *Verwandlungen: Tübinger Poetik Vorlesungen* (1998/2001). Tawada's oeuvre in German encompasses critical essays and fictional work in a variety of genres, and a fluidity of reciprocal influences between her theoretical writing and her fictional texts characterizes her work in a multitude of ways.

As a writer in Japanese and German, (and as many other contributors note) Tawada occupies an unparalleled position in the literary traditions of both cultures. Her writings in German (and Japanese) examine notions of culture, tradition, language, translation, nation, gender, and identity. Tawada uses German literary language in complex ways, negotiating an effort to transmit a linguistic and cultural heritage. She formulates this through simultaneous acts of memory and a critical engagement with the Japanese and German historical and cultural traditions. Tawada's writing style does not configure (given) cultural paradigms in an assumed order, but rather questions and deconstructs expectations. Readers are left with reconfigured, new, images, and with words, voids, and ongoing processes of transformations. Her texts increasingly challenge the categorization of literature according to national boundaries—and not only those of Japan or Germany. Her collection of prose pieces *Überseezungen* (2002), for example, represents a more explicit expansion from her earlier bicultural focus on the two countries and their respective languages. "If language is the single most important determinant of national identity," as some people argue, then narratives are assumed "to support national myths and to shape national consciousness."[1] What happens when the domain of national language is occupied by nonnative writers? Azade Seyhan, who discusses these and related themes, claims that many authors who write "between borders and languages plot complex strategies of translating in an effort to negotiate their loyalties to nation, language, ethnicity, class, and gender."[2] Tawada, however, is also an author who writes in her native language and negotiates her "outside" view of Japan and the bilingualism in her Japanese texts.[3] Her writing, in my view, radicalizes the instance of intercultural dialogue, rare between the East and the West. But since this literature— transnational at least in the German context—operates outside of the German canon and often represents a double or multiple vision by the writer, it not only seeks other ways of aesthetic expression but also asks different questions and opens up new approaches to revise conceptualizations of literature, culture, and even nation, none of which are easy to understand and to engage in. Tawada often disrupts and breaks open conventional use and meaning of language in its varied forms, and challenges the reader to review their perspectives and language use critically. Her texts from the 1990s are unparalleled in German for the unsettling kaleidoscopic view of personal recollection and interpretation of experiences in the world that they contain. The author not only reflects upon and plays with Eurocentric notions of the East, but also deconstructs images of (Asian) female identity.[4] In this vein, Tawada subverts common binary (European) images and literary styles through a practice of mimicry and parody.[5] Seyhan describes in her study that nonnative writers work and live with a plurality of cultural experience which "gives rise to an awareness of simultaneous dimensions."[6] And because of the negotiation of various contrapuntally occurring dimensions represented in their writing, these transnational writers often step, in Seyhan's view, into the "role of an itinerant cultural visionary," sensitizing the reader to the (strategic) use and power of language, and "its capacity to mark cultural difference."[7]

In Tawada's multi-layered texts we can trace aesthetic influences and intertextual references of twentieth-century German-speaking theorists and writers such as Walter Benjamin, Paul Celan, and Ingeborg Bachmann as well as French thinkers such as Roland Barthes. Tawada's literary essay on Paul Celan's poetry in "Das Tor des Übersetzers oder Celan liest Japanisch" presents key aspects of her narrative strategy: her conceptualization of the work(s) of translation, her understanding of the alterity of language, and her own poetological understandings as a writer.[8] Miho Matsunaga discusses the dimension of translation in Tawada's Japanese and German works and defines it as a permanent process of her bilingual writing,[9] in which the author does not translate literally or in a narrow sense (even in editions that come out in Japanese and in German), but transforms and reformulates (*umdichten*) the language in the texts at hand.[10] Tawada expresses her realization while reading the translated poems of Celan that, "The more intensively I read, the stronger my impression became, that Celan's poems *grasped Japanese.*"[11] Contrary to the conventional simplistic notion that "good literature" is often distorted in translation, Tawada saw that the poems were not only translatable, but that the translator had poetically conveyed certain meanings to a Japanese readership. Or, the author wonders, did Celan have the capability to express various *fremde Denksysteme* (foreign systems of thought) in his writing that went beyond the concrete language he used. A translation is not just a copy in Tawada's view, but through it, meanings conveyed in the original receive new bodies, not only made up of different sounds, but of a different body of signs (and thoughts): another script.[12]

For Walter Benjamin—whose thoughts on translation resonate strongly in Tawada's essay—it is clear that "a specific significance inherent in the original manifests itself in its translatability."[13] At the same time though, through a translation an original could attain "its ever-renewed latest and most abundant flowering (*umfassende Entfaltung*)."[14] Benjamin also insists that in "the afterlife—which could not be called that if it were not a transformation and a renewal of something living—the original undergoes a change."[15] For Benjamin it is this renewal of language and its ongoing transformation in or through a translation, which can give eternal life to a work of art. Yet it is also possible to detect a disjunction between content, language, and form of the original and its translation. Importantly though, what counts in a well-done translation is the production of "the echo of the original, because deep down in any translation lies the "foreignness of languages" in which a transfer can never be total.[16] It is this ambivalent movement that defines a work of cultural translation which Homi Bhabha calls a "disjunctive play of symbol and sign" across cultural sites.[17] Bhabha argues that drawing from Benjamin's perspective on the foreignness of languages it becomes possible to confront existing incommensurable differences and through apprehending those differences one is able to "perform the act of cultural translation."[18] In asking herself how Celan's translated poetry could reach this other world (Tawada as a Japanese reader before she knew any German) outside of the German language context, she imagines the existence of a gap, an abyss, between languages in which words tumble down: "There has to be an abyss between languages, into which all words plunge."[19] It is here in this gap and in this site that Tawada dwells as a writer and critic as well that new thoughts and understandings are pondered and demanded. In her second lecture in the Tübingen series "Schrift einer Schildkröte oder das Problem der Übersetzung" (Script of a Turtle or the Problem of Translation), Tawada takes up thoughts on translation again: "Literary translations have to confront untranslatable aspects with unconventional means to question and break open traditional aesthetics and transform a text into the new translated text."[20] She finds it significant that a reader is able to trace the existence of another language in the translated text.[21] She also turns Benjamin's ideas around when she assumes that a literary text can find its original from which it was translated and she goes further to claim that several originals exist alongside each other in different cultural realms and that they might find each other across national and cultural boundaries.[22] Languages and cultures through the medium of a text can have corresponding transnational—translational for that matter—and cultural connections that a reader may discover.

Tawada's insight into Celan's translated Japanese poems (through the ideogram used in their translation) as open gates through which something new is revealed as if in a short flash is an image that, in my view, captures a very important element of her work:

> The title of the third poem "Flash" contains the ideogram |閃| (Flash) that also has the radical "gate." Here one sees how a person |人| is standing under a gate |門|. I had never thought about why the combination of a gate and a person can produce a flash. Maybe one who stands under a gate (or on a threshold), is especially capable of receiving a flash from an invisible world.[23]

In such moments, in which a short flash (*erleuchtet*) illuminates, a new consciousness, a different thought, a transformation is disclosed, or a linguistic or cultural riddle is offered to the reader. Tawada does not look for specific German traits in a (German) poem, but rather, contemplates poems as gates or receivers of light (*ein Gedicht als einen Strahlenempfänger*), as always conceiving *etwas Fremdes und niemals sich selbst* (something foreign and never itself).[24] Poems, literature, and translations that can attract these flashes of revelation bear "foreign" elements in them, which in turn reveal the interstitial and unstable aspects of a text making new understandings possible. This is more than just a coming to terms with the foreignness of languages, which Benjamin discusses in his essay.[25] Tawada's radical difference from Benjamin lies in her suggestion of the meeting between the original text with its translation at the time of the genesis of the original, not later. This, she argues, can only be understood if one imagines time not temporally (linear), but rather spatially—as an in-between space, *einem Zwischenraum auf einer Schwelle* (an in-between space on a threshold).[26] And this space, significantly, is under a gate as she explains of her own reading experience: "I started to view Celan's poems as gates and not as houses . . . Celan's words are not containers, but openings. I walk through the opening of the gate every time I read them."[27]

This interpretation of Celan's translated words as gates or thresholds that can open up new meanings and let the reader wander into this site to experience a disorientation or a revelation can be taken further in reference to Tawada's own writing. She too writes from a transitional or an "in-between space" in which the concrete German language usage and the literary reflections on it are informed, removed, and newly or differently inscribed by signs and symbols of cultural difference and cultural hybridity that cannot easily be translated and understood. Homi Bhabha asks us to "remember that it is the 'inter'—the cutting edge of translation and negotiation, the *in-between* space—that carries the burden of the meaning of culture."[28] For him, "'these in-between' spaces provide the terrain for elaborating strategies" that "initiate new signs of identity, and innovative sites of collaboration, and contestation" important for a redefinition of our times and emerging societies.[29] New aspects enter a text through translation or through a liberating or distancing from the mother tongue and mother script. Seyhan describes this working of a bilingual writer on the threshold as if a text crosses a border, flies over barriers, from fiction to metafiction, from one language to the other: "The memory of the (m)other tongue will not be erased and transfigures its new medium."[30]

Unsettling gaps of knowledge of this literature written from the "Zwischenraum" become part of the reading and listening experience—an effect the author intends to create. Tawada's texts and plays are, as the German Studies scholar Leslie Adelson has characterized Turko-German literature: "*Orte des Umdenkens* (Sites of Reorientation), that is to say, imaginative sites where cultural orientation is being radically rethought."[31] These sites are filled with unpredictability and disorientation, they are "spaces of transgression," because familiar categories of language and social structure are left behind and questioned.[32] Tawada does not analyze Celan's poems as marking a border between two places, but rather interprets them as thresholds and gates (*Zwischenraum, Tor, Schwelle*) where something new flashes into sight, and a change of consciousness occurs. It should come as no surprise that Tawada senses an affinity with Paul Celan, who had chosen German as his literary language, worked as a poet and translator, and was always in search for—on the basis of his multilingual, multicultural background and personal experiences during and after the Shoah—new aesthetic expressions in his poetry.[33] Celan inscribed onto the German language nuances, voices, atmosphere(s), and words that he retrieved from other cultural contexts, he then took apart, reassembled, or invented words so that his language usage brought forth new semantic content, new images, and new forms to decipher.[34] Tawada has written three critical essays in German on different aspects of Celan's poetry; these were all written later than the text *Ein Gast* that I will discuss shortly.[35] These three essays present distinct notions about writing, translating and reading a work of art. The depth and understanding of her reading of Celan's work is very much embedded in the idea of a "translating space" on the threshold she herself as a writer moves in, around, and out of. Linguistic and semantic assignments that other readers might see as fixed, are dismantled and newly assigned or left open as in a magical play with the combination of letters of the alphabet and the system of punctuation by Tawada in her discussion of Celan's poems in "Rabbi Löw und 27 Punkte." Her knowledge of Japanese is essential for her readings of Celan and she artistically reveals hidden aspects and connections in his poetry while at the same time discussing the notion of a different and important visual acknowledgement of poetry and translation: namely the translator acting also as an *Augen-Übersetzer* (eye-translator).[36] She argues for a reading that is not only phonetic, but also visual and that takes into account the alphabetic script as a form of graphic designs that might hide secret meanings and transformations. Matsunaga points out that Tawada seems to have become increasingly aware of, what Matsunaga calls, the "autonomous force of script" (of individual signs and letters) and its visual effect on the reader as well as its hidden messages.[37] These different but interconnected aspects have influenced Tawada's own fictional writing, albeit before she articulated them in these interpretative essays.

In an interview as part of a workshop on writing in connection with her short novel *Ein Gast* (1993), Yoko Tawada voices the view that her writing always expresses a translation in a broader sense: "wenn ich schreibe, ist das immer eine Übersetzung in weiterem Sinne."[38] In this interview one can see how a bilingual writer experiences the connection between language, literature, and translation. Tawada's notion of the poetic process as always "translating" from an imaginary (or formerly lost) language is echoed in this interview. She developed this idea further in the essays on Celan's poetry. She also speaks about the moment of the in-between and space of the gap, which for her is most important:

> And this moment is very important for me, that the emotion or life or the written piece is also something different in the mother tongue. That there is an abyss, in-between, into which one can fall. And this space in-between is very important to me. And in order to reveal this—I want to write in such a way that this space becomes visible.[39]

Tawada's major concern is, as she says, to make visible what is invisible and repressed in the language we use in our daily life.[40] And this process of word for word and even letter for letter deconstruction and reformulation can best happen in writing from and about the in-between space on a threshold. The image of the "Kluft" (the abyss) is again evoked, as it was in the essay on Celan,[41] as a place between languages and cultures into which words and people (can) fall into. Tawada as a female and bilingual writer is consistently trying to trace and then disclose this space on the edge, often hidden and/or not accounted for, into which words and letters (might) tumble. The German literary critic Sigrid Weigel speaks about the in-between space, especially for women writers, where the activity of creative anticipation takes place:

> In order to survive in the in-between space, in the "not any longer" and the "not yet" without becoming insane or wild, women must learn the cross-eyed view which means bringing the contradictions into discussion, seeing and understanding them, living in and with them—and gathering strength from the rebellion against a Yesterday and from the anticipation for a Tomorrow.[42]

Here the feminist and the postcolonial discourses connect in the characteristic place (or displacement) of the "beyond," "third space," or in-between.[43]

It is also this "edgy" space the main protagonist inhabits in the text entitled *Ein Gast.*[44] This is not a novel in the traditional sense, even though it is named so on the book cover. It is more like a story told in twelve short episodes or "Prosabilder" in which the chapters are loosely connected but the text as such does not flow along a causal or logical storyline.[45] The reader cannot always make out the increasingly absurd development of the narrator's life. At the same time the style of language is not difficult and the perspective is similar to that of a confused child who discovers the world for the first time. Certain contexts are not explained and complex differentiations are left out. Yet this seemingly naïve perspective of the narrator is what produces a different, complementary process in which perceptions are intensified, challenged, and unseen things are revealed.[46]

The first person narrator is an unnamed Japanese woman living in Germany trying to read, understand, and also reconstruct her environment. The title itself alludes to various types of guests: the narrator herself, other visitors she is confronted with in her apartment, as well as a voice from a tape recorder she listens to: "I have no visitor, but it happens at times that a woman is suddenly there and I mean not a woman, but a female voice."[47] The narrator herself seems like a different kind of a "translator," mediating aspects of German culture to a Japanese readership: she writes short articles about Germany for a Japanese women's journal. As a subtext the author also performs as a type of "translator," transforming and articulating her vision to the readers in Germany through this text. When the protagonist is asked by her editor to write about German cultural festivals and daily customs in a non-academic style, to supposedly make it easy to follow for the readers, the narrator at first is apprehensive and does not see herself as an anthropologist. Yet she takes up this work for financial reasons. To write about different customs and also to try to explain them to an unfamiliar audience is a task she sees herself unfit for. The narrator doubts her work, precisely because, as she claims, she is not trained as an anthropologist and she cannot explain why the customs are as they are. Her editor does not mind the lack of explanations, since superstition in her opinion cannot be explained anyway: "ich brauche nichts zu erklären, denn Aberglaube lasse sich meistens nicht erklären."[48] This is just one of the twists and acts of deconstruction of the Eurocentric view that Asians or others might be superstitious, while Germans certainly would not see themselves in these terms. Ironically, the Japanese editor does. In this text the narrator lives in a difficult (in-between) space and tries to make sense of her surroundings in a way that is new, amusing and/or irritating to the reader. The female character living in Germany increasingly battles with the German language and its alphabet/script. In the twelve short chapters the protagonist reports about her daily life, the people she meets and the writing she is trying to accomplish, while at the same time this very life becomes more inexplicable and confusing to her. More and more the narrator finds herself in doubt about formulating and writing her assignments and this language-crisis unfolds into her life.

The text begins with the protagonist on her way to the ear-doctor, because she is supposedly suffering from an ear infection. On the way, the contours of her surroundings, the voices and bodies of others are seen and felt as if in a dream or in a fever-like condition, are blurred and become indistinct. Many of Tawada's texts deal with the phenomena of dream-world, underworld, and "reality"; often it is not clear when the characters are in which world or which state of mind. Many times the movement from one state into the next is not clearly marked. This narrative strategy evokes the imaginary spaces of the in-between, which is always dynamic and in flux, while at the same time it also problematizes the limits of writing and language.[49] As the narrator walks through a flea-market on her way to the doctor, she tries to understand the lay-out and the hidden meaning of and connections among various items for sale. This is a theme that weaves itself also through other stories by Tawada. Each time, the narrator stands in front of the item or holds the item in question and gazes at it, in order to solve what seems like a mystery—the relationship between things, the gender of an object—to the protagonist: "I remained so long in front of it, until I had found a solution."[50] A solution not in the logical sense, but a solution that provides an explanation for the troubled and curious narrator who is assuming a relationship between the items she sees. The underlying subtext here is written from the critical perspective of the writer and it engages the notion of an ethnologically informed viewpoint that displaces an original meaning; it likewise shows the possibility of the mere arbitrariness of signs and reveals the absurdity that is often behind such explanations as the protagonist's. It also stresses the search for new meanings in altered circumstances. As Sigrid Weigel has noted Tawada consistently re-stages the moment in which signs become symbols, gestures become social acts, and things or images become script: under this gaze the world becomes a book in which everything can be read.[51] But this process of a different reassembled representation also confuses the linear order of storytelling, reading, and understanding. It calls into question not only what the narrator in *Ein Gast* does not comprehend or want to confront, but also what the reader might have taken for granted as well.

In the essay "Erzähler ohne Seelen," Tawada wonders what it would be like to imagine a "fictive writer" in contrast to an author who imagines a fictional story.[52] Roland Barthes, in his essayistic text "Empire of Signs," imagined a fictionalized (constructed) Japan to theorize. But in an act of mimicry and parody,[53] of shifting images—"eine Verschiebung zwischen den Bildern"[54]—and radical rethinking, Tawada offers as a narrative strategy an alternative view of a storyteller when she shifts the attention from the story as a fictional construct to an author who is "fictive/fictional." In her essay she explicitly refers to such a writer as an outsider, whose culture is not very well known and therefore "fictional" to the mainstream. How would such an observer see the world around him/her as "our" world?[55] In *Ein Gast* the first person narrator, as in other stories by Tawada, enacts the role of the fictive observer, who is an outsider viewing her—"our"—immediate world.

In various stories and essays, as in the case in *Ein Gast*, Tawada plays with the physiognomy and materiality of the letters of the Roman alphabet. When she reads the script or other cultural signs, she often searches for the unknown, the hidden, the magical, and/or the mysterious within these symbols of her European environment. Landscapes, things, words, and individual letters, as well as individual characters in a story, gain different associative powers and meanings through this shifted perspective. Tawada describes this as an attempt at "fiktive Ethnologie" (fictional ethnology), in which it is not what is written about that is fictional, but the writer.[56] In a later theoretical work she explains how in her own analysis of German literary texts she wants to "redirect the ethnological model" of the past, in which the cultures of the East or of Africa were interpreted by Westerners. Tawada then develops her own "ethnological poetology" (*ethnolo-*

gische Poetologie) in which German literature is viewed through a different lens, seen as the "other."[57] This approach by Tawada, together with her various intertextual references and critical reformulations, connect closely to an evolving discourse within Western Literary and Cultural/Postcolonial Studies since the 1980s, in which texts are examined ethnologically and anthropologically in a multitude of ways reflecting cultural practices and power structures.[58] Not only is a literary text a constructed entity, but as Tawada makes us aware, the author reflects the constructedness of her shifting identity in the process of writing and re-visioning. Even though the narrator in *Ein Gast* complains about not being able to work like an anthropologist, and she declares that she despises the work involved in such writing, she nevertheless captures various situations in detail and with laconic irony. In result, Germans are viewed through a different lens. The narrator even recognizes with a feeling of guilt that she only finds interest in those things around her that she could view like an anthropologist.[59] She wants to return the gaze that she is so often confronted with in her daily life.

At a flea-market the narrator buys what she took to be a book. It captures her attention because of its round form and the letters all written in a circle: "Ich sah auf dem Umschlag Buchstaben, die nicht von links nach rechts, sondern im Kreis geschrieben waren."[60] It turns out that it is a tape-recorded book in which a female voice narrates as the protagonist states an uninteresting plot: "Even though the plot did not interest me at all, I walked into the novel, as you enter a house without a door and walls, by accident. I had not seen a threshold, to make me think about, if I wanted to enter or not." The voice is what intrigues and holds the attention and also scares the protagonist at first. But as if there were no choice, since no threshold (*Schwelle*) was visibly experienced, the narrator finds this new experience also liberating from the difficult process of having to decipher the alphabet of the written novels she has been trying to read.[61] The female voice on tape gives her relief, since this voice is without expectation, without eyes to observe and frame her, and ears to listen, a voice in which the spoken language as well as the language of the body are of no consequence.[62] The individual and collective form of letters of the alphabet have felt to the narrator like a wall she always has to fight when reading a German text. She describes how the alphabet remained a *Gitter* (a bar) in front of her eyes while reading. She wonders if the recorder and with it the spoken word was indeed the "gesuchte Zaubermittel" (sought-for magic formula) she was searching for, in order to extinguish the individual letters of novels and to read with greater understanding.[63] In her lecture series, Tawada expresses her personal liking of stories told on tapes and heard on the radio. Language seems to be closer and more easily understood for the author then, when read out loud.[64]

The female voice from the tape becomes a constant "visitor" and even when the narrator believes she has turned off the machine, the voice continues to talk as if under a surreal spell and increasingly disorients and alienates the protagonist from her neighbors and surroundings. She starts to feel obsessed by this voice. The voice is at times an ambivalent metaphor for inspiration, erotic attraction as well as distraction, displacement, and harassment. What at first seemed to be liberating for the narrator, becomes overwhelming and paradoxically hinders her from hearing (and reading) with a wider understanding.[65] The metaphor of the "Gitter der Buchstaben" reoccurs later when the protagonist wants to find the book version of the cassette, because now she wishes to imprison the voice behind the wall (behind bars) of written letters.[66] The alienation of the narrator increases so that even the real voices by guests at a party in her apartment bother and hurt her physically: "On this night I found the sounds of the foreign sentences especially unbearable . . . But it (the sound) intruded into my body, as if it were not distinguishable from its content."[67] The conversations at the party are felt as violent and the whole atmosphere is so painful to experience that the narrator wishes to become a stone, in order to interrupt the flow of conversation. She wants to become a stone to throw herself against the sound of words, so that they would be destroyed or show themselves differently. Is this why the narrator starts out with an ear infection? Is she so tired of listening? Or is this the abyss in which the words tumble before they can be reclaimed? The experiences the narrator undergoes with the other language and its sounds are described as very physical and often on the verge of moving from a pleasurable feeling towards a frightening or even deadly sensation: "Especially when I was lying down, it (the voice) came in a surprising way to me. First it carefully caressed my neck. . . . I was also frightened, that it would elegantly strangle me in this way."[68] As much as the voice becomes a sensually experienced being, language itself transforms into a physical experience. The narrator cannot make out the words from the letters once she finds the written novel of her cassette and she seems to be confused by the spoken word at the party just the same.[69] The physical pain of this bewilderment and confusion in not being able to read the book but also not wishing the voice to be back, that she is trying to keep behind bars—the bars of the written letters—expresses itself in "Schmerzen im Unterleib" (pains in her abdomen) and a whole range of ambivalent feelings she cannot explain. This pain is a metaphor for rape: the violence of a language the narrator is trying to understand or at least "imprison." Here the rape stands for the conquest of the narrator's life by the new language and the new environment and her fight to reestablish her (own) identity and some clear vision of what to say and do. Weigel sees this clash of the materiality of letters and their magical entities in Tawada's writing not only as a process of amazement but also as one of fright and terror. All too often the poetic language play in Tawada's text(s) include(s) a split moment of transformation from affirmation to distress; the reader then is left to seek an orientation and wonder about the language and the depiction in question. A moment of beauty and devotion turns into one of harassment. Things are just not as they seem(ed). In this process of what Weigel calls "the anthropomorphization of language that makes the hidden traces of violence visible again"[70] through marking and transforming metaphors, characters, and images in the physicality of language itself, Tawada's fictional explorations reveal the hidden trace of violence in language.

Towards the end of the story, the narrator is made to assist her neighbor—known only as Z—during his therapy sessions with different women that come to him. In these sessions the narrator acts as a stone or a box (*eine Truhe*), that sucks up the voices of the women Z is allegedly drawing out of them in order to heal. She even colors her face with beige make up, so that the women do not recognize her while she is lying there silently to absorb their sounds and super-fluous voices (mostly of their mothers). Finally she has become a stone, some-thing she has yearned for earlier. Yet, at one point in a liberating moment, the narrator feels anger and lust at this procedure and breaks out in laughter, breaks out of feeling like being a stone, of only being the passive receiver. She actually transforms into the kind of stone she anticipated earlier, a stone that can throw itself and change the scenery.

In the end, the protagonist is not able to formulate coherent sentences or to write about any topic. Instead she types words on the typewriter that come to her spontaneously. The words are all written in the shape of what could be a poetic bar (*Gitter*) the way they are separated on paper without straight lines, but rather in a zigzag motion, as if they are performing many little *z* shaped letters:

Schmut z ig
Wur z eln
Schwit z en
Her z schlag
Kreu z
Ar z t
Schmer z tabletten
Blit z schalg
Net z haut
Z erplat z en[71]

(Dirty
Roots
Sweating
Heartbeat
Cross
Doctor
Painkillers
Lightning
Retina
Explode)

The last word of the whole text is "Z erplat z en" — to explode,[72] an action that corresponds with the wish of the main character: to fight the tone of the (deadly) everyday language in order to destroy this mode or to see a different, trans-formed face behind it.[73] The protagonist wanted to become a stone to smash the ordinary language around her. And the narrator notes how she feels satisfied by writing down these broken words as if she has written something important. The last words organized like a non-linear poem are split up before or after the letter z. This letter is also the last letter of the alphabet and can be read upside down also as a z. If one explores its visual effect and remembers that these words burst

in un-grammatical ways, they give way to new little open spaces between the
divided syllables. It seems to me that the significance is not so much based on
the specific letter z and the word division itself, but rather that the dissolution
(explosion) of letters and words are a means by the author to make us aware of
the alterity, the construction, and the transformative aspect of language, which
we might not be fully aware of (even if or because it is our mother tongue).
Language play can open up this magical space in which the script is recognizable, but the individual letters are pulled apart and are "fleeting as shadows."[74]
Even when the division of words into meaningless syllables has no direct message, poetic language is still being used and can grow from this experiment.[75]
The narrator in the story is faltering in her readings of her immediate surroundings—"our" world—and she had to divide things up, let them burst into the
abyss, so to speak, in order to realign them anew (similar to the process at the
flea-market), so that other developments and realizations can happen. Such a
transformative attempt is, as Tawada says, not always possible to represent in
linear stories: "Because of the impossibility of a transfer productive gaps arise
everywhere in the text."[76] And the text as well as its ending provides us with this
kind of a productive gap, between the letters as well as in the text itself, from
which new things and thoughts may arise, but a definitive interpretation cannot
be given. More than anything, it seems to be the opening process (bursting) that
counts.

    Tawada's text *Ein Gast* is infused with the "foreign" elements, referred to
by Benjamin, Bhabha, and Tawada herself, that deconstruct original structures
of reference and sense of communication "not simply by negating it, but by negotiating the disjunction in which successive cultural temporalities are preserved."[77] Her writing is informed by the following conceptual approaches and
poetological reflections: the beautiful image of the open gate as a space in which
(new) signs and symbols are negotiated and discovered; in which the languages,
both original and in translation, correspond (spatially) almost magically and
reveal their dynamic ambivalences, unsettling gaps, and transformative powers;
and in which the role of the narrator is seen as fictional and is challenged, just as
the text is. In her prose collection *Überseezungen* (2002) a female narrator in the
story "Bioskoop der Nacht" also wants to be freed from the linear and logical
structure of language.[78] She decides to follow the language of her recurring
nightly dreams, and travels to South Africa.[79] This is a playful twist to the conventional assumption that the language of dreams is done in the mother tongue
or/and the language(s) one is embedded in mentally. Yet in "Bioskoop" the narrator does not dream in either of these languages, but in one that is at first unfamiliar to her. In this search for another language (different as it is in *Ein Gast*)—
a utopian language—and for another way to communicate, the character discovers seemingly with ease and lightheartedness, that she has "many souls and
tongues."[80] But also in this story, it is often unclear in what space (of dream or
reality) the narrator is moving. But the emphasis is not any more on the German
language and a life in Europe as a "borderline" experience. The character—just

like the writer—faces complex realities and fictions and has to consistently negotiate the multiple aspects and simultaneous awareness of her identity.

In Tawada's experimental texts, she goes beyond the body of language
(*Sprachkörper*) to incorporate the language of body (*Körpersprache*) very often
to challenge the former. Peter Pörtner explains how script and body of the reader
as well as the writer in Japanese are in a close reciprocal relationship and even a
reciprocal representational relationship,[81] which seem to be reinscribed but also
displaced or removed in Tawada's writing in German. Stories of dreams and
visions and different perceptions of the life of the characters and individual letters and objects are revealed in an associative process often on equal terms.[82]
Tawada relates, envisions, dreams of, questions, illuminates, and reconstructs
(new or) other meanings of language usage, script, and translation, as well as of
the life of the dead, animals, voices and things, and (their) transformed
faces/beings. The distinction between reality and dream, male and female and
the relationship between inanimate and animate objects to one another is obscured, blurred, and remaining an ongoing process of reformulation. The de- and
re-construction of terms, perceptions, and memories are a constitutive part articulated in Tawada's writings that not only portray the world around us in ever
changing and new images, but also critically intervene in the discourse on language, gender, nature, nation, Western and Eastern Civilizations and their relationship.[83] The narrator in *Ein Gast* lives, in metaphorical terms, on a threshold
in search of a different language and new forms of communication and understanding, and because of that she has to undergo various transformations herself
that then again are projected onto the last lines, leaving the space open for the
(different) reader's investigation. The reader in a reversed mirror image to the
narrator undergoes another process of alienation, wonderment, and transformation mainly due to Tawada's language and the narrator's disorienting experiences and culturally critical perceptions albeit presented from a seemingly un-
knowing perspective.

For Tawada, as she explains in her lecture series, the capability to transform, for example, as it is reflected in Ovid's *Metamorphoses* reminds us how
transient and how fictional many "fixed" definitions are, although they are often
taken for granted.[84] To write as a poet, in Tawada's view, is therefore to "translate" an imaginary, magical or lost language as from a dream or another realm
(as the world of the dead and spirits) into its written (trans)form(ation) for us to
read, to decipher critically, and to discover something new, unique, captivating,
and again transformative.

Notes

1. Azade Seyhan, *Writing Outside the Nation* (Princeton, N.J.: Princeton University
Press`, 2001), 8.
2. Seyhan, *Writing*, 8.
3. Miho Matsunaga, "'Schreiben als Übersetzung.' Die Dimension der Übersetzung
in denWerken von Yoko Tawada," *Zeitschrift fur Germanistik* 12, no. 3 (2002): 539. As

an example of this, Matsunaga discusses an episode from Tawada's Japanese novel *Aru-fabetto no kizuguchi*. In it, a translator is translating a (German) text into Japanese by ignoring Japanese syntax and punctuation. The translator organizes the sentence pieces according to German syntax. Thus, it becomes unclear where the sentences begin or end. Optically, the translated piece is being pulled apart and resembles a sick body.

4. Sabine Fischer, "'Verschwinden ist schön': Zu Yoko Tawada's Kurzroman *Das Bad*," in *Denn du tanzt auf einem Seil. Positionen deutschsprachiger MigrantInnenliteratur*, ed. Sabine Fischer and Moray McGowan (Tübingen, Germany: Stauffenburg, 1997), 101.

5. Claudia Breger, "Mimikry als Grenzverwirrung. Parodistische Posen bei Yoko Tawada," in *Über Grenzen. Limitation und Transgeression in Literatur und Ästhetik*, ed. Claudia Benthien and Irmela Marei Krüger-Fürhoff (Stuttgart, Germany: Metzler, 1999), 189.

6. Seyhan, *Writing*, 14.

7. Seyhan, *Writing*, 14.

8. Yoko Tawada, "Das Tor des Übersetzers oder Celan liest Japanisch," *Talisman: Literarische Essays*, (Tübingen, Germany: Konkursbuch, 1996), 121-134. In the following quoted as "Tor." All translations into English from this text are mine.

9. Matsunaga, "Schreiben," 534.

10. Matsunaga, "Schreiben," 541.

11. Tawada, "Tor," 126.

12. Tawada, "Tor," 126, 134.

13. Walter Benjamin, *Illuminations*, ed. Hannah Arendt, trans. Harry Zohn (New York: Harcourt, Brace &World, Inc., 1968), 71.

14. Benjamin, *Illuminations*, 72.

15. Benjamin, *Illuminations*, 73.

16. Benjamin, *Illuminations*, 75-76.

17. Homi K. Bhabha, *Location of Culture* (New York: Routledge, 1994), 163.

18. Bhabha, *Culture*, 164.

19. Tawada, "Tor," 122.

20. Yoko Tawada, *Verwandlungen: Tübinger Poetik-Vorlesungen* (Tübingen, Germany: Konkursbuch, 1998/2001), 35.

21. Tawada, *Verwandlungen*, 35.

22. Tawada, *Verwandlungen*, 39.

23. Tawada, "Tor," 126-7.

24. Tawada, "Tor," 127.

25. Benjamin, *Illuminations*, 75.

26. Tawada, "Tor," 129.

27. Tawada, "Tor," 130.

28. Bhabha, *Culture*, 38-39.

29. Bhabha, *Culture*, 1-2.

30. Seyhan, *Writing*, 148.

31. Leslie A. Adelson, "Against Between: A Manifesto," in *Unpacking Europe: Towards a Critical Reading*, ed. Salah Hassan and Iftikhar Dadi (Rotterdam: NAI Publishers, 2000), 247.

32. Adelson, *Between*, 249.

33. Enzo Traverso, "Paul Celan: Dichtung der Zerstörung," in *Auschwitz denken. Die Intellektuellen und die Shoah*, trans. from the French by Helmut Dahmer (Hamburg, Germany: Hamburger Edition, 2000), 214.

34. Traverso, "Dichtung," 217.

35. The two other essays are "Rabbi Löw und 27 Punkte—Physiognomie der Interpunktion bei Paul Celan" and "Die Krone aus Gras. Zu Paul Celans 'Die Niemandsrose.'"

36. Tawada, "Krone," 174.

37. Matsunaga, "Schreiben," 543.

38. Hugo Dittberner, ed., *Mit der Zeit erzählen? fragt er. Marcel Beyer—Heiner Egge—Gundi Feyrer, Yoko Tawada. Das zweite Buch* (Göttingen, Germany: Wallstein, 1994), 197.

39. Dittberner, *Mit der Zeit*, 198.

40. Dittberner, *Mit der Zeit*, 198.

41. Tawada, "Tor," 122.

42. Sigrid Weigel, "Der schielende Blick. Thesen zur Geschichte weiblicher Schreibpraxis" in *Die verborgene Frau. Sechs Beiträge zu einer feministischen Literaturwissenschaft* (Hamburg, Germany: Argument, 1988), 105.

43. Bhabha, *Culture*, 38-39.

44. Yoko Tawada, *Ein Gast. Roman* (Tübingen, Germany: Konkursbuch, 1993). In the following quoted as *Gast*.

45. Sibylle Cramer, "Zwischen den Sprachen und Worten. Yoko Tawada als Erzählerin, Essayistin und Dramatikerin," *Frankfurter Rundschau*: January 8, 1994. ZB 4.

46. Andrea Krauß, "*Talisman*—Tawadische Sprachtheorie," in *Migration und Interkulturaliät in neueren literarischen Texten*, ed. Aglaia Blioumi. (Munich, Germany: Iudicium, 2002), 58.

47. Tawada, *Gast*, 22.

48. Tawada, *Gast*, 27.

49. Krauß, "Talisman," 60-61.

50. Tawada, *Gast*, 9.

51. Sigrid Weigel, "Transsibirische Metamorphosen. Laudatio auf Yoko Tawada zur Verleihung des Adalbert-von-Chamisso-Preises 1996," *Frauen in der Literaturwissenschaft* 49 (1996): 5.

52. Yoko Tawada, "Erzähler ohne Seelen," *Talisman: Literarische Essays*, (Tübingen, Germany: Konkursbuch, 1996), 24.

53. Breger, "Mimikry," 200.

54. Dittberner, *Mit der Zeit*, 196.

55. Tawada, "Erzähler," 24.

56. Tawada, "Erzähler," 24.

57. Yoko Tawada, *Spielzeug und Sprachmagie. Eine ethnologische Poetologie* (Tübingen, Germany: Konkursbuch, 2000), 14.

58. Doris Bachmann-Medick, ed., *Kultur als Text. Die anthropologische Wende in derLiteraturwissenschaft* (Frankfurt, Germany: Fischer, 1996), 15; Krauß, "Talisman," 61.

59. Tawada, *Gast*, 42.

60. Tawada, *Gast*, 9.

61. Tawada, *Gast*, 20.

62. Tawada, *Gast*, 41-42.

63. Tawada, *Gast*, 19-20.

64. Yoko Tawada, *Verwandlungen: Tübinger Poetik-Vorlesungen* (Tübingen, Germany: Konkursbuch, 1998/2001), 26.

65. Tawada, *Gast*, 33, 41-42.

66. Tawada, *Gast*, 45. The image of "Gitter"—a grating, a bar—is also used by Celan in "Sprachgitter," for example. In Tawada's reading of Celan's poetry in her essay

"Die Krone aus Gras" she pays close attention to the graphic form of the letter *t* and the magical hidden meaning it entails for her interpretation when connected with Japanese ideograms (172). The word "Gitter" in her text *Ein Gast* could be read as enhancing the sensation of imprisonment the narrator feels optically for the reader, since the two *t*'s in the word itself could be seen as bars.

67. Tawada, *Gast*, 35-36.
68. Tawada, *Gast*, 41.
69. Tawada, *Gast*, 49.
70. Sigrid Weigel, "Transsibirische Metamorphosen. Laudatio auf Yoko Tawada zur Verleihung des Adalbert-von-Chamisso-Preises 1996," *Frauen in der Literaturwissenschaft* 49 (1996): 6.
71. Tawada, *Gast*, 78.
72. Tawada, *Gast*, 78.
73. Tawada, *Gast*, 37.
74. Tawada, "Krone," 176.
75. Tawada, "Krone," 181.
76. Tawada, *Verwandlungen*, 38.
77. Bhabha, *Culture*, 227-228.
78. Yoko Tawada, "Bioskoop der Nacht," in *Überseezungen* (Tübingen, Germany: Konkursbuch verlag, 2002), 61-91.
79. Tawada, "Bioskoop," 68.
80. Tawada, "Bioskoop," 70.
81. Peter Pörtner, "Zeichen—Setzen: Zur Sino—Japanischen Schrift und Ihrer Geschichte," in *Über den Umgang mit der Schrift*, ed. Wende Waltraud (Würzburg, Germany: Königshausen & Neumann, 2002), 74.
82. Albrecht Kloepfer and Miho Matsunaga, "Yoko Tawada," *Kritisches Lexikon zur deutschsprachigen Gegenwartsliteratur* 64 (2000), 3.
83. Breger, "Mimikry," 191.
84. Tawada, *Verwandlungen*, 54-55.

Bibliography

Adelson, Leslie A. "Against Between: A Manifesto." Pp. 244-255 in *Unpacking Europe: Towards a Critical Reading*, edited by Salah Hassan and Iftikhar Dadi. Rotterdam: NAI Publishers, 2000.
Bachmann-Medick, Doris, ed. *Kultur als Text. Die anthropologische Wende in der Literaturwissenschaft*. Frankfurt, Germany: Fischer, 1996.
Barthes, Roland. *Im Reich der Zeichen*. Translated by Michael Bischoff. Frankfurt: Suhrkamp, 1981.
Benjamin, Walter. *Illuminations*. Edited by Hannah Arendt. Translated by Harry Zohn. New York: Harcourt, Brace &World, Inc., 1968.
Bhabha, Homi K. *Location of Culture*. New York: Routledge, 1994.
Breger, Claudia. "Mimikry als Grenzverwirrung. Parodistische Posen bei Yoko Tawada." Pp. 176-206 in *Über Grenzen. Limitation und Transgeression in Literatur und Ästhetik*, edited by Claudia Benthien and Irmela Marei Krüger-Fürhoff. Stuttgart, Germany: Metzler, 1999.
Cramer, Sibylle. "Zwischen den Sprachen und Worten. Yoko Tawada als Erzählerin, Essayistin und Dramatikerin." *Frankfurter Rundschau*. 8 January 1994, section ZB 4.

Dittberner, Hugo, ed. *Mit der Zeit erzählen? fragt er. Marcel Beyer—Heiner Egge—Gundi Feyrer, Yoko Tawada. Das zweite Buch.* Göttingen, Germany: Wallstein, 1994.

Fischer, Sabine. "'Verschwinden ist schön': Zu Yoko Tawada's Kurzroman *Das Bad*." Pp. 101-114 in *Denn du tanzt auf einem Seil. Positionen deutschsprachiger MigrantInnenliteratur*, edited by Sabine Fischer and Moray McGowan. Tübingen, Germany: Stauffenburg, 1997.

Kloepfer, Albrecht and Miho Matsunaga. "Yoko Tawada." *Kritisches Lexikon zur deutschsprachigen Gegenwartsliteratur* 64 (2000): 1-17.

Kosta, Barbara, and Helga Kraft, eds. *Writing against Boundaries. Nationality, Ethnicity and Gender in the German-speaking Context.* New York: Rodopi, 2003.

Krauß, Andrea. "'Talisman.'—'Tawadische Sprachtheorie.'" Pp. 55-77 in *Migration und Interkulturaliät in neueren literarischen Texten*, edited by Aglaia Blioumi. Munich, Germany: Iudicium, 2002.

Matsunaga, Miho. "'Schreiben als Übersetzung.' Die Dimension der Übersetzung in denWerken von Yoko Tawada." *Zeitschrift fur Germanistik* 12, no. 3 (2002): 532-546.

Pörtner, Peter. "Zeichen—Setzen: Zur Sino-Japanischen Schrift und Ihrer Geschichte." Pp. 66-75 in *Über den Umgang mit der Schrift*, edited by Wara'Wende Waltraud. Würzburg, Germany: Königshausen & Neumann, 2002.

Seyhan, Azade. *Writing Outside the Nation.* Princeton, N.J.: Princeton University Press, 2001.

Tawada, Yoko. "Die Krone aus Gras. Zu Paul Celans 'Die Niemandsrose.'" In *Text und Kritik. Zeitschrift für Literatur*, edited by Heinz Ludwig Arnold. 2002. Vol. 53/54, 3rd edition: 170-183.

———. *Ein Gast. Roman.* Tübingen, Germany: Konkursbuch, 1993.

———. "Erzähler ohne Seelen." In *Talisman: Literarische Essays.* Tübingen: Konkursbuch, 1996. 16-27.

———. "Rabbi Löw und 27 Punkte—Physiognomie der Interpunktion bei Paul Celan." In *Arcadia: Zeitschrift für Allgemeine und Vergleichende Literaturwissenschaft*, edited by John Neubauer and Jürgen Wertheimer. Berlin and New York: Walter de Gruyter: 1997. Vol. 32.1: 283-286.

———. *Spielzeug und Sprachmagie. Eine ethnologische Poetologie.* Tübingen, Germany: Konkursbuch, 2000.

———. *Talisman: Literarische Essays.* Tübingen, Germany: Konkursbuch, 1996.

———. *Überseezungen.* Tübingen, Germany: Konkursbuch, 2002.

———. *Verwandlungen: Tübinger Poetik-Vorlesungen.* Tübingen, Germany: Konkursbuch, 1998/2001. 23-40.

Traverso, Enzo. "Paul Celan: Dichtung der Zerstörung." In *Auschwitz denken. Die Intellektuellen und die Shoah*, translated by Helmut Dahmer. Hamburg, Germany: Hamburger Edition, 2000. 214-237.

Weigel, Sigrid. "Der schielende Blick. Thesen zur Geschichte weiblicher Schreibpraxis." In *Die verborgene Frau. Sechs Beiträge zu einer feministischen Literaturwissenschaft.* Hamburg, Germany: Argument, 1988. 83-137.

———. "Transsibirische Metamorphosen. Laudatio auf Yoko Tawada zur Verleihung des Adalbert-von-Chamisso-Preises 1996." *Frauen in der Literaturwissenschaft* 49 (1996): 5-6.

Chapter Seven
Tawada's Multilingual Moves: Toward a Transnational Imaginary

Yasemin Yildiz

The idea of a common language is instrumental in the imagination of the nation as a community, as Benedict Anderson has argued. As a result of massive migrations, increased mobility, and the growth of exile and diasporic communities in the twentieth century, however, languages have become dislocated from national territories to an unprecedented degree. This dislocation, and the emergence of new hybrid languages which frequently accompanies it, has created a situation in which the ideological equation of language, territory, and national identity has become increasingly difficult to maintain. In the cultural realm, this situation has led to the emergence of bilingual and multilingual writers who explore the connections and disconnections between languages, territories, and nations in innovative and critical ways.[1]

I suggest that we read Yoko Tawada's bilingual oeuvre in this light as producing and providing insight into new transnational imaginaries.[2] By transnational imaginaries I mean the mental maps that negotiate the diverse social, cultural, political, and psychic forces that interact with a heightened intensity today and that are not limited to any given national context.[3] As is well known, Tawada, a Japanese-born writer who has been living in Germany since 1982, writes award-winning prose, poetry, theater and radio plays as well as literary essays in Japanese and in German.[4] Her German texts,[5] on which I primarily focus in this paper, frequently employ a displaced female Japanese narrator in Europe, who observes the oddity of rituals and details of everyday life in a sort of ethnography.[6] Rather than developing coherent plots, the texts usually consist of a series of loosely related vignettes and observations. In addition to her literary work, Tawada has completed a doctoral dissertation on German literature, and so is also fluent in the "languages" of theory and philosophy.[7]

While Tawada is the author of a bilingual oeuvre in Japanese and German, I argue that one of the most important aspects of her writing is in fact her multilingual writing practice *within* each of these languages. In both her German and her Japanese texts other languages are invoked and inscribed.[8] As I will demonstrate in more detail below, many of Tawada's texts develop a varied multilingualism that derives from moving between languages and from switching per-

spectives on the language at hand. In her German texts, she frequently defamiliarizes German language habits by taking words or grammatical concepts, such
as grammatical gender, literally. Her attention to the shape of alphabetic letters
and the confrontation of the Roman alphabet with Japanese and Chinese script
likewise serves to defamiliarize the very material of writing. This defamiliarization, aided by another language's presence, but not fully explained by it, puts
into question the supposed identity of a language and the notion of clear-cut
boundaries between languages.

Multilingualism in literature is not a new form in itself, as the pioneering
study of Leonard Forster, *The Poet's Tongues* (1970), already documents. Yet
the recent increase in titles on literary multilingualism indicates that this form is
expanding into new directions and at the same time receiving growing critical
attention.[9] I suggest that this attention is due to its significance as an aesthetic
site for thinking cultural interaction in a globalizing world.[10] I therefore propose
that we consider Tawada's multilingual form not only as a site where the contours of national language(s) are made porous but also as partaking in a larger
reimagination of language subjects and affiliations. In the often playful move
beyond the separateness of national languages, Tawada begins to offer a linguistic imagination that invokes realms beyond categories such as the nation.

Tawada's texts proceed in this reimagination by subtly questioning the
naturalized links between subjects and languages. Since the mother tongue is a
central figure of claiming such links as natural, it is not surprising that her texts
repeatedly turn to this term. In the 1996 prose text "Von der Muttersprache zur
Sprachmutter" (From the Mother Tongue to the Language Mother) in the collection *Talisman*, Tawada deconstructs the notion of the mother tongue most explicitly. I examine the implications of her specific form of deconstruction,
namely the turn away from organic to inorganic modes of belonging, and finally
to a utopian realm outside language. The very notion of the subject and subjectivity are not left untouched in this deconstruction, but are rather themselves
deconstructed. In the short prose piece "Eine leere Flasche" (An Empty Bottle,
2002) the move away from the national context of origin and its language into a
new language realm is figured as a move to a new "I" beyond restricted ground-
ing. That text suggests that a transnational move allows for a liberation from
nationality, history, as well as gender identity. The volume *Überseezungen*
(Overseastongues, 2002), in which it is featured, as a whole introduces an ex-
tended transnational realm. This book marks a step beyond the heretofore dominant East-West axis in Tawada's writing and towards a reorganization of her
imaginary topography that now includes an engagement with the North-South
axis. The story "Bioskoop der Nacht" (Bioscope of the Night), set in the section
on "South African Tongues" provides a compelling constellation of languages
and histories in this regard. By constructing a first-person narrator who is a
Japanese woman living in Germany but dreaming in Afrikaans, a language unknown to her conscious self, Tawada explodes the binary of existing either in
the mother tongue or in the foreign language. Her turn to dream-language in

general and to Afrikaans in particular has implications for imagining transnational subjects and their historical entanglements.

Mother Language—Language Mother: Organic and Inorganic Kinship

As a deeply ideological concept, the mother tongue has been used to make political claims about belonging and nationality since the late eighteenth century. While the issue of the mother tongue appears in a number of Tawada's texts, it is most programmatically treated in the 1996 volume *Talisman* in her story-essay "Von der Muttersprache zur Sprachmutter" (From the Mother Tongue to the Language Mother—or more literally, preserving the German title's chiasmic structure: From the Mother Language to the Language Mother.) Written for a German-speaking audience, this text relates the Japanese narrator's linguistic experiences while working in a German office shortly after arriving in Germany.

How does Tawada stage belonging with regard to the "mother tongue," a concept that invokes language affiliation as a result of birth and kinship? In Tawada's text the figure of kinship does not relate to the "mother tongue" itself, but to what the narrator calls her "language mother." Instead of invoking an organic mother, this term refers to a machine. The narrator explains that in order to learn the grammatical gender of German nouns, she imagined them as male or female objects.[11] By taking the notion of grammatical gender literally and conflating grammatical gender with human gender (or even sex), that is, treating it as if it was a natural dimension of the object, the text paradoxically denaturalizes the grammatical category. The literal-mindedness, a seemingly naïve stance, reminds the reader of a dimension of the language that is normally not perceived.[12] This reminder does not change the grammatical order of the German language, but it defamiliarizes the language to its speakers and readers and thereby does alter it nonetheless.

In the text, this shift leads to a sexualized desk, where the narrator finds herself surrounded by male—even masculine—seeming objects, such as pens and pencils: "the pencil, the ballpoint pen, the fountain pen—the male shapes lay there in a manly way and also got up in a manly way when I took them in my hand."[13] The only "female" object on this desk is *die Schreibmaschine* (the feminine article typewriter): "This female machine which gave me the gift of language I called a language mother."[14] The machine functions as a "mother" insofar as a new language subject originates from it. Kinship is transferred to a mechanical process of repetition and reproduction. This shift does not lead to a second mother tongue, though, since for the narrator the typewriter "did not change the fact that German is not my mother tongue."[15] The machine does not reproduce a mother tongue, but supplements it. What it changes is the notion of kinship itself: that term is no longer limited to organic relationships but designates inorganic relationships which can "adopt" subjects as well.[16] Why the mother tongue needs to be supplemented in this manner is only explained at the end of the text:

In the mother tongue words are attached to people so that one cannot playfully enjoy language. There, the thoughts cling so closely to the words that neither the former nor the latter can fly freely. In a foreign language, however, one has something like a staple remover: it removes all the things that are attached to each other and cling to one another.[17]

The mother tongue is associated with too tight a relationship, a form of belonging that requires strategies of detachment. What is removed is the inevitability and supposed naturalness of the relation between word and referent. The desire for distance from the mother tongue is not presented as based on cultural rejection but rather on the desire for cultural space not smothered by nativity. Thus Tawada's title—"From the mother language to the language mother"—appears as a programmatic stance on affiliation, indicating a shift from a discourse of a naturalized relationship to language to an inorganic one.

While the typewriter—interpellated as the "language mother"—occupies a privileged position through its titular appearance, it is in fact the staple remover, the *Heftklammerentferner*, that functions as the ultimate model: "its wonderful name embodied my yearning for a foreign language."[18] The staple remover is outside of the chiasmus of the title; it detaches what the chiasmus still holds together, namely kinship figured through both the mother language and the language mother. This utensil, not able to write or erase, is fully detached from the act of writing itself. It is "illiterate"[19] and does not function to reproduce language or writing. In contrast to the other objects on the desk, this item is also not imagined as male or female in a human sense. Rather, it is said to resemble a snake's head with teeth.[20] The auxiliary alignment of an object's grammatical gender and its "sex" in the narrator's imagination is interrupted. With that the object breaks the chain of human reproduction and even alternative modes of kinship. The desire for a "foreign language"—rather than German—gestures to a realm beyond the human, the one that is supposed to be distinguished by language. In this text, Tawada moves from an organic to an inorganic model of kinship, only to abandon it altogether as a restrictive model. Rather than kinship and belonging, the text envisions detachment as a desirable process and quality of being. This detachment is enabled by a multilingual environment, not because any specific language is preferred over another one, but because multilingualism can defamiliarize the very language structures in which we exist. With this positive definition of detachment as libratory, Tawada suggests a perspective on multilingual transnational encounters as positive and productive rather than as a site of loss or grievous alienation.

Redefining the Subject

Whereas in the "Muttersprache" text the gender system of the German language is used as a point of departure, the short prose piece "Eine leere Flasche" (An empty bottle) from the 2002 volume *Überseezungen* (Overseastongues)[21] takes up the gender system inherent to Japanese, in order to problematize subjects and belonging from a different perspective. In a number of her German texts,

Tawada refers to the Japanese system of pronouns in which gender is built into the "I." In "Eine leere Flasche" the Japanese narrator tells German-language readers of the different Japanese terms of self-reference and their gendered and age-specific character. She explains that these terms range from the young girls' self-reference as *atashi* and the boys' self-reference as *boku* or the older boys' *ore"* to the ungendered adult term *watashi*. Tawada's elaboration emphasizes that children are strongly gendered until they reach adulthood and have the option of using a gender-neutral term for "I". The narrator of this brief text—like the first-person narrator in the earlier novel *Das Bad* (The bath, 1989)—tells us that as a child she was uneasy with all these terms for "I" because she did not feel gendered in as clear a way as the terms demanded.[22] She further tells us of a girl who refers to herself with the young boys' "I," namely "boku." That girl defines her gender, her *gefühltes Geschlecht* (felt gender) as *boku*.[23] In contrast to that grammatical gender crossing, the narrator identifies neither as a girl-I nor as *boku*.[24]

This text stresses the relationship between "I" and gender particularly in a Japanese-language childhood. Given that determinative relationship, a language which does not force the speaker to identify herself in terms of gender every time she refers to herself is seen as desirable and libratory. This liberation is linked to a spatial move and a linguistic change:

> I lost sight of the problem of self-reference. Because I moved to Europe and found the word "I" which does not force you to have such considerations. An "I" does not need to have a specific gender, or age, or status, or history, or attitude, or character. Anyone can call themselves simply "I." This word consists only of the fact that I speak at all. . . . "I" became my favorite word.[25]

The "European" word is described as an empty sign that takes on meaning only in the act of speaking itself and is thereby idealized for its lack of baggage.[26] The narrator of this text consequently favors the word *ich* for similar reasons as the narrator of "Muttersprache" privileges the staple remover, namely they both serve as sites of detachment. This is based on a linguistic understanding of pronouns as shifters, though in that field this characterization is not limited to European languages. This notion—that in Europe a subjectivity can be expressed that is not circumscribed by gender, age, status, or history—is enabled by the focus on a structural understanding of language, rather than a historical one.

However, in the end of the text, both the "I" and the verb "to be" are offered in an altered sense that relies precisely on Japanese in order to be a space of possibility:

> I also like that an I (*ich*) begins with the letter *I*, a simple line, like the beginning of a brush stroke which touches the paper and simultaneously proclaims the opening of speech. *Bin* [first person present tense of "to be"] is also a beautiful word. In Japanese there is also the word *bin*, that sounds exactly the same and means "a bottle." When I begin telling a story with the two words *ich bin* (I

am) a space opens up, the I is the beginning of a brush stroke and the bottle is empty.[27]

Comparing the *I* in *ich* to the stroke of a brush implicitly evokes calligraphy and relocates the "European" letter to the realm of Japanese writing art. The pleasure is derived in the calligraphic opening of speech. The possibility of a Japanese phonetic understanding of *bin*, that is, the German first-person form of the verb "to be" as *Flasche* (bottle) supplies another dimension of meaning. The text translates the parts of *Ich bin* (I am) into a calligraphic opening stroke and a bottle respectively. Though seemingly unrelated, those two associative and phonetic meanings are combined into a new understanding. What is transformed is the deeply philosophical articulation of existence and subjectivity that is encapsulated in *Ich bin*. In the Japanese-inspired but ultimately primarily associative, creative, and "subjective" version of *Ich bin* this expression becomes one of openness, possibility, space, lightness, and emptiness. These words are translated from German to Japanese and back to German until we end up with an idiosyncratic and object-filled image.

The story "Eine leere Flasche" that began with the problem of the Japanese self-reference does not end with a shift to the "European" alternative but uses the European version as an occasion to combine and reimagine both German and Japanese. This reimagined form of "I am" is thus multilingual in its multiple moves between these two languages. The multilingualism resides in the fact that we do not simply encounter two different languages. Rather, in the series of translations and reimaginations it is the narrator's association which provides the rewriting. This association is the third term in the interchange of the two languages. The gender aspect is "overcome" not only by growing up and moving to Europe but, as this ending implies, also by the replacement of human subjectivity with writing utensils and acts of writing (the calligraphic stroke) as well as other non-human objects (the bottle). In that sense it performs a similar shift to the one in "Muttersprache" where the gendered objects including the "language mother" itself are ultimately transcended by the name of an object that is not imagined in human terms, namely the *Heftklammerentferner* (staple remover). This vision of forms of detachment leads us to the question of history. Does Tawada completely eschew history in her multilingual, transnational imaginary?

Dream Language and the Topography of Transnational Imaginaries

What happens after the staple remover detaches papers from each other and lets them reorganize or "fly freely"? As I indicated earlier, Tawada's more recent writing undergoes such a reorganization with respect to the maps underlying her "imaginary topography," to borrow Sigrid Weigel's term. Whereas "Europe" is a frequent reference point for Tawada in many earlier texts, most notably in *Wo Europa anfängt* (Where Europe Begins, 1991), her 2002 collection *Überseezungen* expands this topography. The text "Eine leere Flasche," for example, is situated in the section on "Eurasian Tongues." Here for the first time we no longer have a binary between East and West, between Asia and Europe, but rather the melded geographical entity "Eurasia." The rewriting of "I am" into "an empty bottle," an image that is also neither simply "European" nor "Japanese," brings those codes together through multilingualism. At the same time, the palimpsest-like layering that is the basis of this particular rewriting provides an alternative model to that of melding or undifferentiated convergence that the term "Eurasia" otherwise might seem to suggest. This Eurasia is now one part of an expanded world map that includes "South African Tongues," and "North American Tongues." With the appearance of the latter two, Tawada supplements the previously dominant East-West axis with the North-South one and begins telling different stories and histories.

The relatively long prose piece "Bioskoop der Nacht" (Bioscope of the Night)[28] is the only text in the section on South African tongues. The text engages with the dislocation of language, territory, and national identity that I described earlier through its own dislocations and displacements. In a series of vignettes, we shift between surreal dream sequences on the one hand, and the first-person narrator's attempts to find an answer to the question in which language she dreams, on the other. This question, we learn, is imposed on the narrator, who is once again a Japanese woman living in Germany, by complete strangers. The assumption behind it is explicitly articulated when someone admonishes her: "But one dreams in the language of the country in which the soul resides."[29] According to this logic, the dream reveals the soul's true residence in such a way that language, territory, and soul correspond to each other and profess a singular and clear-cut affiliation. The unconscious and involuntary articulations of dreams are treated as identifiable as a specific, national, language.

Instead of rejecting the nationalization of dream-language, Tawada offers a seemingly affirmative response. Yet contrary to expectations, the dream-language is identified neither as Japanese nor as German. In the course of party small talk, the narrator describes her dreams to a Dutch psychoanalyst who responds unambiguously: "That is Afrikaans."[30] In the first of the story's dream sequences, the narrator had encountered a man who referred to himself in a confusing gender. He pointed to himself and proclaimed: "Die Mann" (feminine article man). The analyst explains: "Die man, die frou, die kind." (Man, woman, child. Everything is feminine."[31] Now that the protagonist realizes that elements of her dream correspond to Afrikaans, she is able to decode them. For example, the man's statement "ich arbeite in einem Winkel" (I work in a corner) as he stands in a small shop derives from the Afrikaans word *Winkel* for shop rather than the German meaning of *Winkel* as corner. That this shop is immediately identified by the narrator as a *Kolonialwarenladen* (a colonial goods store)[32] in which the goods have images of Dutch women in traditional costumes also points to South African colonial history.[33] This dream-language, which the narrator claims not to know, neither corresponds to her nationality nor to her adopted home, but rather follows its own logic of displacement, a logic which subsequently leads the narrator to journey to South Africa to begin learning the language, in order to translate her own dreams.[34]

Two questions arise at this point: Why does Tawada stage disaffiliation from national alternatives through dreams? And secondly, Why Afrikaans? Tawada's use of the dream is no doubt on the one hand parodic. It ridicules the essentialist logic of this indeed ubiquitous question, as any bilingual or multilingual person can attest. On the other hand, taking up the dream as a form points to something more complicated about affiliation and belonging. Tawada does not dismiss the idea that dreams are productive sites of investigation. In contrast to the interlocutors' assumption that the dream will transparently reveal something about the dreamer, however, the story reminds us that dreams are overdetermined. As we recall from Freud, dreams mobilize multiple mechanisms of displacement and condensation. These mechanisms help us to explain what to make of the shift to Afrikaans.

As I suggested earlier, Afrikaans as the third term displaces the German-Japanese binary. Yet because of the language's inextricable association with colonialism and racism, this displacement does not lead to an untainted alternative. In the story, the displacement offers an occasion to reflect on the legacy of apartheid. It prompts the narrator, for example, to recall high school discussions on Japan's relationship to the apartheid regime and its implication in it.[35] The narrator's journey to post-apartheid South Africa further highlights the aftermath of racist policies, as in a visit to a township.[36] The question of how Japanese people would have figured in the racial categorizations of apartheid preoccupies the protagonist repeatedly. Would she have been one of the *Blankes*, the Whites?[37]

The uncanny presence of violence is even inscribed into the textbook that the protagonist reads in her Afrikaans language course in Cape Town. In the form of a ghost story, the text incorporates a narrative that deals with the demands of the dead and of justice. The interpolated story tells of the ghost of a murdered girl whose corpse periodically appears by the side of the road until the police finally resolve her murder, some one hundred years after the deed. The story's closure comes with the act of locating the bones of the murder victim at the site where she reappeared.[38] In contrast to the transnational moves that the framing text otherwise stages, this recounted story insists on marking the exact place of a violent death and a reconstruction of the events that led to it. Though the textbook story ends with a resolution, the murdered girl nevertheless makes her way to the present of the classroom: "The murdered girl sat in our classroom, she interfered, although she did not belong to the class. . . . The girl wanted to tell us her story, her encounter with her murderer." The girl's presence affects the language that the students produce in trying to respond: their sentences are "krumm, lückenhaft und durcheinander" (crooked, full of gaps, and confused). Yet these sentences are "befriedigend" (satisfying)[39] since they are part of a conversation, rather than an empty exercise. In the students' response and in the structure of the "Bioskoop" story, the uncanny quality of the inserted story is replaced with satisfaction where Afrikaans sentences come out crooked, that is, marked by an ongoing, paradoxically lively conversation with the dead.

Tawada's story suggests an altered perspective on the language. In fact, despite its association with apartheid, a word that literally means separateness, Afrikaans is a site of heterogeneity. Though derived from Dutch, Afrikaans is actually a hybrid language which has incorporated lexical and syntactical structures of German, English, Portuguese, Malay, Xhosa, and various other African languages. That is, this language which is inextricably associated with a racially purist regime, is in fact hybrid. Its linguistic elements record its history. Malay influences, for example, index the importation of Asian slaves to South Africa.[40] The language thus functions as a site of the condensation of both languages and multiple histories. Though we do not receive such a history of Afrikaans from Tawada, her story still marks an engagement with history through a new constellation of multilingualism that includes Afrikaans. Ultimately then, and in contrast to the notion of detachment, the logic of displacement that the dream form enables actually functions to connect different histories. Transnational dislocation as represented here does not liberate from history, it does not escape the violence of national contexts, but rather makes visible a more implicated relationship between seemingly separate languages, histories, and national contexts.

Conclusion

The German language stories by Yoko Tawada that I have discussed in this paper suggest a productive shift from nativity to inorganic modes of belonging and beyond and from narrowly national contexts to transnational imaginaries. They also help us to see, I would argue, that Tawada is not merely operating "between" two languages, cultures, or national contexts. Rather, her writing playfully opens up languages from within and introduces links to other languages that are not determined by "natural" connections. Though from extratextual sources we know that Germany and Japan are main reference points for Tawada's biography, the textual evidence does not line up with those national categories. Germany, for example, does not seem to play any role as a national context, but is subsumed under "Europe," a phantasmatic site of greater importance in her work. Even that category, though, undergoes change, one that is accompanied or even enabled by a multilingual rewriting.

As my readings have also revealed, these rewritings are significantly linked to questions of gender. Among the seemingly "organic" forms of belonging that are dislodged in Tawada's texts is the belonging to a gender. In these texts, gender does not just appear as an issue for embodied subjects, but is evoked as the very structuring principle of language and thus as inscribed into the material out of which subjectivities are shaped in the first place. In the form of the mother tongue, gender is also linked to kinship, another organic category that is deconstructed. Because of the nature of the ideology of the mother tongue, the form of kinship that is reproduced through the mother tongue is linked to the nation. We can thus speculate that the refusal of organic kinship is also the refusal of restrictive, national belonging. In Tawada's writing these categories, namely language, gender, kinship, and national context, are interrelated. Because of this inextricable relationship, it is necessary to rethink all of them simultaneously, as Tawada does.

While the first two stories I discussed emphasize detachment as positive and liberating, the third one acknowledges that this is not so easily possible. The forms of detachment envisioned in the earlier texts are enabled by an attention to the *structures* of language, rather than by historical considerations. As both language and subjects exist simultaneously at the nexus of synchronic and diachronic axes, however, questions about historical location also demand to be considered. When Tawada does this, it happens through the unlikely route of the dream. With the stimulating figure of "dreaming in Afrikaans," Tawada suggests both the dislocations as well as the powerful forces that govern language, territory, and nation.

Notes

1. While the terms of this description, and especially the emphases on dislocation and languages, are mine, my understanding of the larger situation is based on the work of scholars of cultural globalization, especially anthropologist Arjun Appadurai and his important book *Modernity at Large*.

2. I follow the convention of her German publications from which I will be drawing in writing Tawada's name in this order.

3. Besides Appadurai, who emphasizes the importance of imagination as an active agent in the process of cultural globalization, I draw on the work of other members of the Center for Transnational Studies who are also associated with the journal *Public Culture*. See the special issue of that journal on "New Imaginaries," edited by Dilip Parameshwar Gaonkar and Benjamin Lee.

4. See Matsunaga on the distribution of genres according to language and her list of Tawada's "parallel texts," that is, texts available in both languages, though they might not be entirely identical. As Matsunaga demonstrates, Tawada prefers some languages for some genres. Thus, so far at least, she writes poetry solely in Japanese and literary critical essays solely in German. We are therefore not dealing with an entirely parallel and symmetrical literary production across two languages, but one in which form and language seem to influence each other.

5. It is, of course, not so easy to draw the boundaries of Tawada's "German" and "Japanese" oeuvre. Her first book publications occurred in Germany, in bilingual editions or in translation. That is, the poems and texts were written in Japanese, but published in German translation, and only circulated in Germany. Are those texts then part of her "German" or her "Japanese" work? The prose texts that are only available in German translation without a published Japanese original put pressure on such facile categorizations.

6. For readings of Tawada's take on ethnography, see the essays by Claudia Breger and Andrea Krauß.

7. Among others, the thought of Walter Benjamin is a frequent reference point for her. See her published dissertation *Spielzeug und Sprachmagie* (2000) which she wrote under the direction of one of Germany's leading literary and cultural critics, Sigrid Weigel. The fact that the dissertation was published by her long-time German literary pub-

lisher, Konkursbuchverlag Claudia Gehrke, also indicates the fluidity between her literary and her critical oeuvre.

8. For information on literary strategies in her Japanese texts I rely on Matsunaga as well as Kloepfer and Matsunaga. Matsunaga cites for example the odd syntax in some of Tawada's Japanese texts (538), such as in *Arufabetto no kizuguchi* (1993). With *Hikon* (1998), Tawada has produced a Japanese text that deliberately uses as many Chinese characters as possible (Kloepfer and Matsunaga 14).

9. See for example Kellman; Schmeling and Schmitz-Emans; Sommer.

10. See also my essay on the influential Turkish-German bestseller *Kanak Sprak* by Feridun Zaimoglu, where I demonstrate how that text's multilingualism—which consists of a defiant and provocative mixture of languages, slangs, dialects, and registers rendered in a hip hop inflected style—is a site where the local, nonnational, and transnational are negotiated.

11. She elides, however, the neuter and operates as if only two genders exited in German, rather than three: female, male, and neuter. That third gender appears later in the text in its indeterminate form as "es." As Krauß demonstrates, Tawada's evocation of the "es" indicates a larger philosophical and psychoanalytic discourse. The "es" as a grammatical placeholder in sentences without a subject (as in "es regnet" "it rains"), its god-like function, and also the Freudian term of the "Es" for the unconscious or Id are all negotiated in this seemingly simple text.

12. Krauß describes the staged naiveté that also enables this scene as a critical tool in Tawada's poetics. Breger's elaborations on the critical potential of mimicry offer another perspective on this scene. By excessively mimicking native speakers who are said to feel the grammatical gender of an object naturally, the narrator in Tawada's text subverts the notion of a natural link between grammar and referents and between language and subjects.

13. It is barely necessary to point to the phallic quality of the pen that psychoanalysis first identified. What is more noteworthy is the fact that Tawada's text reads at times like a translation of psychoanalytic terms into images and scenes (see also Krauß on this point). While the "other" language in this text could in one reading be identified as either Japanese—the language not spoken—or as German—the narrator's foreign language—psychoanalysis also is a translated presence here and hence functions as an element of the text's multilingualism.

14. Yoko Tawada, "Von der Muttersprache zur Sprachmutter," in *Talisman*. (Tübingen, Germany: Konkursbuchverlag Claudia Gehrke, 1996), 13.

15. Tawada, "Muttersprache," 12.

16. Tawada, "Muttersprache," 13. A similar move is evident in the text "*Sieben Geschichten der sieben Mütter*" (Seven Stories of the Seven Mothers) in the same volume, where none of the seven "mothers" refers to a biological mother. Instead, all vignettes rewrite conventional notions of motherhood and mothering. Among the mentioned "mothers" are for example a female doctoral advisor, in German literally "doctoral mother," and mother-of-pearl "Perlmutter."

17. Tawada, "Muttersprache," 15.

18. Tawada, "Muttersprache," 14.

19. Tawada, "Muttersprache," 14.

20. Tawada, "Muttersprache," 14.

21. The title, *Überseezungen*, is a difficult to translate condensation of multiple words, including overseas, sole (the fish), tongues, and translations.

22. Yoko Tawada, "Eine leere Flasche," in *Das Bad*, (Tübingen, Germany: Konkursbuchverlag Claudia Gehrke, 1989), 53.

23. Tawada, *Das Bad*, 55.
24. Tawada, *Das Bad*, 53.
25. Tawada, *Das Bad*, 56-57.
26. It is significant for an exploration of transnationalism that Tawada speaks of "ich" as a "European" rather than a "German" word. The national category of German is elided in favor of a continental scale. This phenomenon reoccurs in many places in Tawada's writing. "Europe," which in many discourses, both in Japan and outside it, functions similarly to the trope of "the West" (see Naoki Sakai for a forceful critique of the binary of Asia and the West), is clearly a phantasmatic category, just like the notion of a "European" "I."
27. Tawada, *Das Bad*, 57.
28. "Bioskoop" is the Afrikaans word for cinema and movie theater and still in use in South Africa. In German, the word "Bioskop" refers to an early cinematographic apparatus. As "Bioskoop of the Night" it is part of yet another mechanical metaphor, this time for dreams.
29. Tawada, "Bioskoop der Nacht," 70.
30. Tawada, "Bioskoop," 65.
31. Later in the text, the protagonist's Afrikaans teacher in South Africa remarks that some see the language as ungendered since a differentiation between genders requires the existence of multiple genders (76). As in the story "Eine leere Flasche" we encounter a constellation where the feminine gender is confronted with the possibility of unmarked gender. The tensions around gender thus seem to be more about the relationship between feminine and ungendered, than between feminine and masculine.
32. Tawada, "Bioskoop," 62.
33. This is also reminiscent of Tawada's story "Das Fremde aus der Dose," (published in English as "Canned Foreign") in which the image of a Japanese woman in traditional costume on a tuna can sold in German supermarkets plays an important role. Kader Konuk reads that story as Tawada's engagement with the circulation of the images of the ethnic female on the literary market (39).
34. Tawada, "Bioskoop," 76.
35. Tawada, "Bioskoop," 68. Given Japan's still repressed colonial history, one might also speculate whether this is a displacement of a discourse on Japanese colonialism.
36. Tawada, "Bioskoop," 77-80.
37. Tawada, "Bioskoop," 74-75.
38. Tawada, "Bioskoop," 88-89.
39. Tawada, "Bioskoop," 90.
40. Tawada, "Bioskoop," 75. This fact also appears in the story in a conversation between a policeman and the protagonist.

Bibliography

Anderson, Benedict. *Imagined Communities: Reflections on the Origin and Spread of Nationalism*. London: Verso, 1983.
Appadurai, Arjun. *Modernity at Large: Cultural Dimensions of Globalization*. Minneapolis: University of Minnesota Press, 1996.
Breger, Claudia. "'Meine Herren, spielt in meinem Gesicht ein Affe?' Strategien der Mimikry in Texten von Emine S. Özdamar und Yoko Tawada." In *Aufbrüche: Kulturelle Produktionen von Migrantinnen, Schwarzen und Jüdischen Frauen in*

Deutschland, edited by Cathy Gelbin, Kader Konuk, and Peggy Piesche. König-stein/Taunus, Germany: Ulrike Helmer, 1999, 30-59.

———. "Mimikry als Grenzverwirrung. Parodistische Posen bei Yoko Tawada." In *Über Grenzen: Limitation und Transgression in Literatur und Ästhetik*, edited by Claudia Benthien and Irmela Marei Krüger-Fürhoff, 176-206. Stuttgart, Germany: Metzler, 1999.

Forster, Leonard. *The Poet's Tongues: Multilingualism in Literature*. London: Cambridge University Press, 1970.

Gaonkar, Dilip Parameshwar, and Benjamin Lee, eds. "New Imaginaries." Special Issue of *Public Culture* 14, no. 1 (2002).

Kellman, Steven G. *The Translingual Imagination*. Lincoln: University of Nebraska Press, 2000.

Kloepfer, Albrecht, and Miho Matsunaga. "Yoko Tawada." *Kritisches Lexikon der Gegenwartsliteratur* 64 (2000): 2-17.

Konuk, Kader. "Crossing Borders. 53rd Annual Meeting of the South Central Modern Language Association." *Rundbrief Frauen in der Literaturwissenschaft* 49 (1996): 38-40.

Krauß, Andrea. "'Talisman.' 'Tawadische Sprachtheorie.'" In *Migration und Interkulturalität in neueren literarischen Texten*, edited by Aglaia Blioumi, 55-77. Munich, Germany: Iudicium, 2002.

Matsunaga Miho. "'Schreiben als Übersetzung': Die Dimension der Übersetzung in den Werken von Yoko Tawada." *Zeitschrift für Germanistik* 12, no. 3 (2002): 532-546.

Sakai, Naoki. "'You Asians': On the Historical Role of the West and Asia Binary." *SAQ: The South Atlantic Quarterly* 99, no. 4 (2000): 789-817.

Schmeling, Manfred and Monika Schmitz-Emans, eds. *Multilingale Literatur im 20. Jahrhundert*. Würzburg, Germany: Königshausen und Neumann, 2002.

Sommer, Doris, ed. *Bilingual Games: Some Literary Investigations*. New York: Palgrave, 2003.

Tawada, Yoko. *Arufabetto no kizuguchi*. Tokyo: Kawade Shobo Shinsha, 1993.

———. *Das Bad*. Tübingen, Germany: Konkursbuchverlag Claudia Gehrke, 1989.

———. *Hikon*. Tokyo: Kodansha, 1998.

———. *Spielzeug und Sprachmagie in der Europäischen Literatur : Eine Ethnologische Poetologie*. Tübingen, Germany: Konkursbuchverlag Claudia Gehrke, 2000.

———. *Talisman*. Tübingen, Germany: Konkursbuchverlag Claudia Gehrke, 1996.

———. *Überseezungen*. Tübingen, Germany: Konkursbuchverlag Claudia Gehrke, 2002.

———. *Wo Europa anfängt*. Tübingen, Germany: Konkursbuchverlag Claudia Gehrke, 1991.

Weigel, Sigrid. *Bilder des kulturellen Gedächtnisses: Beiträge zur Gegenwartsliteratur*. Dülmen-Hiddingsel, Germany: Tende, 1994.

Yildiz, Yasemin. "Critically 'Kanak': A Reimagination of German Culture." In *Globalization and the Future of German*, ed. by Andreas Gardt and Bernd Hüppauf. Berlin: Mouton de Gruyter, 2004.

Chapter Eight
Traveling without Moving: Physical and Linguistic Mobility in Yoko Tawada's *Überseezungen*
Christina Kraenzle

Travel, in its many forms—for example, (im)migration,[1] tourism,[2] colonial expansion[3]—has been one of Yoko Tawada's most persistent thematic preoccupations. Many of Tawada's German-language works are, in a broad sense, travel stories and offer up a veritable catalogue of travellers with varying relationships to the privilege of motion.

Her writings subsequently raise a number of intriguing questions about the interconnections of space, subjectivity and mobility: for example, how is space productive of subjectivity or, conversely, how might subjects have a hand in producing the spaces they inhabit? How is travel bound up with the production of knowledge of the cultural Other and how are cultural identities formed in acts of travel? Finally, what models of subjectivity are made possible by the constant travel across spaces, cultures, and—most importantly for Tawada—languages?

Indeed, it is the experience of linguistic mobility which constitutes another of Tawada's primary investigations. *Talisman*, for example, explores the linguistic consequences of the narrator's move from Japan to Germany and the resulting clash of linguistic sign systems that make up her daily reality. The protagonist in *Das Bad* (*The Bath*) returns to her native Japan after a long sojourn in Germany and must reflect on her new, and at times distanced, relationship to her mother tongue.

While many of Tawada's writings consider the consequences of linguistic as well as geographic dislocation, in *Überseezungen* travel through language becomes not a side-effect but a substitute for travel through space. Embedded in *Überseezungen*'s dual focus on geographic and linguistic dislocation are wider implications about the nature of modern communication and travel, arguably resulting in Tawada's most sustained reflection on the interconnectedness of mobility, geography, language, and identity to date.

Published in 2002, *Überseezungen*'s neologistic title and layout announce these thematic concerns. As many review articles were quick to point out,[4] the title can be understood in two ways. Read as a compound consisting of *Übersee* (overseas) and *Zungen* (tongues), the title reflects the collection's consideration of foreign places and foreign languages; the word *Zungen* also suggests a link between language and the body, or between sound and its physical production. Alternatively, if the stress is allowed to fall on the second syllable, the title bears phonetic similarity to the German word *Übersetzungen* (translations). The typography of the book cover suggests the latter: there is a barely perceptible italicization of the second syllable on the front cover, suggesting that the stress should fall there. The fourteen essays are arranged cartographically into three sections, entitled "Euroasiatische Zungen" (Eurasian Tongues), "Südafrikanische Zungen" (South African Tongues) and "Nordamerikanische Zungen" (North American Tongues); each chapter title page displays a black and white graphic resembling a torn scrap of paper shaped like the geographical region in question and covered with typewritten symbols and characters from various alphabets. Together, the book's title, the chapter headings and the graphics reflect the various themes that run through each text: language, translation, travel, geography, and the embodied self.

Many essays describe trips made to various locations within these three regions. Most often the traveller seems to be Tawada herself: she describes, for example, her stay in Boston as the Max Kade Distinguished Visitor at the Massachusetts Institute of Technology (1999) and her visit to Toronto for the International Festival of Authors (2001).[5] The collection thus blurs the boundaries between essay, autobiography, travelogue, and short story. Consequently, the reader must always consider how truth and fiction are interwoven in each text.

Tawada's travelogues take up a variety of forms of physical and virtual mobility, from plane travel to the flow of information along telecommunications highways, considering how modern technology may alter perceptions of distance or reorganize the interactions between community members. Furthermore, her texts consider how the increasing uniformity of modern-day transportation turns travel into immobility. Consequently, even some forms of physical travel—for instance, airplane travel—take on the qualities of virtual travel. This observation prompts her to question what is really "in motion" in contemporary journeys, for example, to ask what is altered for the travelling subject and how it is changed. Tawada concludes that as travel between places can in some instances become less distinct, it is travel through language in which the most compelling journeys take place. In *Überseezungen* language takes on the qualities of space, and it is the experience of linguistic, not physical, mobility that has the most radical effect on subjectivity and embodiment.

Virtual Travel

While many physical journeys take place in this collection, the essays also contemplate forms of virtual mobility: the travel of information via internet technology, email, or communications technology. This is not a new concern for Tawada: in "E-mail für japanische Gespenster" (Email for Japanese Ghosts) she considers how computer technology erases the materiality of handwritten script, as characters on the computer screen appear "gespenstischer als Pinselschrift auf Papier, denn sie sind da und doch nicht da" (more ghostly than pen marks on paper, for they are there and yet not there).[6] These characters can disappear or materialize in distant places via electronic communications, erasing time and distance "so wie Geister es können" (like ghosts can).[7] In *Überseezungen*, however, Tawada investigates how communication, information, and transportation technology affect our perception of space and our sense of community.

"Die Ohrenzeugin" (The Earwitness), for example, takes up the impact of communications technology. The essay describes an afternoon in the department of foreign languages and literature at MIT. Appropriate to her subject, Tawada paints a linguistic portrait, piecing together the languages, voices, scraps of conversation, non-verbal human sounds (laughter, footsteps, coughing) and the noises of machinery (e.g., the ring of the telephone, the whir of the photocopier, the click of computer keyboards) that the narrator hears from her office. She describes the department hallway as a row of similar offices that resemble *gehörorgan*" (auditory organs) through which the narrator can take in the sounds that comprise her workplace.[8]

This level of attentive listening provokes reverie; the narrator contemplates a number of subjects, offering numerous reflections on language, communication, and technology. She muses about how she communicates with her colleagues—how often, via which media, and over what distance—and about how these factors affect her relationships and her sense of physical proximity to each member of the department. Narrative devices encourage this line of thought. While constant references to the passage of time arrange events chronologically, repeated statements about the location of her colleagues' offices in relation to her own prompt the reader to consider the web of communicative events in spatial terms.

The telephone conversations, voice messages, and emails that the narrator describes are remarkable not for their content, but for what they reveal about how the medium shapes the parties' sense of distance or community. For example, a colleague on another floor is reached by telephone rather than in person since "eine andere Etage bedeutete eine andere Welt" (another floor constituted another world).[9] Similarly, colleagues in another building communicate with each other by email thus intensifying their sense of distance from one another.

Tawada here comments on how telephone and email are used not only as devices for communicating with those who are geographically remote, but also as a medium of exchange with those in close proximity. They thus bridge, but also maintain distances. The narrator notes her skepticism about claims that modern geographies of telecommunications networks collapse space, arguing instead that they may reinforce distance between individuals:

Man sagte mir, die Welt sei vernetzt, die Entfernung spiele keine Rolle mehr. Es schien mir aber so, als ob nicht die Entfernung, sondern die Nähe keine Rolle mehr spiele. Auch jemandem, der nebenan sitzt, kann man eine E-Mail schicken. Ist die Welt wirklich vernetzt oder ist die vielleicht verletzt?[10]

(I was told the world is interlinked; distance no longer mattered. However it seemed to me that it was not distance but proximity that no longer mattered. You can send an email even to someone sitting next to you. Is the world really interlinked or is it perhaps injured?)

In this instance, the convenience of email keeps people who are in fact in close proximity distant from one another. Nevertheless, technology can also unite people. The narrator confesses that technology disempowers her and, thus, requires her to seek human assistance, especially when technical problems arise:

Je mehr ich mit technischen Geräten zu tun hatte, desto mehr menschliche Hilfe brauchte ich. Die Technik entmündigt Menschen wie mich, darin besteht die Menschlichkeit der Technik: Technische Probleme verbinden Menschen miteinander oder erzeugen neue Geschichten, die dann von Mund zu Mund weitererzählt werden.[11]

(The more contact I had with technical devices, the more human assistance I required. Technology incapacitates people like me. Therein lies the humanity of technology: technical difficulties connect people with one another or produce new stories that are then recounted from one mouth to another.)

Taken together, these mundane telephone conversations display the multiple uses of technologies. For example, technologies may be employed in a variety of ways depending on the social context in which they are used. They can create a sense both of proximity and of widening distances, and can prevent or simulate movement, or render it superfluous altogether. In this vein, the narrator's recollection of the work of Joseph Beuys can be read as a commentary on her ambivalent reactions to these multiple uses and effects of modern communication systems:

Ich erinnerte mich an das ‚Erdtelephon' von Joseph Beuys, ein Lehmklumpen, vermischt mit vertrocknetem Gras, und unmittelbar daneben stand ein schwarzer Telefonapparat aus den fünfziger Jahren. Heutzutage sind die meisten Telefonhörer handlich und federleicht. Warum soll das Telefonieren nicht mehr an die Erde gebunden sein?[12]

(I recalled Joseph Beuys' *Earth Telephone*, a lump of clay mixed with dried grass and directly next to it stood a black telephone from the 1950s. Nowadays most telephones are easy to carry and light as feathers. Why should telephoning no longer be earthbound?)

Beuys' *Erdtelefon* can be interpreted in a number of ways. It may offer a statement on the rupture between nature and modernity, or reflect on the power of technology to shape our conception of the natural world. Alternatively, communication and communication technologies might be taken in Beuys' work as the substance to be molded, reminding the viewer that such organization or reorganization can be actively negotiated. The narrator's question about why the phone should not be earthbound is similarly ambiguous: it might serve as a critique of the present reconceptualisation of distance where "proximity no longer matters," or it might be interpreted as a reminder that the current order of things needn't be accepted passively. Either way, her statements remind us that geographies of communication networks have the power not only to affect perceptions of distance, but also to influence social and cultural definition.

Technologies of Motion

While "Ohrenzeugin" deals primarily with the virtual travel of voices and emails between relatively immobile individuals housed in various offices on the MIT campus, "Eine Scheibengeschichte" (A Disk Story) concentrates on physical travel, describing the narrator's flight to Toronto. Its position in the collection directly after "Ohrenzeugin" is significant: in "Scheibengeschichte" Tawada explores how real and virtual travel may in some instances have much in common. Reflecting on a transatlantic flight, Tawada reminds the reader that to travel by plane is to remain immobile and disconnected from the landscape below. More specifically, she considers how our experience of airplane travel has resulted in a shift in spatial parameters and affected our relationship to space and place, suggesting that modern-day travel often constitutes a break between the traveller and the space through which she moves.

In this regard, Tawada seems to echo the insights of Michel de Certeau offered in *The Practice of Everyday Life*, where he comments similarly on the effects of modern modes of transportation. In his chapter "Railway Navigation and Incarceration" de Certeau considers the interface between subject, vehicle, and space, pointing out the disconnection between subject and landscape and the relative immobility of the passenger within the space of the train compartment. De Certeau maintains that the enclosed capsule of the train creates a sense of stable identity for the travelling subject where the "self could believe itself *intact* because it was surrounded by glass and iron."[13] While passenger and landscape remain still, it is only the vehicle, the "rationalized cell," which travels, where "everything has its place." This "closed system" creates "a bubble of panoptic and classifying power, a module of imprisonment that makes possible the production of an order, a closed and autonomous insularity–that is what can traverse space and make itself independent of local roots."[14]

De Certeau maintains that the production of internal order and independence from the terrain through which one travels can be increased through other modes of transportation. Airplane travel offers the subject a "position that is more abstract . . . and more perfect" than that afforded by train travel precisely because it withholds the melancholic pleasure of "seeing what one is separated from."[15]

Tawada briefly alludes to similar phenomenon in "Bioskoop der Nacht" (Bioskope of the Night). Here she contemplates the hermetically sealed space of the airport, where the gateway to the airplane becomes the passage to foreign territory:

> Das Tor zwischen Warteraum und Flugzeug heißt hierzulande »Ausgang««. Man wird zum Ausgang Nummer soundso gebeten und geht hinaus ins Ausland.[16]

> (In these parts the gate between the waiting room and the plane is called "Ausgang." You are called to gate number so and so and you exit into foreign territory.)

Like de Certeau, Tawada posits airplane travel as abstract. It disconnects passengers from the terrain through which they move, erasing any sense of the distance to be travelled.

In "Scheibengeschichte," she focuses on the space of the plane itself and on how, as in virtual travel, the traveller is rendered relatively motionless. Unlike de Certeau, however, Tawada does not posit the intactness of subjectivity. Rather, that intactness is threatened as soon as language comes into play:

> Wenn ich im Flugzeug sitze, habe ich keinen Raum für Körperbewegung. Mein Rücken wird steif, die Füße und Waden schwellen an, das Steißbein sitzt nicht mehr richtig, und die Haut trocknet aus. Nur die Zunge wird immer feuchter und elastischer. Sie bereitet sich auf die Begegnung mit einer Fremdsprache vor.[17]

> (When I sit in the plane I scarcely have room to move my body. My back gets stiff, my feet and calves swell, my tailbone no longer sits properly, and my skin dries out. Only my tongue gets moister and more elastic. It prepares itself for the encounter with a foreign language.)

In de Certeau's model, the fixedness of the vehicle's interior allows for the creation of order. In Tawada's model, the order of the plane cabin is less rigid; despite her own physical immobility things are nevertheless shifting through the intervention of language. More specifically, the confrontation with a foreign language provides a greater sense of dislocation than the actual plane journey. Tawada elaborates on this phenomenon in a radio interview for Joachim Büthe's review of *Überseezungen*:

> Es gibt nichts bewegungsloseres als Sitzen im Flugzeug. Aber in dem Moment, in dem ich eine andere Sprache spreche, im Flugzeug wird man ja z.B. von jemandem plötzlich angesprochen in irgendeiner Sprache, und man versucht dann zu antworten und spricht eine andere Sprache. Dann merkt man sofort, vom Körperinneren, erst mal von der Zunge, die versucht, diese fremden Laute auszusprechen, wie eine Verwandlung, eine Veränderung stattfindet. Um eine Sprache zu sprechen, muss man ja auch Muskeln im Gesicht ganz anders be-

wegen, als wenn man andere Sprachen spricht. Und das ist für mich eigentlich die Reise.[18]

(There is nothing more motionless than sitting in an airplane. But in the moment I speak another language [e.g., in the plane you are of course suddenly spoken to by another person in some language and you then try to answer and you speak a different language. Then you immediately notice, from inside your body, first of all from your tongue which tries to pronounce these foreign sounds, that a transformation, a change is taking place. To speak a language you must move the facial muscles totally differently than when you speak other languages. And that, for me, is actually the journey.])

In this interview, Tawada summarizes the main points of her more poetic reflections in "Eine Scheibengeschichte" where she explores the modes of subjectivity open to the airplane passenger. Like de Certeau, Tawada posits that the motionless interface of subject, space, and vehicle offers a stability of identity. But language offers another sort of journey altogether, a linguistic journey in which the subject may be transported—or more properly, translated—into another system of sounds and significances.

Language and Corporeality

While *Überseezungen* shows how the physicality of motion can go missing in some modes of travel, the linguistic journeys documented in *Überseezungen* are nevertheless intensely physical, requiring, but also increasing, a bodily relationship to language. This fact is announced by the collection's title, where the presence of the word *Zungen* (tongues) not only evokes the themes of translation and language, but also alludes to the symbolic organ of speech and hence the body's role in the production of sound.

In the interview cited above, Tawada comments on the physical transformation that takes place when switching from one language to another: crossing over into another language can heighten the speaker's awareness of the physical exertion inherent in speech, especially when the languages in question are phonetically distinct. In *Überseezungen*, Tawada not only considers the corporeal component of speech, but also the traversal of the body by language. In "Eine Scheibengeschichte," the narrator recalls a conversation with her Canadian host and considers how the body may be differently coded in a foreign language. When her host uses the English word "disks" to explain why one suffers from backache after a long flight, the narrator is taken aback:

Ich habe keine Diskette in meinem Körper, weder eine floppy disk noch eine Musik-CD, erst recht keine CD-Rom, erwiderte ich. Mag sein, daß CDs in einer anderen Sprache nichts mit den Bandscheiben zu tun haben, aber wenn wir Englisch sprechen, haben wir Disketten in der Wirbelsäule. Darin sind alle Körperhaltungen gespeichert, die man im Leben eingenommen hat. Und immer, wenn eine Diskette aus der Wirbelsäule herausspringt und auf der Nervensaite reibt, wird eine schmerzhafte Musik gespielt.[19]

(I don't have any diskettes in my body, neither a floppy disk nor a music CD, and certainly no CD Rom, I replied. It could be that in other languages CDs have nothing to do with intervertebral disks, but when we speak English, we have diskettes in our spine. All the postures we have taken up in life are saved there. And every time a diskette slips in our spine and rubs against the strings of our nerves, a painful music is played.)

This encounter with the English language creates a new and unexpected sense of her own embodiment. Later the narrator sums up her journey as a bodily metamorphosis: "Eine Reise kennt keine Bewegung, aber sie macht die Zunge feucht. Wenn sie spricht, verwandelt sich der Körper" (A journey knows no motion, but it moistens the tongue. When it speaks, the body is transformed).[20] While there is no motion or kinesis in Tawada's depiction of plane travel, in crossing over from one linguistic territory to another, the speaking body is nevertheless doubly transformed, both through a renewed sense of the bodily exertion inherent in speech acts and through a recoding of the body in the foreign language.

Tawada has considered this sort of linguistic transformation elsewhere. In *Verwandlungen* (Metamorphoses), for example, she notes how an awareness of her speaking body was absent in her native Japanese and contrasts this corporeal erasure with the materiality and permanence of script.[21] When linguistic borders are crossed, however, the voice is decentred and defamiliarized, and thus takes on a new materiality. Words are imagined as living creatures: "Es ist, als würde man nicht Wörter sondern Vögel ausspucken" (It's as if you are not spitting out words, but birds).[22] The adoption of a new language results in the same kind of linguistic metamorphosis described in *Überseezungen*. Vowels and the signs of punctuation permeate the body, transforming the speaking subject:

> Was macht man, wenn man von fremden Stimmen umgeben ist? Einige Menschen versuchen bewußt oder unbewußt, ihre Stimme der neuen Umgebung anzupassen. Tonhöhe und Lautstärke werden korrigiert, der neue Sprachrhythmus wird nachgeahmt und auf das Ein- und Ausatmen geachtet. Jeder Konsonant, jeder Vokal und vielleicht auch jedes Komma durchlaufen die Fleischzellen und verwandeln die sprechende Person.[23]

> (What does one do when one is surrounded by foreign voices? Some try, consciously or unconsciously, to adapt their voices to the new surroundings. Pitch and volume are corrected, the new speech rhythm is imitated and attention is paid to inhalation and exhalation. Every consonant, every vowel and perhaps every comma pass through the flesh cells and transform the speaker.)

Überseezungen bears witness to this radically physical experience of language throughout, as Tawada attempts to reinstate the presence of the corporeal or material in her texts,[24] attributing substance to the symbolic and reinvesting words with the power to evoke physical sensation. For example, in "Eine leere Flasche" (An Empty Bottle), the word *atakushi*, the Japanese first-person singular pronoun indicating privileged social status, bears the fragrance of *Zypressen-holz* (cypress), that is, the scent of wealth, luxury, or comfort.[25] In "Bioskoop der Nacht," she compares the laborious acquisition of Afrikaans to a cutting out of her tongue.[26] Paradoxically, as physical travel creates an impression of immobility, movement from one linguistic territory to another provides a new sense of embodiment.

Travel, Translation and Territory

While many physical journeys are undertaken in *Überseezungen*, the emphasis on linguistic dislocation has prompted one reviewer to refer to the collection as a series of "spracherlebnisse" (linguistic experiences) in another of Tawada's many "sprachexpeditionen" (linguistic expeditions).[27] In her review, Sabine Treude similarly refers to the *Überseezungen* essays as "linguistic adventures" ("Sprech—und Sprachabenteuer"). Both descriptions focus on Tawada's interest in language and space, where languages are imagined as territories that can be navigated and explored. Within such a model languages become sites through which the individual can move, locations where identity can reside, or bounded spaces demarcating belonging or exclusion. This vision leads Tawada to consider the relationship between language and territoriality. A shared language, she reminds us, can create the same feelings of belonging and loyalty as a common geography can: linguistic identities can be as powerful as national ones. Consequently, the individual who moves between languages, particularly ones that are as removed from one another as German and Japanese, may be a particular object of scrutiny or even suspicion.[28] This idea is explored in "Bioskoop der Nacht" where Tawada confronts the question often posed to the multilingual subject: "In welcher Sprache träumen Sie?" (In which language do you dream?).[29]

The story begins with a sequence from one of the narrator's dreams and introduces the reader to the unusual language of her dream world. Some readers might recognize the influence of Afrikaans in the structure of some utterances (e.g., double negation, the absence of the *Sie*-form, the system of gender); in some lexical items (e.g., *tot*, *Winkel* or *lecker* in contexts atypical of German); or in the word *Bioskoop* (cinema) in the story's title. Others may recognize the horizontal *Y* on a green, red and blue background as the South African flag. Or the unique linguistic mix and symbols might remain alien—as they do to the narrator at this point—and, therefore, be reminiscent of the distortion of language and the indecipherable symbols characteristic of dreams.

The narrator of "Bioskoop der Nacht" experiences such an alienation, which is exacerbated by the tendency of those she meets to insist on interrogating her linguistic identity. A series of vignettes follow, in which the narrator is questioned about the language of her dreams, something she registers as "ein qualvolles Spiel" (an agonizing game) because she is never able to answer with the certainty demanded of her:

In ihren Augen leuchtete Erwartung, ich wußte aber nicht, was sie von mir erwarteten.
»Ich weiß das leider nicht. Es ist eine Sprache. Ja, es ist sicher eine Sprache, aber eine Sprache, die ich nie gelernt habe, deshalb verstehe ich meine eigene Traumsprache nicht.«[30]

(Their eyes shone with expectation, but I didn't know what they expected from me.
"I unfortunately don't know. It's a language. Yes, it's certainly a language, but a language I've never learned. Therefore I don't understand my own dream language.")

Here Tawada problematizes the commonly held notion that dreams reveal the degree of a subject's connection to a particular language, that is, where intimacy of a certain language is measured by whether or not one dreams in that language. The narrator cannot quite fathom the belief that, by submitting to this line of questioning, she will be forced to conclusively locate her linguistic identity.

These lines express unease at the expectation that identity should reside firmly in one language and, furthermore, that this language should be accessible in dreams. Later, at a party, it is suggested that the protagonist's dream language is a result of the struggle between her first and second languages. It is thus implied that the individual can exist only in one language:

Eine Gymnasiumslehrerin fragte mich wieder, in welcher Sprache ich träumen würde. Ich erzählte von meinen Träumen. Ich gab zu, daß ich nicht wüßte, in welcher Sprache ich träumte. Ein Mann [. . .] sagte, die Sprache, die ich beschrieben hätte, sei eindeutig die deutche Sprache, jedoch völlig deformiert. Diese Mißgestalt nähme sie an, weil sie in meinem Kopf ständig von der mächtigen Muttersprache unterdrückt werde. Es sei eine Zumutung, daß zwei erwachsene Schwestern ein kleines Kopfzimmer teilen müßten.[31]

(A highschool teacher again asked me which language I dreamt in. I recounted my dream. I admitted that I didn't know which language I dreamt in. A man . . . said the language that I had described was clearly German but completely deformed. It took on this misshapen figure because it was constantly suppressed by the powerful mother tongue in my head. It was unreasonable that two grown sisters should share a small head space.)

Here Tawada works overtly with images of territory and language. According to the model of linguistic identity held by the fellow guest, Japanese and German battle for the space of the narrator's psyche.

It is not until a third party that a Dutch woman finally identifies the dream language as Afrikaans. While the protagonist welcomes this revelation, unfortunately it does not help her to negotiate better the dreaded question. In fact, it seems to make matters far worse: she has neither visited Africa nor studied Afrikaans. One guest in particular refuses to accept this complete lack of correspondence between cultural identity, place, and language, insisting: "[m]an träumt doch in der Sprache des Landes, in dem die Seele wohnt" (one dreams in the language of the country in which the soul resides).[32] Undaunted, the narrator refuses to reduce her identity to any one location, claiming, "ich habe viele Seelen und viele Zungen" (I have many souls and many tongues).[33]

This passage reveals the expectations embedded in the questions about the Japanese woman's dream language. It is hoped that if she submits to this line of questioning, she will be forced to declare her ultimate allegiance, not simply to language, but also to place, to the country "in which the soul resides." To declare one's linguistic ties is thus akin to producing identity papers.

"Wolkenkarte" (Cloud Card) makes this link between language, territory, identity, and document explicit. Ostensibly about supermarket client cards that offer consumer rewards while tracking customer purchases, the essay provides a number of insights regarding language, regional dialects, geography, and belonging. Asked to show one of these cards in a supermarket in Basel, the narrator does not understand the cashier's request at first. The situation calls to mind a similar episode in Boston:

Es war auch an der Kasse eines Supermarktes gewesen, und die Kassiererin hatte mich gefragt, ob ich die ›starcard‹ hätte. Ich verstand die Frage zuerst nicht, die Kassiererin wiederholte sie. Dann verstand ich sie, aber die Karte besaß ich nicht. Es kam mir vor, als ginge es um einen Ausweis, den man braucht, um zu dem Ort zu gehören. Ich besaß keine Sternenkarte in Boston, also war ich von einem anderen Planeten. Und was für eine Karte sollte ich hier in Basel haben? [. . .] Wenn ich nach einem Ausweis gefragt worden wäre, hätte ich meinen Reisepaß oder meinen Fahrausweis [. . .] zeigen können.[34]

(It was also at a supermarket checkout, and the cashier had asked me if I had the "starcard." At first I didn't understand the question; the cashier repeated it. Then I understood, but I didn't have the card. It seemed to me as if the whole thing was about a document which one required to belong to that place. I didn't have a starcard in Boston, so I was from another planet. And what sort of a card was I supposed to have here in Basel? . . . Had I been asked for a piece of ID, I could have shown my passport or my driver's license.)

The narrator considers how the names of such cards vary from place to place, and then ponders the lexical items that are indigenous to particular locations. She recalls, for instance, that in Switzerland there are approximately seventy-five variants of the word for ladybug. When asked whether she has a bicycle (*Velo* in Swiss German) she relates language and document:

Eine Woche später fragte mich eine Frau:
Haben Sie ein Velo?
Ich war erschrocken, denn Velo klingt fast genauso wie ein japanisches Wort, das Zunge bedeutet. Haben Sie eine Zunge? Das ist eine wichtige Frage. Haben Sie die Zunge, die man braucht, um hierher zu gehören?[35]

(A week later a woman asked me, "Do you have a Velo?"

I was alarmed, for "Velo" sounds almost the same as a Japanese word that
means tongue. Do you have a tongue? That's an important question. Do you
have the tongue required to belong in this place?)

In this passage Tawada repeats the question that begins her essay ("Haben
Sie eine . . . Karte?"), altering only the final word ("Haben Sie ein Velo?"). Each
question prompts a consideration of how the object in question legitimates presence in a particular place. The phonetic similarity between the Swiss German
word *Velo* and the Japanese word for tongue reminds the narrator how a shared
language creates a sense of belonging and community. The structural similarity
of the questions asked as well as the responses given sets up an equivalence between the words *Karte* and *Velo*; the latter can, therefore, also be regarded as a
sort of document, required "to belong in this place." The essay concludes with
the statement that all new Swiss acquaintances are asked to reveal their particular regional variant for the word "ladybug." This question can be likened to the
question in "Bioskoop der Nacht" where the answers are expected to reveal a
speaker's linguistic, and therefore national or regional, identity.

In "Bioskoop der Nacht," however, Tawada counters the notion that the self
must choose a linguistic home, opting instead for the travel between places, languages, and identities. Thus begins yet another of *Überseezungen*'s many journeys. The narrator decides to book a trip to Cape Town because, as she puts it,
"die Sprache, in der geträumt wird, muß besucht werden" (the language in
which one dreams must be visited).[36] The essay continues to mimic the structure
of dreams, interspersing realistic episodes with more surreal elements; for instance, characters appear unexpectedly or seem inexplicably changed and the
narrator has no firm sense of the passage of time or the relationship between
events.[37] The fragmentary nature of the essay allows for disjointed reflections on
everything from the sounds and structure of Afrikaans and Xhosa, a language
the narrator encounters in a nearby township, to the history of South African
apartheid. Despite the narrator's desire to embrace multiple linguistic identities,
however, many people she encounters insist that one language must prevail over
all others. The narrator's contention that she in fact has "many souls and many
tongues" is repeatedly discounted and mistrusted.

"Porträt einer Zunge" (Portrait of a Tongue) explores this idea of a single,
restrictive linguistic identity further. Here, an encounter with the German word
Eingeborene (literally "a person born into," i.e., a native) leads the narrator to
consider how languages create spaces of belonging or enclosure:

> Ich hatte ganz vergessen, daß es dieses deutsche Wort gab. Wenn man eine
> »native American« als »Eingeborene« bezeichnen kann, könnte man unter ei-
> nem »native speaker« jemanden verstehen, der in eine Sprache hineingeboren
> wird. Ich war also ins Japanische hineingeboren worden, wie man in einen Sack
> hineingeworfen wird. Deshalb wurde diese Sprache für mich meine äußere
> Haut.[38]

(I had totally forgotten that this German word existed. If you can call a "Native American" an "Eingeborene" then you could understand a "native speaker" to be someone who is born into a language. So I was born into the Japanese language, the way one is thrown into a sack. That's why this language became like an outer skin for me.)

Linguistic identity seems to be fixed, where the metaphor of an "outer skin" casts such identities as natural and permanent.

If languages create spaces of belonging, however, then concomitantly they also create barriers of exclusion. The narrator muses that in Germany, she will always be considered an outsider who can approach the German language only from its outer borders: "In Deutschland wurde ich immer als eine Fremde betrachtet, die die Sprache der Einheimischen von außen antastet" (In Germany I was always regarded as a foreigner who encroaches on the language of the locals from the outside).[39] She counters this notion with another body metaphor: "Die deutsche Sprache jedoch wurde von mir hinuntergeschluckt, seitdem sitzt sie in meinem Bauch" (I, however, gulped down the German language; ever since it has sat in my belly).[40] Language, she maintains, can indeed be adopted or internalized.

But this clearly makes some people uncomfortable. If languages create boundaries, then to translate oneself into another idiom might be regarded as an act of transgression. This is illustrated in the narrator's recollection of conversations with the American author Ian Levy, who claims that while Japanese society and culture are closed to non-natives, the Japanese language is nevertheless open: everyone may write it. The narrator, however, holds that a majority of Japanese would reject such a notion and instead seek to secure their national identity precisely through the "Unantastbarkeit der heiligen Muttersprache" (inviolable nature of the holy mother tongue).[41] Drawing a parallel to the German situation, the narrator points out that native German speakers may also have proprietory instincts about their native language:

[I]ndirekt geben sie einem immer wieder zu verstehen, daß die Sprache ein Besitztum sein muß. Sie sagen zum Beispiel, daß man eine Fremdsprache nie so gut beherrschen könne wie die Muttersprache. Man bemerkt sofort, daß das Wichtigste für sie die Beherrschung ist.[42]

(Indirectly they always give you to understand that language must be a possession. For example, they say that one can never master a foreign language as well as a first language. You notice right away that, for them, the most important thing is mastery.)

The metaphor of ownership (*Besitztum*) that the narrator employs underscores the territorial notions of identity she encounters, where crossing into another linguistic space is cast as a violation of another's native language. Within such a framework, switching linguistic allegiances might be regarded as suspicious or treacherous:

Andere sagen, nur in der Muttersprache könne man authentisch seine Gefühle
ausdrücken, in einer Fremdsprache lüge man unwillkürlich. Sie fühlen sich bei
ihrer Suche nach dem authentischen Gefühl gestört, wenn sie ihre Sprache auf
fremden Zungen sehen.[43]

(Others say that only in the mother tongue can one authentically express one's
feelings; in a foreign language one lies involuntarily. They are disturbed in
their search for authentic feeling when they see their language on foreign tongues.)

For some, translation constitutes treachery, a distortion of intended meaning.

Throughout her writing, however, Tawada has persistently negated the notion that there is any possibility of unmediated—and therefore genuine or
authentic—expression of emotion in any language, be it "native" or "foreign."
Asked in an interview about the publication of translations of her original works
and the possible danger that in translation her original ideas might be *verfälscht*
(distorted), Tawada rejects the notion that an authentic rendering is possible in
either language:

|D|ieses Moment ist für mich sehr wichtig, daß das Gefühl oder Leben oder das
Geschriebene auch in der Muttersprache etwas anderes ist. Daß dazwischen so
eine Kluft ist, wo man auch hineinfallen kann. Und dieser Zwischenraum ist für
mich sehr wichtig. Und |. . .| ich möchte so schreiben, daß dieser Zwischen-
raum sichtbar wird.[44]

(This moment is very important for me: that emotion or life or written langauge
is also different in the first language. There is a kind of gulf between them that
you can fall into. And this inbetween space is very important for me. And . . . I
would like to write in a way that renders this inbetween space visible.)

Tawada thus casts doubt on the notion of a subject who can master the signs
of language. She points instead to the gulf that exists between perception and
language, a space that she wishes to illuminate in her own writing. Later in this
interview, she demonstrates how translations from one language to another can
help render this space more clearly visible.[45] We can therefore read the presence
of the word *Überseezungen* in the collection's title as a reference not simply to
translation between first and second languages, but to acts of translation of many
kinds: the move from lived experience, emotion or cognition to language; from
written to spoken language (and vice versa); and, in "Bioskoop der Nacht," from
the workings of the subconscious to the language of dreams.

Tawada's *Überseezungen* offers numerous reflections on these various acts
of translation. "Ein Chinesisches Wörterbuch" (A Chinese Dictionary), for example, considers the intersections of German and Chinese. This brief text consists simply of German to Chinese translations, where both entries are rendered
in German, but the Chinese translations are literally expressed. Graphically
highlighted on the centre of the page is the word *Tintenfisch* (squid) which in
Tawada's rendering exhibits an identical structure and evokes similar connota-

tions in both languages; both allude to the presence of ink (*Tinte*).[46] The other entries, however, do not mirror each other in this way. The word "computer," for example, is translated as *Elektrisches Gehirn* (electric brain); *Kino* (cinema) is translated as *Institut für elektrische Schatten* (literally "institute for electric shadows").[47] Each entry therefore shows a gap between the two languages. "Ein Chinesisches Wörterbuch" becomes, then, less about simple translation than about untranslateability: the blank spaces that exist between words, the gaps characteristic of lives lived in the intersections of languages and signifying systems.

Another example of the disconnection between language systems occurs in "Eine leere Flasche" (An Empty Bottle), an investigation of the many ways to render the first person singular in Japanese. Factors such as gender, age, social status, and the relationship between speakers affect the choice between the many possibilities: *boku, ore, atashi, watashi, atakushi, watakushi*. The essay revolves around a childhood memory about a young girl who referred to herself as *boku*, a masculine pronoun. This prompts reflection on the various subject positions available in Japanese, a problem that is non-existent in German:

> Das Mädchen, das sich als »boku« nannte, verlor ich irgendwann aus den Augen. Das Problem der Selbstbezeichnung verlor ich auch aus den Augen. Denn ich zog nach Europa und fand das Wort »ich«, bei dem man sich keine solchen Gedanken mehr machen mußte. Ein Ich muß kein bestimmtes Geschlecht haben, kein Alter, keinen Status, keine Geschichte, keine Haltung, keinen Charakter. Jeder kann sich einfach »ich« nennen. Dieses Wort besteht nur aus dem, was ich spreche, oder genauer gesagt aus der Tatsache, daß ich überhaupt spreche.[48]

> (At some point I lost sight of the girl who called herself *boku*. I also lost sight of the problem of self reference, for I moved to Europe and found the word "I" which no longer required such considerations. An "I" requires no particular gender, no age, no status, no history, no attitude, no character. Anyone can simply call themselves "I." This word is comprised only of that which I speak, or more properly, of the fact that I speak at all.)

As in "Ein Chinesisches Wörterbuch," this essay points to a gap between signifying systems, which, in this instance, is viewed as positive: "»Ich« wurde zu meinem Lieblingswort. So leicht und leer wie dieses Wort wollte ich mich fühlen." ("'I' became my favourite word. I wanted to feel as light and empty as this word").[49] The essay's title, "An Empty Bottle," functions as a metaphor for this space between languages as well as the space of the self; the metaphor is aided by the fact that the German verb *bin* (am) phonetically corresponds to the Japanese noun for bottle:

> Auch »bin« ist ein schönes Wort. Im Japanischen gibt es auch das Wort »bin«, das klingt genau gleich und bedeutet »eine Flasche«. Wenn ich mit den beiden Wörtern »ich bin« eine Geschichte zu erzählen beginne, öffnet sich ein Raum, das Ich ist ein Pinselansatz, und die Flasche ist leer.[50]

("Bin" is also a beautiful word. Japanese also has the word "bin" which sounds
exactly the same and means "a bottle." When I begin to tell a story with the two
words "ich bin" [I am] a space opens up: the "ich" is the beginning of a brush-
stroke and the bottle is empty.)

The image of the empty bottle offers a metaphor for the use of the German
first-person pronoun, which is emptied of the many markers of age, gender,
status, etc. demanded in Japanese. Tawada thus reminds us how movement
across geographical boundaries may involve the translation of the self into another linguistic medium. Here translation from one language to another offers a
liberating space of altered subject positions where the self is freed of the numerous self-identifications required in Japanese.

Überseezungen does not, however, concentrate simply on translations from
one language to another; in several essays Tawada considers the relationship
between the written and the spoken word. In "Der Apfel und die Nase" (The
Apple and Nose), Tawada explains the act of typing in Japanese where, because
the keyboard cannot contain the wealth of ideograms present in the Japanese
language, lexical items must be rendered phonetically: "In Wirklichkeit schreibt
man ein Wort so, wie man es ausspricht" (In reality you write a word as it is
pronounced).[51] This leads her to contemplate the relationship between two separate moments of language, between writing and speech: "Natürlich kann man
nicht so schreiben wie man spricht, wie man auch eine Suppe nicht so malen
kann, wie sie schmeckt" (Of course you can't write the way you speak, just as
you can't draw a soup the way it tastes).[52] Here translation from the spoken to
the written word constitutes loss, as the voice is erased through its representation
in the signs of written language.

Ultimately, though, all these essays consider the theme of the translated
self, the multilingual subject who continually moves across linguistic borders.
The finest and most sustained example of this theme is "Portrait einer Zunge."
In this essay Tawada draws an acoustic portrait of P, a German woman living in
Boston and lecturing in German at Harvard. Like the narrator, P lives between
locations and languages. We learn nothing of her appearance, although a photo
is taken at the outset of the narrative. Instead, P's portrait consists of her turns of
phrase, diction, and accents; the qualities of her voice and pronunciations; the
languages she speaks (American English, German, and French); and these languages' unique intersections in transplanted accents, neologisms, and her angli-
cized German. "Porträt einer Zunge" thus reminds the reader of the power of
words to evoke memory: while memories of place fade, linguistic memories
remain powerful. The narrator can no longer remember where certain conversations with P took place. Back in Berlin, however, the sudden appearance of one
of P's anglicisms in the narrator's speech has the power to evoke her memory:
"Das Wort kam unerwartet aus meinem Mund, wie ein Stück Erinnerung" (The
word came out of my mouth unexpectedly, like a slice of memory).[53] Language
thus transports her to another place and time in a way that visual memory cannot.

Überseezungen thus reminds us of the double meaning of translation, which is at once to render the spoken or written word from one language in another, but also to move or carry from one place to another, a dual meaning that is perhaps more immediately present in the German *übersetzen*. This duality of language and mobility, translation and transportation is everywhere visible, from the collection's title and chapter headings, to the essays which embed reflections on language and translation in narratives of travel, to the graphics combining alphabetic characters and cartographic images that introduce each of the collection's three chapters. Tawada reflects on travel and translation of various sorts: the geographic displacement of speaking subjects, the translation of lived experience and cognition into acts of speech and writing, the carrying over of significance from one language into another, and the translation of the subject into another cultural or linguistic medium. As the interview with Büthe suggests, it is in these acts of translation that Tawada locates the most compelling journeys: "And that, for me, is actually the journey."

But while Tawada's reflections on physical and virtual mobility may echo much contemporary thought about the collapsing of distance or the increasing uniformity of place, her focus on language and territoriality tells another story altogether, where regionalisms and nationalisms flourish. Tawada thus suggests the fallacy of the notion of a world without borders: even as geographical borders may seem increasingly insignificant, linguistic boundaries may nevertheless remain intact. In fact, the crossing from one linguistic territory to another may, in some cases, prove a more radical change of environment than mere physical displacement.

Notes

1. Several of Tawada's German-language works contain Japanese narrators residing in German or European locales: e.g., *Talisman, Das Bad, Ein Gast, Überseezungen, Das nackte Auge*.
2. The *Talisman* essay "Rothenburg ob der Tauber" and the drama *Till* both depict Japanese tour groups visiting medieval German cities and reflect much contemporary theory about leisure travel and the social construction of tourist sites.
3. Siberia's colonial past forms an important subtext of the short story "Wo Europa anfängt."
4. See, for example, Büthe or Treude.
5. I am referring here to the piece "Eine Scheibengeschichte" which recounts the narrator's flight to Toronto. Although the essay does not refer to the occasion for, or the date of, the visit, in her on-stage interview at the International Festival of Authors Tawada related the details of her arrival in Toronto and the ensuing conversation with her interviewer, who had picked her up from the airport. These are the very same details that form the premise of her essay.
6. Yoko Tawada, *Verwandlungen* (Tübingen, Germany: Konkursbuch Verlag Claudia Gehrke, 1998), 42. All translations from the original are my own.
7. Tawada, *Verwandlungen*, 42.
8. Yoko Tawada, "Die Ohrenzeugin," in *Überseezungen* (Tübingen, Germany: Konkursbuch Verlag Claudia Gehrke, 2002), 97.

9. Tawada, "Die Ohrenzeugin," 99.

10. Tawada, "Die Ohrenzeugin," 101.

11. Tawada, "Die Ohrenzeugin," 99-100.

12. Tawada, "Die Ohrenzeugin," 98-99.

13. Michel de Certeau, *The Practice of Everyday Life*, (Berkeley: University of California Press, 1988), 114.

14. de Certeau, *Everyday Life*, 111.

15. de Certeau, *Everyday Life*, 113-114.

16. Yoko Tawada, "Bioskoop der Nacht," in *Überseezungen* (Tübingen, Germany: Konkursbuch Verlag, 2002), 71.

17. Tawada, "Bioskoop," 115.

18. Yoko Tawada, "Review of *Überseezungen*," interview by Joachim Büthe, *Deutschlandradio*, 23 September 2002.

19. Yoko Tawada, "Eine Scheibengeschichte," in *Überseezungen* (Tübingen, Germany: Konkursbuch Verlag, 2002), 115-6.

20. Tawada, "Eine Scheibengeschichte," 117.

21. Yoko Tawada, *Verwandlungen* (Tübingen, Germany: Konkursbuch Verlag Claudia Gehrke, 1998), 10.

22. Tawada, *Verwandlungen*, 7.

23. Tawada, *Verwandlungen*, 8.

24. It is likely this interest in reevaluating the corporeal component of language that has led Tawada to look beyond textual media for expression. While drama has always been one part of Tawada's German-language production, in recent years she has also explored the potential of the performance of the spoken word. *Diagonal* offers selections from her live performances with Japanese pianist and composer, Aki Takase, where the spoken texts are set to Takase's original piano compositions. Many of these texts originate from previous publications, nevertheless taking on a new quality in the act of performance where the physical production of sound is foregrounded. In many of these performances, the stress patterns of words and the intonation of sentences are non-standard, drawing attention from the lexical or semantic to the phonetic level of language.

25. Yoko Tawada, "Eine leere Flasche," in *Überseezungen* (Tübingen, Germany: Konkursbuch Verlag, 2002), 53.

26. Tawada, "Bioskoop," 89.

27. Karl-Heinz Ott, "Babylonische Exkursionen," review of *Überseezungen*, by Yoko Tawada, *NZZ-Online. Neue Zürcher Zeitung*. 9 July 2002.

28. Yoko Tawada, "Review of *Überseezungen*," interview by Joachim Büthe, *Deutschlandradio*, 23 September 2002.

29. Tawada, "Bioskoop," 63-64, 70. In *Verwandlungen* (*Metamorphoses*), Tawada takes up this same subject when she writes: "Es gibt eine beliebte Frage zur Sprache im Traum: „In welcher Sprache träumen Sie?" Es ist aber nichts Besonderes, wenn man im Traum eine fremde Sprache spricht. Die gesprochene Sprache kann schnell in den Mund hineinschlüpfen und wieder aus ihm herausspringen. Man muß sich eine Sprache nicht einverleiben, um sie in einem Traum verwenden zu können" ("There is a popular question about the language of dreams: 'In which language do you dream?' It is, however, nothing special when one speaks a foreign language in a dream. Spoken language can quickly slip into your mouth and jump out of it again. It is not necessary to absorb a language to be able to use it in a dream," 39). In her essay, Tawada problematizes the notion that the linguistic medium of one's dreams can ultimately reveal anything about one's cultural allegiances, since dream language is often in some way a distortion.

30. Tawada, "Bioskoop," 63.

31. Tawada, "Bioskoop," 64.
32. Tawada, "Bioskoop," 70.
33. Tawada, "Bioskoop," 70.
34. Tawada, "Wolkenkarte," in *Überseezungen* (Tübingen, Germany: Konkursbuch Verlag, 2002), 51-52.
35. Tawada, "Wolkenkarte," 52.
36. Tawada, "Bioskoop," 68.
37. Tawada, "Bioskoop," 85, 87, 74.
38. Tawada, "Porträt einer Zunge," in *Überseezungen* (Tübingen, Germany: Konkursbuch Verlag, 2002), 103.
39. Tawada, "Porträt," 109.
40. Tawada, "Porträt," 103.
41. Tawada, "Porträt," 109.
42. Tawada, "Porträt," 110.
43. Tawada, "Porträt," 109-110.
44. Hugo Dittberner, ed., *Mit der Zeit Erzählen? fragt er Marcel Beyer, Heiner Egge, Gundi Feyrer, Yoko Tawada: das zweite Buch* (Göttingen, Germany: Wallstein, 1994), 197-198.
45. Dittberner, *Erzählen*, 197-198.
46. Yoko Tawada, "Ein Chinesisches Wörterbuch," in *Überseezungen* (Tübingen, Germany: Konkursbuch Verlag, 2002), 31.
47. Tawada, "Wörterbuch," 31.
48. Yoko Tawada, "Eine leere Flasche," in *Überseezungen* (Tübingen, Germany: Konkursbuch Verlag, 2002), 56-57.
49. Tawada, "Flasche," 57.
50. Tawada, "Flasche," 57.
51. Yoko Tawada, "Der Apfel und die Nase," in *Überseezungen* (Tübingen, Germany: Konkursbuch Verlag, 2002), 15.
52. Tawada, "Apfel," 15.
53. Tawada, "Porträt," 140.

Bibliography

de Certeau, Michel. *The Practice of Everyday Life*. Translated by Steven Rendall. Berkeley: University of California Press, 1988.
Dittberner, Hugo, ed. *Mit der Zeit Erzählen? fragt er Marcel Beyer, Heiner Egge, Gundi Feyrer, Yoko Tawada: das zweite Buch*. Göttingen, Germany: Wallstein, 1994.
Ott, Karl-Heinz. "Babylonische Exkursionen." Review of *Überseezungen*, by Yoko Tawada. *NZZ-Online. Neue Zürcher Zeitung*. 9 July 2002.
Takase, Aki, and Yoko Tawada. *Diagonal*. Tübingen, Germany: Konkursbuch Verlag Claudia Gehrke, 2002.
Tawada, Yoko. *Das Bad*. Trans. Peter Pörtner. Tübingen, Germany: Konkursbuch Verlag Claudia Gehrke, 1993.
———. *Das nackte Auge*. Tübingen, Germany: Konkursbuch Verlag Claudia Gehrke, 2004.
———. *Ein Gast*. Tübingen, Germany: Konkursbuch Verlag Claudia Gehrke, 1993.
———. *Orpheus oder Izanagi. Till*. Tübingen, Germany: Konkursbuch Verlag Claudia Gehrke, 1998.
———. "Review of *Überseezungen*." Interview by Joachim Büthe. *Deutschlandradio*. 23 September 2002.

——. *Talisman*. Tübingen, Germany: Konkursbuch Verlag Claudia Gehrke, 1996.
——. *Überseezungen*. Tübingen, Germany: Konkursbuch Verlag Claudia Gehrke, 2002.
——. *Verwandlungen*. Tübingen, Germany: Konkursbuch Verlag Claudia Gehrke, 1998.
——. *Wo Europa anfängt*. Tübingen, Germany: Konkursbuch Verlag Claudia Gehrke, 1991
Treude, Sabine. Review of *Überseezungen*, by Yoko Tawada. *Prairie*. 12 April 2002.

Chapter Nine
The Unknown Character: Traces of the Surreal in Yoko Tawada's Writings
Bettina Brandt

In this essay, I propose to read Tawada's writings in the context of a particular modernist thought and practice: within the frame of surrealism. Here her writings can then be seen as illustrative of a particular avant-garde aesthetics that Rosalind E. Krauss defined as follows: "Surreality *is*, we could say, nature convulsed into a kind of writing."[1] This particular aesthetic strategy is also one we can use to characterize quite a few, if not all of Yoko Tawada's writings; an aesthetic in which reality is always already constituted as a sign. In this specific sense then Tawada's texts, which regularly have been branded as surreal but have never been actually analyzed as such, can indeed be read as contemporary developments in a well-established modernist tradition.[2] Within the context of that tradition I will suggest a theoretical and aesthetic model that—similar to Simmel's concept of the stranger—emphasizes the mobile, innovative and experimental aspects inherent in the writings of the most literary of these strangers.

Tawada's German and Japanese writings form, quite literally, a textual corpus; a theoretical body of fiction in which particular titles can be connected to specific body parts and each of the senses is closely inspected for its role in the production of pleasure and of knowledge about the self and the other. The body in Tawada's texts is never a mere object; it is itself a site of transformation that, with the help of the senses, converts mere sensitiveness into sense and sensibility. The early short novel *The Bath* (written in Japanese but first published in German in 1989 and referenced in Tawada's introductory essay in this volume), for example, is devoted to the sensuousness of a (rather flaky) skin; the story "Persona," written in Japanese, highlights the face; her recent German novel *The Naked Eye* (2004) focuses on the (cinematic) eye and the German essay collection *Overseastongues* (2002) explores that moveable organ attached to the bottom of our mouth which so easily gives us away when we travel. In her first German novel entitled *A Guest* (1993), which is central to this essay, it is the ear in and around which the text sinuously coils.[3]

Addressing how a local population perceives a stranger and how this stranger, in turn, attempts to decipher the cultural particularities of an unfamiliar

111

place, A Guest explicitly raises questions about the very possibility of reading and writing the other. Commissioned to write a series of articles about German celebrations and traditions for a Japanese woman's magazine a young, female Japanese narrator is struggling to produce her essays. Continuously disrupted by her German neighbors and other unsolicited guests, fighting with tape recorders, radios and other technological inventions that enhance hearing, she has trouble writing even a few coherent sentences. At the end of the novel the narrator informs us that she has written only "a series of meaningless words."[4] This particular kind of writing where the textual geography or spacing contributes to the semiotic breakdown of the word while accenting each individual letter is the only activity that pleases the narrator because it makes her feel as if she had "notated something important."[5]

This story line, at first glance, seems to offer a rather negative assessment about the possibility of producing a narrative description let alone an analysis of a foreign, unknown culture. I will argue, however, that A Guest—and this is not, by far, the only Tawada text which can be read in this mode—in fact suggests a new language with which to experiment in this realm. The vocabulary, the oneiric grammar and, above all, the poetics of surrealism offer Tawada and other Germanophone and polyglot writers both a discourse and a script with which to experiment in the realm of critical ethnography and experimental poetics.

The Trouvaille

We first encounter the narrator hoping to distract herself from a pounding earache while strolling amongst old posters, used jackets and coats, greasy, stained paperbacks, a pair of ice skates and a clock, and other discarded objects that are on display at a local flea market. A flea market is, of course, a surrealist place par excellence. It is, as André Breton explained in Mad Love, a place where "objects that, between the lassitude of some and the desire of others, go off to dream."[6] For Breton this kind of marketplace was one of the sites within every day life where out-of-the-ordinary experiences could occur and where reality could be transformed into surreality.

The flea market is the locus for the surrealist trouvaille, often translated as "the found object" or "the lucky find." The trouvaille was for the Surrealists a "cipher of freedom," as Peter Bürger phrased it, because the found object presents a moment of chance where the human being subjects himself or herself "to the entirely heteronomous." Arguing that in the trouvaille the production of meaning, proper to the human subject, surfaces as a product of nature which only needs to be deciphered, Bürger explained why the Surrealists whose fundamental project, as Margaret Cohen has argued, was "to release unconscious forces that leave their imprints on the visible world but that nowhere appear as such," were so fond of the found object.[7]

The trouvaille, Breton suggest, is important because this object from the outside world functions as a portent. The object is a sign that mysteriously attracts the subject because it has something to tell; it personally addresses the subject who attempts to read the sign. What the found object brings to the subject is some kind of a solution; a solution to a question that the subject himself could not yet even formulate as such.[8] In the surrealist novel *Nadja* (1928) the *trouvaille* often illuminates a previous thought or situation. In *Mad Love* the *trouvaille* can also be an object, as we see when Breton describes how an uncommon iron mask, found at a Parisian flea market in St. Ouen, suggested a facial shape to Alberto Giacometti when the sculptor was in the midst of thinking about the features of a statue-in-progress.

Inside The Ear

A Guest has numerous features of a dream landscape. Besides the explicit references ("the people standing on either side of the aisle inspecting the items offered for sale looked to me as though they'd come from a dream"[9]), it is, first of all, the location of Tawada's flea market that particularly suggests that we are, from the beginning, in a dream site. Situated in a subterranean pedestrian passage "that led from a subway station to a street with many shops,"[10] the flea market—this marginalized marketplace outside the institutionalized paths of economic exchange—also functions in Tawada's text as an opening into the narrator's body. It is, to be precise, both the entrance into the narrator's ear canal and the entrance into an outmoded shopping arcade. Problematizing the distinction between inner and outer and producing a sensation of uncanniness in the process, the Tawadian labyrinthine ear—like other bodily openings that share these characteristics—can, I argue, hence also be called a surrealist organ.

The fictional tale of *A Guest*, in other words, unravels inside the narrator's body and when events do take place outside in the city—in an arcade, in a doctor's office or in an apartment—they are, like stimuli from the outside world incorporated into the dream, turned into sensations that, each in their own way, relate to the body. Everyday German expressions, for instance, following the narrative logic of dreams, have been transformed into images that tell their own story and structure the narrative through condensation and displacement. To give but one example, the dream image of the "flea," with which we are already familiar from the flea market, seems to be jumping around in the text. The narrator also believes that "a flea living in her ear," is responsible for her ear infection. Following the particularities of dream language the image of a flea living in a human ear, when translated back into German words, points to a German saying: "to put a flea into somebody's ear," which means to slip a thought or a wish into somebody, which then no longer leaves the person alone. In the narrator's case, the thought that no longer leaves her alone is, as we will see, an (animated) object that she finds at the flea market. This object is some kind of book. *Flöhe*, the plural of fleas, is also a jargon word in the book business where it then refers to discounted paperbacks.

An Illustrated Encyclopedia

The narrator, however, describes the flea market, not primarily as a dream site but somewhat surprisingly perhaps, first and foremost, as a site of knowledge. When describing the market Tawada uses a simile—a poetic figure appropriate to the context of dreams where nothing is exactly the same though everything appears familiar—she writes: "the flea market was like an illustrated encyclopedia."[11] In *A Guest*, in other words, the flea market is presented as a reference book, as a compendium through which the stroller can browse at leisure, to consult an unknown topic or read up on something or someone. The flea market offers a repository of words and images and provides comprehensive information about all or specialized areas of knowledge.

But at the flea market knowledge is not presented in a traditional encyclopedic manner. The objects on display have been freed from the straightjacket imposed by the alphabetic order were they in an actual reference book; yet they are not positioned according to any other obvious "logical" category either. Quite on the contrary, each flea market visitor has to discover his own set of interpretative tools while strolling through the site. The flea market, Breton wrote, is a place that houses "objects that can be found nowhere else; old-fashioned, broken, useless, almost *incomprehensible*, even *perverse*—at least in the sense that I give to the word and which I prefer."[12] The flea market then suggests a surrealist alternative to the assumptions about representation inherent in realist aesthetic codes. In *A Guest* Tawada's narrator informs us:

> An iron and a candle stick stood side by side, as though there were some relation between them. I was even able to think how this proximity might be deciphered; the iron produces heat and the candlestick light. Each takes the place of the sun, which from the underground passage is never visible. . . . A pair of ice skates and a clock lay side by side, as though challenging me to guess their relationship. I stood before them until I had found the solution: ice skates and clock—both turn in circles. When ice skaters twirl, they look like the dolls in music boxes, which you wind like a clock.[13]

As the narrator is walking towards the end of the subterranean pedestrian passage in which the flea market is being held—still pondering the order of things as she passes by other remarkable visual compositions—she chances upon two famous surrealist objects; she notices an umbrella next to a sewing machine at one of the stalls. When presented together on a third plane (here the flea market) these two particular objects turn into the best-known surrealist image of all, which can be traced back to Lautréamont's infamous long prose poem *Les Chants de Maldoror*. When first published, the novel went almost unnoticed but was rediscovered, first by Huysmans, and later again by Breton who praised it as an extraordinary piece of experimental writing. In *Maldoror* this unusual image is used to describe the physical appearance of a young man who was "as handsome . . . as the fortuitous encounter upon a dissecting-table of a sewing machine and an umbrella."[14] Breton cherishes this particular image because it perfectly illustrates one of the principles of surrealist poetics: the fortuitous juxtaposition of two terms—here the sewing machine and the umbrella—which create a poetic spark when brought together in close quarters. It is this well-known Lautréamontian image that seems to draw Tawada's narrator closer to one of the last vendor's booths and it is while examining this Lautréamontian image up close that she suddenly finds her own enigmatic *trouvaille*, framed by that most celebrated surrealist figure of poetic composition.

> At the end of the passage I discovered a book between a black umbrella and a sewing machine with a treadle. I don't know why this book in particular drew my attention. I picked it up, and noticed its slight warmth in the palms of my hands. On the book's cover I saw letters that were written not from left to right, but in a circle.[15]

This key passage of which, for the moment, I only present the first few lines, deserves our critical attention for several reasons. First of all it introduces an important character, in many ways *the* main antagonist of *A Guest*: a surrealist found object—in this case a book—that mysteriously attracts the narrator ("I don't know why this book in particular drew my attention") and which the narrator purchases to take home, though she is not entirely sure what she has bought. Upon closer examination, once inside her apartment, the book turns out to be "a book on tape," one in a German literary series in which contemporary writers record their own poems or novels in their own voice. The content of the recorded novel is deemed of no interest and is never revealed. This voice of the other (author) creates both a pleasant (invisible but physical erotic) presence and an actual disturbance in the narrator's daily writing routine.

As we are dealing with a surrealist "found object," we immediately suspect that this recorded voice also functions as a portent and has an important message for the narrator, even though probably she herself—in line with the surrealist tradition—might not know yet what it is that she hopes to solve. So what is it that turns out to be plaguing Tawada's Japanese narrator in the German environment? The narrator who has trouble writing her ethnographic pieces on Germany and the Germans—she starts with a piece on birthday celebrations and is planning articles on Christmas and German Unification Day but has difficulties finding "explanations" for certain cultural rituals—also has difficulties reading. Something, she explains, in her reading experience has changed in Germany as well:

> It's been years since I last read a novel in which I could make the letters disappear. This probably has nothing to do with me, but with the city; the only books here are written in a foreign script. As long as I've lived here I've been unable to enter novels. I read and read, but the alphabet never vanishes before my eyes, but rather remains like iron bars or like sand in salad or like the reproduction of my face in the window of a train at night. How often my own reflection in the glass has kept me from enjoying a nocturnal landscape. Even when there was nothing to see, I would have liked to gaze into the darkness, not into my own mirror image. *Why had it never occurred to me that a tape recording could be the magic means for erasing the letters in a novel?*[16]

The surrealist *trouvaille* of the flea market functions for the narrator as a magic medium to make letters disappear, offering her the possibility of losing herself in a novel. The narrator apparently found what she wanted at the flea market: "Finally I had succeeded in eliminating the alphabet. I should have been happy." So why isn't the narrator content? Is it perhaps, to speak with Breton in *Mad Love*, because a found object always offers "an answer in excess?" And what might that excess be in the narrator's case?

If in the process of transcription from speech to writing the subject's body disappears, it should, in contrast, reappear when a written text is vocalized again. This is the case in *A Guest* where the recorded voice of the book-on-tape, effectively blowing away the letters of the alphabet, soon starts to become a (invisible) physical presence that matters. The narrator informs us: "it [the voice] came to me in surprising ways. First it stroked my neck cautiously. This tended to go on too long for my taste, and I was afraid it might elegantly strangle me. I never understood what it wanted from me, if it wanted anything at all."[17]

Though still able to turn the tape recorder off and on, the narrator no longer controls the recorded voice that seems to have a speed and a will of its own. When the narrator, who is increasingly desperate to finish her writing assignment, resists the putative primacy of speech over the written word, the recorded automated voice slowly turns into the stranger we know from Simmel's essay: a potentially mobile but now residential human being who is experienced sometimes as an interruption and sometimes as liberating instance.

Tawada, it is important to point out, rewrote Lautréamont's poetic image for her own purposes. Positioning her *trouvaille* "between" the black umbrella and the old-fashioned sewing machine, the placement of the book object offers an indication about the particular method that the narrator uses in her attempt to gain knowledge about the cultures and the people living in the unknown locale. Entering into direct contact with the reality captured during the moment of the encounter, the found object represents a way of being *amidst* rather than standing before the world. Hence, it makes sense that the narrator's *trouvaille* is a "book-on-tape," an object that is directed towards the (absorbing) ear rather than to the (mastering) eye. Georg Simmel had already pitched these two senses against each other to argue that, though the ear can formally be seen as the most egoistical of all organs because it takes everything in but gives nothing back, it has an unusual relationship to private property. As Simmel phrased it: "Generally speaking, one can only possess the visible, what is only audible, in contrast, ceases to be as soon it comes into being and does not have the potential to become 'property.'"[18]

This book-on-tape then presents itself as the new poetic spark, as a charged, erotic explosive, that is the result of the meeting between the umbrella and the sewing machine.[19] The book object, as a result of this surrealist encounter, still even has a "slight warmth," which the narrator senses when she picks up the item. In this fashion Tawada's found object can then literally be interpreted as an aesthetic "offspring" of the famous surrealist encounter, as a surrealist product that first appears at the antiquated market but leaves with the narrator to start an new aesthetic existence in a contemporary intercultural context.

Tawada, of course, altered not only the position of the found object, she changed the location of the poetic meeting as well. Transforming Lautréamont's "operating table" into a flea market which "was like an illustrated encyclopedia," Tawada argues not only, as we have seen, that a flea market can be read as a place of knowledge where information presents itself and solutions can be found, but she also and equally important argues the reverse, namely that an illustrated encyclopedia, like a flea market, is a surrealist space. In an encyclopedia, or in a dictionary, random, semantically and historically unrelated words are forced together by the order and the logic of the alphabet as Foucault has argued. They come together on the same page or, perhaps more accurately, on the same *table* if we understand this word both in its common usage and as *a tabula*, as an arrangement of information or data into columns or a condensed list.[20] Tawada's table, as we will see in what follows, is a self-cleaning surface of inscription.

Writing the Illegibile

The recently found object with the unusual script is eventually likened to the narrator herself. Though it is not immediately clear to the reader what exactly, if anything, the foreign narrator and the book might have in common, the German vendor, for one brief moment acting like a Surrealist himself, brings the two together. The narrator who is intrigued by the unknown script addresses the local vendor with a question:

> I asked the man who was standing there hawking his wares in what language the book was written, since I don't know any language whose letters are arranged in a circle. *He shrugged his shoulders* and said *it wasn't a book, it was a mirror.* I glanced at the thing he was calling a mirror. Maybe it isn't a book at all, I conceded, but I would still like to know what's going on with this writing. The man grinned and replied; *to our eyes you look exactly like this writing.* That's why I said it was a mirror. *I rubbed my forehead from left to right, as if rewriting my face.*[21]

Here the flea market is suddenly no longer only a place where information can be consulted; it has also become a site where knowledge is *created*, where the narrator experiences how the local reads her physical presence and where she can react to this information, adding her knowledge to the compendium as well.

While Tawada's narrator at the flea market, like the Surrealists, ponders the only seemingly familiar—the object looks like a familiar object, a book, but on closer inspection it has an "unknown" script—and enjoys the irruption of otherness and the unexpected, the local vendor uses the opposite approach; he attempts to render the strange and the stranger comprehensible by reducing the unknown to the known.[22] Having no answer to the narrator's question ("he shrugged his shoulders"), the local right away connects one inexplicable object—the book with the unfamiliar script—to another—the Japanese narrator in front of his eyes—making the two rather disparate objects fit into the crude category of "the unknown," before turning both unfamiliar objects into a mirror. Reading the other as a mirror, we know from Lacan, might be a necessary developmental stage in the attempt to create a coherent self, but has precious little to offer as a device that might produce knowledge about the other. Seeing the stranger as mirror means that we have erased the features of the other to see only a reflection of our familiar self on the flattened surface of the other's face. From her earliest writing onward, Tawada has insisted that in order to let "the strange" and "the stranger" exist in their own right, this type of reading the other should be avoided.[23]

So how does the Japanese narrator react to this representation and interpretation of her body? Choosing not to respond to the market vendor's puzzling comment with words, she gestures, having recourse to a different sign system. This social behavior, I argue, should tell us something. The narrator, we read, "*rubbed* her forehead from left to right, as if *rewriting* her face," or in German—and the original is important here—"ich rieb mir die Stirn von links nach rechts, als würde ich mein Gesicht *umschreiben*."[24]

Umschreiben (to rewrite) has more than a dozen different connotations, depending on the pronunciation of the verb and the context in which it is used.[25] Tawada plays with several meanings of *umschreiben*, when she states that in *A Guest* the narrator is "rewriting" her face. Here, it will suffice to point to those that are most relevant to my argument. I suggest that the narrator is "delineating her face" while "altering" it by "paraphrasing" and "transcribing" it. Attempting to represent her face both "in other words," and in "another image," the narrator, as we will see, picks up her creative surrealist activity one more time.

In a short text entitled "Bilderrätsel ohne Bilder," (Image Riddles without Images) Tawada explained that the Chinese character for "body," is made up of the sign for "human being," and the sign for "book." She then goes on to ask "Does this mean that the body is a book that pretends to be a human being?"[26] I will argue that when the market vendor brings together the Japanese narrator ("a human being") and the object with the unfamiliar script ("a book") the German man is trying to read "the body" of the foreign narrator as a "Chinese character." Failing at his attempt to read the foreign script as a coherent signifying entity (the character has fallen apart into two separate signs) he quickly falls back into transforming her into a reflection of the familiar. When the narrator, in response, rubs her face she changes the function of the mirror that now is no longer just a narcissistic object that human beings use to look at themselves. After erasing the Chinese character with her hands, she has created an empty mirror, a clean surface of inscription on which the narrator then rewrites herself one more time and turns herself into another twisted enigmatic surrealist image.[27] Thus, as we have seen with the umbrella and the sewing machine which Tawada used but only as a framing device, the author makes use of the stockpile of historical surrealist images only to read them against the grain.

Clock Face

In the opening scene of *A Guest* when the narrator is just about to enter the flea market, she briefly takes note of a broken clock, though once in the subterranean tunnel where the market takes place, time no longer seems to play a role:

> Just before the entrance to the passage I'd seen a clock mounted on the side of the kiosk. The clock was missing the numbers three and seven. Beside the clock stood a man who was just taking the missing numbers from his tool kit so as to affix them to the clock's face. The woman inside the kiosk shouted to him how nice it would be to be able to see the correct time again. All at once it seemed strange to me that the numbers were arranged in a circle, since ordinarily numbers are always written from left to right.[28]

At the end of the novel this same clock—or perhaps a similar clock since we are, after all, still in a dream site—now seems to have all its numbers attached and, perhaps, is actually working again. Simultaneously, it is as if the narrator herself has somehow transformed herself into this clock.[29] In other words, the narrator has exchanged her human face—the sight that Simmel has called *the* geometric space of all interpersonal knowledge—for a mechanical face with, as we will see, a surrealist history.[30]

> But no one recognized me because I had plastered my face with light-gray, concrete-like paint. *My nose and mouth looked like two hillocks*, and my eyes were holes. On my cheeks, Z wrote the numbers three and seven. When the women arrived, they generally gave my face a brief glance and *acted as if they hadn't seen anything*.[31]

Rewriting her face, she attempts to make it look more "familiar" with the help of the Roman alphabet, using the "hilly" letters *n* and *m* for her nose and her mouth respectively. The "face clock" narrator now has a certain resemblance both with the wall clock and with the surrealist *trouvaille* from the flea market and its circular inscription, just like the German market vendor had noticed earlier.

This enigmatic, surrealist face-clock image strongly echoes one of Walter Benjamin's mechanical images that appeared in his classic 1929 essay on the historical movement Surrealism, "For the moment only the surrealists have understood its present command. They exchange, to a man, the play of human features for the face of an alarm clock that in each minute rings for sixty seconds."[32] Benjamin's continuously ringing human alarm clock, this image of surrealist shock, has been understood as the collective awakening from "the dream world of mass culture" and the resulting rise of the revolutionary class consciousness.[33] But Tawada—though using and referring to the historical surrealist image and data bank, its "illustrated encyclopedia," so to speak—once again created her own altered contemporary surrealist image. In her rewriting of the surrealist image she highlights, like she did in the case of Lautréamont's famous image, that some of the better known, originally illuminating, images of the historical avant-garde are worn-out a century later. In *A Guest* the Benja-minian alarm clock no longer has the power to interrupt through its shocking ring. The new face clock, like the voice of a local, is invisible (the narrator as an entity seems to now have finally dissolved), but it nevertheless has the imagistic force to interrupt and to create a disturbance. Tawada explains this fatigue and the resulting need of a continuous production of new word (and image) combi-nations in the following passage:

> Words that tire out the air are multiplying all around me. I have to let one word collide against another so that they annihilate each other. During the moment of collision, there is a flash of lightning in the air. This flash of lightning is the only verbal product that interests me. But it is not easy to know which word should be thrown against which other word. Most words have signed a reassur-ance agreement so that they only fight others and not each other. When these words do happen to collide, they hold on to each other in a strong embrace in order not to see each other's face. At that moment the air becomes heavy; noth-ing happens, there is no lightning flash, and the words remain what they have been all along; carriers of meaning. Supposedly they are transporting meaning-ful contents, reinforcing each other and furthering the world in its development. It is almost sad too see which word proudly supports which other word. Two words come together and leave no free space, no freedom: master and litera-ture, voice and democracy, free time and nature. During each of these tiresome combinations my lungs are losing more energy, and there is less air to breath. In order to keep breathing I always have to invent new collisions so that there is a lightning flash again: master and flea, voice and fork, free time and black board. Unfortunately, there is no single combination that, in the long run, can produce a flash of lightning. [34]

This is how and why the thought and practice of Surrealism is still relevant to-day; not as a program, not as code but as a theoretical and aesthetic form that continuously produces a flash of lightning, interrupts our debates and in doing so insists on the unknown character. Tawada's poetic images, like those of the Surrealists, are neither regulated by a dialectical *Aufhebung*, nor are they pro-jected into a utopian horizon where a final unification might occur; the parts are juxtaposed but only to never be fully resolved on a table, a *tabula*, or any other third plane. The enigmatic surrealist image remains ununifiable and, precisely because of that, raises questions of irritation and difference as form. The surreal-ist image, I argue, offers us a theoretical and aesthetic completion that, like Simmel's concept of the stranger, stands in a distant relation to the unknown, mobilizing the whole through its various modes of interruption. Always extend-ing beyond, separating from and disarranging the whole, suggests that this con-cept is itself to be arrested in the context of contemporary transnational and postcolonial studies debates.

Notes

1. Rosalind E. Krauss, *The Originality of the Avant-Garde and Other Modernist Myths* (Cambridge, Mass.: MIT Press, 1985), 113. Emphasis in original.

2. Beate Laudenberg ("Aspekte der deutschsprachigen Migrantenliteratur, dargestellt an Yoko Tawada's Roman "Ein Gast," in *Literatur im interkulturellen Dialog. Festschrift zum 60. Geburtstag von Hans-Christoph Graf von Nayhauss* [Bern, Switzerland: Peter Lang, 2000]), Florian Gelzer ("Wenn ich spreche, bin ich nicht da. Fremdwahrnehmung und Sprachprogrammatik bei Yoko Tawada," *Recherches Germaniques. Revue Annuelle* 29 [1999], 67-91), Claudia Keller ("Deutschland neu lesen. Autoren denken über Heimat und Fremde in der Literatur nach." *Der Tagesspiegel,* 5 May 2000), Sibylle Cramer ("Surreale Puppenwelt," *Basler Zeitung,* vol. 3, no. 1 [1992]) and Albrecht Kloepfer and Miho Matsunaga (*Kritisches Lexikon zur deutschsprachigen Gegenwartsliteratur*), all use "surreal" or "surrealist" as a descriptor when writing about Yoko Tawada's work.

3. Yoko Tawada, *Ein Gast* (Tübingen, Germany: Konkursbuch Verlag Claudia Gehrke, 1993). The English translation "A Guest" is published in *Where Europe Begins,* translated by Susan Bernofsky and Yumi Selden (New York: New Directions, 2002). Scholarly articles focusing on *A Guest* either interpret Tawada's text with the help of feminist insights, situate the text awkwardly within the context of the German migrant literature debate, or read the text through certain linguistic-based theories.

4. Tawada, "Guest," 208.

5. Tawada, "Guest," 208.

6. André Breton, *Mad Love,* trans. Mary Ann Caws (Lincoln: University of Nebraska Press, 1987), 28. Emphasis mine.

7. Peter Bürger, *Theorie der Avantgarde.* (Frankfurt am Main, Germany: Suhrkamp, 1974), 90. See also Margaret Cohen, *Profane Illumination: Walter Benjamin and the Paris of Surrealist Revolution* (Berkeley: University of California Press, 1993), 133. Cohen exams the role of the *trouvaille* in Breton's theoretical writings and points to the psychoanalytic factors at play in the surrealist found object.

8. Breton, *Mad Love,* 13.

9. Tawada, "Guest," 150.

10. Tawada, "Guest," 149.

11. Tawada, "Guest," 150.

12. André Breton, *Nadja,* trans. Richard Howard (New York: Grove Press, 1960), 52. Emphasis mine.

13. Tawada, "Guest," 152-153.

14. Isidore Ducasse Lautreamont. *Les chants de Maldoror* (New York: New Directions, 1965), 263.

15. Tawada, "Guest," 153.

16 Tawada, "Guest," 166. Emphasis mine.

17. Tawada, "Guest," 177.

18. Simmel, "Exkurs," 730. Translation mine. Tawada links the visual display of cultural artifacts in museums to issues of imperialism and cultural dominance.

19. The umbrella and the sewing machine have, of course, frequently been read as sexual imagery. See for instance Jacques Derrida's *Spurs: Nietzsche's Styles,* 129-130.

20. Michel Foucault uses this argument (table as *tabula*) when he talks about Jorge Luis Borges "A Certain Chinese Dictionary" in the preface to *The Order of Things: An Archeology Of The Human Sciences.* New York: Vintage Books. In "The Dictionary

City," published as part of the essay collection *Talisman*, Tawada further developed this idea.

21. Tawada, *Ein Gast*, 9. Translation modified. Italics mine.

22. Tawada's narrators are familiar with this Western approach to knowledge production. "Because I had compared something with which I was unfamiliar to something that had once existed in our country, she knew right away that I was from the 'West' even though I wasn't European or American." From "Das Leipzig des Lichts und der Gelatine" published in *Nur da wo du bist da ist nichts*, p. 9. Translation mine.

23. "I knew at once she couldn't read. Whenever she saw me she gazed at me intently and with interest, but she never attempted to read anything in my face. In those days I often found that people became uneasy when they couldn't read my face like a text. It's curious the way the expression of a foreigner's face is often compared to a mask. Does this comparison conceal a wish to discover a familiar face behind the strange one?" Yoko Tawada, "Canned Foreign," in *Where Europe Begins*, 86.

24. Tawada, *Ein Gast*, 10. Emphasis mine.

25. The verb can be pronounced either as *um*schreiben or as um*schreiben*.

26. Yoko Tawada, "Bilderrätsel ohne Bilder," in *Nur da wo du bist, da ist nichts*, translated by Peter Pörtner. (Tübingen, Germany: Konkursbuch Verlag Claudia Gehrke, 1997), 3. Translation from the German is mine.

27. The image of the "wiped slate" reminds the reader, of course, of Freud's famous "Note on the Mystic Writing Pad," in which he linked the functioning of a certain writing device, the so-called *Wunderblock* to the functioning of the mental apparatus. Both, Freud argued, receive a set of impressions on one of their layers (letters written with a stylus in the case of the *Wunderblock* and a set of stimuli from the outside world or from the body itself in the case of the mental apparatus) but neither surface that received the original imprint carries permanent visible marks of these impressions. Each system presents itself, rather, as "a slate wiped clean": though no longer visible in the location where they were recorded they nevertheless remain in the system as a permanent network of traces. For Yoko Tawada the image of the empty, cleaned slate is related to the activity of dreaming. She writes: "Sleep resembles an endless preview only consisting of advertising; prices, telephone numbers, addresses and dates that do not interest me appear on a slate, and I have to be continuously work with my eraser to wipe them away them." Yoko Tawada, "Die Leere Tafel," *Sinn und Form* 3 (1994), 466-471.

28. Tawada, "Guest," 149. *Ein Gast*, p.5. The numbers three and seven float around, like in a dream, throughout the work.

29. Here Tawada seems to play with a version of the German expression: "die tickt nicht richtig," which literally translates as "she is not ticking correctly," implying that somebody has completely lost it. At the end of the novel the narrator who has become a correctly ticking clock then seems to have her act together again.

30. Simmel, "Exkurs über die Soziologie der Sinne," 725.

31. Tawada "Guest," 203. Emphasis mine.

32. "Surrealism. The Last Snapshot of the European Intelligentsia." Walter Benjamin. *Selected Writings*, Vol. 2, 1927-1934. Trans. Rodney Livingstone and others. Ed. by Michael W. Jennings, Howard Eiland, and Gary Smith. Cambridge, Mass.: The Belknap Press of Harvard University, 1999. "Sürrealismus. Die letzte Momentaufnahme der europäischen Intelligenz," Walter Benjamin, *Gesammelte Schriften*. Band II.I. Werkausgabe (Frankfurt, Germany: Edition Suhrkamp, 1977), 297. See for instance Rainer Rumold, *The Janus Face of the Avant-Garde*, for the significance of this essay in the context of the German avant-garde.

33. See particularly Susan Buck-Morss, "The Dream World of Mass Culture," *The Dialectics of Seeing*, pp. 253-287. Sigrid Weigel's "Die Passage durch den Leib-und Bildraum im Surrealismus," *Enstellte Ähnlichkeit. Walter Benjamins theoretische Schreibweise*, pp. 113-127.

34. Yoko Tawada, "Die Leere Tafel," *Sinn und Form* 3 (1994), 466-471. Translation mine.

Bibliography

Benjamin, Walter. "Surrealismus. Die letzte Momentaufnahme der europäischen Intelligenz," *Gesammelte Schriften*. Band II.I. Werkausgabe, Frankfurt am Main, Germany: Suhrkamp, 1977.

———. "Surrealism. The Last Snapshot of the European Intelligentsia." *Selected Writings*, Vol. 2, 1927-1934. Translated by Rodney Livingstone and others. Edited by Michael W. Jennings, Howard Eiland, and Gary Smith. Cambridge, Mass.: The Belknap Press of Harvard University, 1999.

Brandt, Bettina. "Schnitt durchs Auge. Surrealistische Bilder bei Yoko Tawada, Emine Sevgi Özdamar und Herta Müller." *In Literatur und Migration*. München: Text und Kritik, 2006, 74-84.

Breton, André. *Mad Love*. Translated by Mary Ann Caws. Lincoln: University of Nebraska Press, 1987.

———. *Nadja*. Translated by Richard Howard. New York: Grove Press, 1960.

Buck-Morss, Susan. *The Dialectics of Seeing: Walter Benjamin and the Arcades Project*. Cambridge, Mass.: MIT Press, 1999.

Bürger, Peter. *Theorie der Avantgarde*. Frankfurt am Main, Germany: Suhrkamp, 1974.

Cohen, Margaret. *Profane Illumination. Walter Benjamin and the Paris of Surrealist Revolution*. Berkeley: University of California Press, 1993.

Cramer, Sibylle. "Surreale Puppenwelt." *Basler Zeitung* 3, no. 1 (1992).

Derrida, Jacques. *Le monolinguisme de l'autre*. Paris: Seuil, 1999.

———. *Spurs. Nietzche's Styles*. Translated by Barbara Harlow. Chicago: The University of Chicago Press, 1979.

Foucault, Michel. *The Order of Things. An Archeology Of The Human Sciences*. New York: Vintage Books, 1973.

Gelzer, Florian. "Wenn ich spreche, bin ich nicht da. Fremdwahrnehmung und Sprachprogrammatik bei Yoko Tawada." *Recherches Germaniques. Revue Annuelle* 29 (1999).

Jay, Martin. *Downcast Eyes. The Denigration of Vision in Twentieth-century French Thought*. Berkeley: University of California Press, 1993.

Keller, Claudia. "Deutschland neu lesen. Autoren denken über Heimat und Fremde in der Literatur nach." *Der Tagesspiegel*, 5 May 2000.

Kloepfer, Albrecht, and Miho Matsunaga. "Yoko Tawada." *Kritisches Lexikon zur deutschsprachigen Gegenwartsliteratur* 64 (2000): 1-17.

Krauss, Rosalind E. *The Originality of the Avant-Garde and Other Modernist Myths*. Cambridge, Mass.: MIT Press, 1985.

Laudenberg, Beate. "Aspekte der deutschsprachigen Migrantenliteratur, dargestellt an Yoko Tawada's Roman 'Ein Gast.'" In *Literatur im interkulturellen Dialog. Festschrift zum 60. Geburtstag von Hans-Christoph Graf von Nayhauss*. Bern, Switzerland: Peter Lang, 2000.

Lautréamont, Isidore Ducasse. *Les chants de Maldoror*. New York: New Directions, 1965.

Nacify, Hamid. *An Accented Cinema. Exilic and Diasporic Film Making*. Princeton, N.J.: Princeton University Press, 2001.

Rumold, Rainer. *The Janus Face of the German Avant-Garde. From Expressionism to Postmodernism*. Chicago: Northwestern University Press, 2002.

Simmel, Georg. "Exkurs über den Fremden." In *Soziologie. Untersuchungen über die Formen der Vergesellschaftung*, edited by Otthein Rammstedt. Vol. 2. Frankfurt am Main, Germany: Suhrkamp, 1992.

Tawada, Yoko. "Bilderrätsel ohne Bilder." In *Nur da wo du bist, da ist nichts*. 5th ed. Translated by Peter Pörtner. Tübingen, Germany: Konkursbuch Verlag Claudia Gehrke, 1997.

——. "Canned Foreign." In *Where Europe Begins*, Translated by Susan Bernofsky and Sumi Yelden. New York: New Directions, 2002.

——. *Das Bad*. Translated by Peter Pörtner. Tübingen, Germany: Konkursbuch Verlag Claudia Gehrke, 1989.

——. *Das Fremde aus der Dose*. Graz, Austria: Droschl, 1992.

——. "Die Leere Tafel." *Sinn und Form* 3 (1994), 466-471.

——. *Ein Gast*. Tübingen, Germany: Konkursbuch Verlag Claudia Gehrke, 1993.

——. "A Guest." In *Where Europe Begins*, Translated by Susan Bernofsky and Yumi Selden. New York: New Directions, 2002.

——. *Verwandlungen, Tübinger Poetik Vorlesung*. Tübingen, Germany: Konkursbuch Verlag Claudia Gehrke, 1998.

——. *Wo Europa anfängt*. Tübingen, Germany: Konkursbuch Verlag Claudia Gehrke, 1991.

——. "Zukunft ohne Herkunft." In *Zukunft! Zukunft?* Tübingen, Germany: Konkursbuch Verlag Claudia Gehrke, 2000.

Weigel, Sigrid. *Enstellte Ähnlichkeit. Walter Benjamins theoretische Schreibweise*. Frankfurt am Main, Germany: Fischer Verlag, 1997.

Chapter Ten
Words and Roots: The Loss of the Familiar in the Works of Yoko Tawada

Bernard Banoun

Translated from the French by Joshua Humphreys

> Freedom from the sedentary forms of existence is,
> perhaps, the human way of being in the world.
> —Emmanuel Levinas[1]

Languages and Resting Places

Once I met Clymene at a sculpture exhibition in the warehouse district. The artist had formed sculptures that represented the inner depths of human heads. Each head was as big as a room—and hollow. We went inside the heads and looked at them from within.
"It's really quite thrilling to consider how hollow a head can be."
"The face on the outside, by contrast, is hardly of any interest whatsoever."
"You could actually live fairly well in your own head."
"And languages, where exactly do they live?"
"I was thinking that we were the ones living within languages. That's why I never have the feeling of being homeless, even when I'm moving around for weeks on end."[2]

This dialogue between an unlikely first-person narrator and the linguist Clymene appears in *Opium für Ovid*, Yoko Tawada's novel that probes the lives of several contemporary characters as they circulate through the city of Hamburg. Three positions are put into play here: the extremely contemporary nature of the narrative, the literary absolute, and the radical materiality of language.

Over the course of history—and no more acutely than during a twentieth century marked by repeated uprootings and displacements—language, the poet's "domain," that "pleasant asylum,"[3] has frequently revealed itself to be the writer's only true country. The tragic foundational account of what Peter Huchel once called the "broken bricks of Babel," in a verse of a poem dedicated to Michael Hamburger,[4] cannot be dissociated from the writings of Paul Celan and Nelly Sachs. And as Hilde Domin writes in her essays subtitled *Heimat in der*

Sprache (My Homeland in Language), "Language is for me that last thing that cannot be lost when you realize that everything could very well be lost. It is the final, inalienable, home."[5]

Yoko Tawada is not, neither historically nor literarily, in precisely this same situation. We notice that in this nomadic author, whose native Japanese is by no means the only rest stop over the course of her wanderings, exile has nothing to do with the ordeals and forced upheavals of totalitarianism. Tawada, who writes in both Japanese and German, has migrated across spaces and languages, taking up German after having studied Russian and because this split personality of sorts has made it difficult for her to lay roots in any single linguistic homeland, she has done it all in a movement at once pluralistic and unburdened.

Numerous writers change languages, adopt another or successively two others, before establishing themselves definitively: Conrad, Nabokov, Ionesco, Canetti, Celan. It is a particularly common phenomenon in contemporary German literature.[6] Much rarer are those who continue to use two languages in parallel or to translate themselves from time to time, such as Pessoa, Beckett, Tabucchi or, in the world of Franco-German writers, Georges-Arthur Goldschmidt.

Being bilingual, writing in two languages and living more than one life, has given Yoko Tawada additional strings to play on her Orphean lyre and allowed her to be numbered among these writers who experiment with this kind of self splitting. No question: she seems to possess and to cultivate the languages she uses; these metaphors of domination, taken from the worlds of agriculture and linguistics alike, often describe one's relationship to a particular language in the most innocent, though by no means thoughtless, terms. And yet the opposite is no less true. Whoever speaks, reads and writes languages also becomes possessed by them—this basic critical position of modernity attests to both the arbitrary nature of signs and the gaping hole language opens when it claims to translate or express something precisely at the point where words result in, indeed impose, meaning. This idea is repeatedly at work in Tawada's works, particularly in her first texts published in German. "I feel the thirst for power of those who want *to master* languages in order to be able to use them like tools. But these people don't realize that the languages are writing them, rather than the other way around."[7] Tawada, however, forges this initial intuition only to go beyond it. She situates her writing in this break between being and language, in the absence of any familiarity or identity given from the outset. A person generally believes that speaking is natural, and one speaks the language of a nation which is itself supposedly aligned etymologically with the native and nature.

The Strange Foreignness of Language

In *Le Monolinguisme de l'autre*, Jacques Derrida takes his particular, personal situation as a point of departure: a French-speaking Jew from Algeria, caught between languages, the local Arabic and the French of Metropolitan France, both of which are foreign and thus neither of which gives him access to the basic rights of citizenship and property. At the heart of this contradiction, Derrida defines what he means by the monolingualism of the other: language is a law that we must appropriate, and even though we act as if we give ourselves this law, it remains, like the essence of any law, heteronomous. This basic definition can be seen as the political dimension of the *Sprachskepsis* of Viennese modernity. "We speak only one language," Derrida writes, "yet we do not *have* it,"[8] not only in the sense that language possesses and acculturates us when we think we are possessing and cultivating it, but also because we are colonized by the intermediary of language. That something else has become lodged within us. This leads Derrida to highlight the essential strangeness of language, the strange foreignness that makes the balancing act between cultures and sign systems apparent in a way that one could never really avoid.

The two aspects are indissociable. To feel within one's mouth words that have not been assimilated from childhood makes one wonder whether the physical presence of language, even your native language, is something natural. In "Das Fremde aus der Dose" (Canned Foreign), an essay describing her early difficulties with German, Tawada explains this phenomenon with reference to the body.[9]

> Most of the words that came out of my mouth had nothing to do with how I felt. But at the same time I realized that my native tongue didn't have words for how I felt either. I only discovered this once I'd begun to live in a foreign language.
> Often it sickened me to hear people speak their native tongues fluently. It was as if they were unable to think and feel anything but what their language so readily offered up to them.[10]

The opposition between native and foreign languages and, beyond that, between native and foreign lands thus shows itself to be unfruitful, and the idea that one territory is superior to another, that some great potency is to be found in a sense of rootedness in a particular place and that there are benefits to be drawn from this umbilical connection, is also rendered illusory.

This appears to be even more the case when it comes to the question of voice: voices, your own voice, the voices that you carry within yourself do not belong to you like personal property. Tawada explores this question in the first of her Tübingen lectures on poetics, "Stimme eines Vogels oder Das Problem der Fremdheit" (The Voice of a Bird, or the Problem of Foreignness). The study begins with an observation: when one speaks while in a foreign country, the voice is isolated, bare and drifting, each sentence is exact, stripped down to the essence of the message to be communicated. Either one tries to acclimate one's voice, or one savors this newfound foreignness. The latter is what the narrator herself prefers to do. While the voice that one has in one's native language is imperceptible, the new accent and the process of forming words in one's mouth provides an embodied-ness. And this detour that one must take through the foreign voice reverberates back upon one's own voice, which can then liberate itself in turn:

If I refer to "foreign voices" here, I do not proceed from the assumption that each person who only speaks his or her native language is keeping his or her original voice. For we do not keep the voices with which we were born. The tension between integration and foreignness of voices is an inevitable part of socialization.[11]

Numerous German texts by Tawada make apparent, in precisely this way, things that are not obviously so. What might be understood, in the way that a signifier belongs to a signified, suddenly becomes strange. Meanings become sharper, and the subject detaches itself from what had seemed self-apparent. And this is a gain, not a waste, because "generally one remains blind in a situation that one otherwise masters."[12]

Among the numerous texts in poetry criticism where Tawada traces this process of losing the familiarity of language, the most explicit is "Der Schrift-körper und der beschriftete Körper" (The Body of Writing and the Body Written), where she describes the movement from one language to another:

Most writers stop writing in one language once they have begun to write in another. This makes perfect sense to me since one language seeks to destroy any other that tries to develop within the space of the same head. Whenever I have worked intensively on a Japanese text, for example, I can no longer write in German. Blind and vulnerable, I crawl arduously back into the German language, which has become newly foreign to me; step by step I grope for words until I find myself able to write once more. But then I feel as if I had never written Japanese in my life. Not a single Japanese word that could possibly move me to write even occurs to me any longer. All words are dead, or rather not the words, but I myself am dead in this language. Nevertheless, I persist in placing Japanese characters on the paper, one after another. In an effort to communicate with the characters, they slowly begin to give rise to pictures, words, and ideas. In this kind of a moment, languages actually seem to want to help people express themselves. I have no faith, however, in languages' good intentions. They are monsters that would rather destroy every "expression." I have gone so far as to use this destructive process as a literary method. At the beginning of each new text I want to be thrown back to the zero point, to the point of speechlessness, to the point at which it is no longer obvious that a sentence can naturally produce a meaning. The literature that attracts me the most is the kind that knows something about this powerlessness of being speechless.[13]

Rediscovering how to speak in a foreign language thus leads to discovering one's "native language as a foreign language."[14] The transition into a foreign language therefore reveals the non-proprietary quality of language and of the absence of language's natural identity with the speaker.

This process is accompanied by a devaluation of the function of language as an instrument of communication based on its referential features, and an accentuation of its poetic and acoustic qualities. The expression "speechlessness," cited in this passage, is thus best understood as an absence from language and in this sense an absence in the world (in the way that one is *absent*-minded): the signifier becomes meaningless in a way that seems disconcerting at times. This is precisely how Tawada brings something new to the German language, in the way suggested by Derrida, who contrasts the quest for origins within language (Heidegger) to the situation of those who write in a language by choice or exile, such as Kafka, Celan, or Levinas. In describing her departure from Japan, the narrator of *Where Europe Begins* evokes the moment when her ship leaves port; as passengers are throwing streamers (which she compares to umbilical cords), she throws a white streamer like a page out of a writing pad, and "it became my memory. . . . In that moment, as my streamer tore apart, my memory ceased to function. That's why I know nothing else about that trip."[15]

The break, the moment of absence, is the condition of a new apprehension of the world, and the momentary amnesia is the condition of writing, just as knowledge of one's origins comes through their loss or by distance. Tawada highlights how she only became aware of certain elements of Japanese culture, such as her newfound recognition of the importance of the Sei Shōnagon texts, for example, by having followed her European detour. Unlearning her native culture through immersion in a different one requires looking hard in the face of the original, but now doing so at a distance. The experience is parallel to that described by Barthes in *Empire of Signs*—a work which, for the French reader at least, seems almost too perfect of an introduction to Tawada's Japan—where the writer describes, in his chapter "The Unknown Language," how traveling through the country provides a way "to undo our own 'reality' under the effect of other formulations, other syntaxes."[16]

The Materiality of Signs

Tawada's linguistic path marks a rediscovery of ways of reading and living, reinforced, perhaps permitted, by the contrast between different systems of writing: the alphabet for German and, for Japanese, a writing that combines *kana*— phonetic characters that serve principally for the purposes of syntax and transcribing words from foreign languages—and *kanji*—pictograms and ideograms taken from Chinese. Difficulties with German are heightened by the fact that one must relearn how to read, on one hand, but also that reading ideograms does not involve pronunciation based on an alphabet. Japanese can be read purely with the eyes, without vocalizing; sound is not even necessarily contained within the sign, nor is any sign always pronounced in one single way.[17]

Tawada describes how at times the quietly and deconstructive analytical reading of the ideogram can interfere with the reading of our alphabet: signs are deployed differently from one language to another, destabilizing certainties and meaning. The letters that make up our western words are devoid of meaning, yet all they yield, when looked at separately, with a pause taken between each one, is emptiness and an absence of meaning. As a reader, Tawada finds herself nearly brought to the brink of madness. She can speak or hear the foreign language, but as soon as it comes to reading, the activity becomes overburdening, obscured by letters that hide the forest of meaning and dam the voice's natural flow.

But Yoko Tawada makes poetic virtue out of necessity. The diffraction and slowness of reading allows her to open the text. And by stopping at each word, shattering the continuum of each sentence, Tawada is able to explore texts, as she does in her illuminating study on the poems of Celan, based on their Japanese translation.[18] The text is no longer a fully-achieved totality, closed, finalized, and it is no coincidence that these analyses resonate with the fascinating and somewhat risky speculations found in Talmudic texts. As Marc-Alain Ouaknine writes in *Lire aux éclats*, a book that brings together ancient tradition and contemporary criticism and considers how one might read in a way that deepens meaning by shattering it, or even making meaning disappear, through a dizzying distillation: "Reading letter after letter is to feel the constitution of things, to learn the spacing that exists between each letter. This stratified reading spaces the text, opens its meaningful depths, liberates it from its gravity and its typographic petrifaction."[19]

This principle of isolating each sign and of interrupting the natural flux of reading can be found in Tawada at the stage of writing because the writing of the signs that have been learned is done letter by letter, making the coherence of lexical meaning and of the sentence itself emerge only with the greatest difficulty. The dread generated by the sign that appears in all its materiality disrupts the spontaneity and natural process of reading and comprehension.

Japan, the West: Surface and Depth

From an "Asiatic" perspective, this break in the conventional relationship between signs and meaning becomes an existential component of the West:

> Europe is a champion of criticism; indeed, critique is one of her essential qualities. When she fails to criticize, she disappears, and non-existence is what she fears more than anything else. I too have tried to criticize her because that's what she demanded of me, but my attempts have proved to be fruitless. At best I could only recapitulate her own self-criticisms. I just could not come up with a better critique. Criticism has still not yet become a creative form of expression for me, whether it be about myself or someone else. For her, however, it is dishonest, deceitful or practically immoral not to criticize oneself and others. She never speaks of a person, an event or an institution without criticizing it. Not because she wants to disparage everything but rather because criticism is the basic form of her thought.[20]

This observation depends on a different conception of reading and of seeing more generally, one in which signs should make themselves understood right away: "The body that wants to be seen and must be seen is a European body. Narcissism need not play a role in this. Rather this need is based much more on the fear that something unseen can disappear at any time."[21]

The subject is caught between being and non-being, between presence and disappearance. The Japanese woman from the streets of Hamburg is a mystery, an illegible text, a sign of other signs, and she writes of an illiterate friend: "Whenever she saw me, she looked at me intensely and with interest, but she never tried to discern anything further from my expression. At the time I often found that people would get restless if they weren't able to read my expression like a text."[22] The "neutral" surface, which simultaneously avoids the gaze, is an incitement to another reading. One could say that for Tawada the sign is at once magnified and abolished in a two-fold movement.

The omnipresence of bodies and fabrics in her texts makes this clear. But in contrast to the bodies obsessively written upon in Peter Greenaway's film *The Pillow Book*, empty surfaces, dresses and skin, bodies and clothes stripped of any writing, become the final authorities, the perfect signifiers, because they *undress* themselves. Thus of one image that often recurs, a piece of material, a cloth draped across the body on which sweat imprints a map, she writes, "Upon her flat chest, the powder and sweat were drawing an atlas," or "The silk absorbed so many sweat stains that the Indian peninsula appeared on her bosom."[23] What appears on the fabric is a new pictogram to decode, a map of the world. Outside of any western religion, the clothing becomes the Holy Shroud, and bodily humors provide the ink for an individual's writing.

When one understands to what extent fabrics and texts are semantically brought together in Tawada's imagination, it becomes impossible to downplay the importance of these images. Not only isolated letters and ideograms but also objects, behaviors, and movements become new and unknown signs. Sounds, forms, colors, and rhythms open the way for apprehending the world, without needing to look for signification underneath or behind the words. Ritually enveloping oneself in fabrics calls for an unveiling. This is no metaphysical revelation however. The processes of coding and decoding are infinite, and meaning is never discovered nor interrupted since there is no stable meaning, first or last, just as there is no original text.[24]

The pieces of fabric suggest depth and secrecy yet paradoxically lead to the pure sign, the surface-level meaning above, without any need to go further "below."[25] But they also reveal a paradigmatic conflict between East and West: between the surface and interiority, banality and depth, disappointment and fulfillment. The foreign world, Europe, northern Germany, is no less an empire of signs than Japan was for Barthes. With her outsider's view, Tawada is able to catch meaning there, to foil German and the Germans and the cult of *Innerlichkeit* (inwardness).[26] It is in this sense that she is "soulless," and thus completely non-Faustian.[27]

But it is also within European languages that Tawada maintains that she was able to obtain a total meaninglessness of the subject. Our western self is filled solid, but grammatically it is empty. In "Eine leere Flasche" (An Empty Bottle), continuing her round-trip voyages back-and-forth between East and West and finding the grammatical subject in Japanese too tightly squeezed into an identity, or at the very least fixed in a social and sexual position, Tawada delivers an ode to the single-syllable subjects *Je*, *Ich*, and *I*:

> When it comes to the subject, there is a huge difference between the two languages [German and Japanese]. An interesting example is the German word *ich*, for which there is no translation in Japanese, or rather there are too many possible translations. . . . Also in Germany a teacher speaks in the classroom as a teacher. With his grandmother he would speak in a completely different way. But the word that he uses is always the same one, *ich*. In Japanese the bearing and position of the speaker are inscribed in the word that means *ich*. . . . Two years later I came to Hamburg, and the German word *ich* moved me like a miracle. Then the word seemed completely empty and light as a feather, free from any social meaning. *Ich* must always be said, regardless of the person with whom you speak, how or where you speak, how old someone is, in which dialect you speak, and whether or not you are the emperor. Women just like men, the elderly and children alike, intellectuals and criminals all use the same word, and with it they all similarly speak of themselves. Like a transparent forefinger, this word identifies the speaker. In that moment the "I" has no gender, no age, no status, no history. It exists exclusively from what he says and, before anything else, that he speaks.[28]

The motif of the disappearance of the subject is essential to the way in which the narrator introduces herself, as the (grammatical) subject of writing, the female subject of the writing or, perhaps more than anything else, subjected to the writing that crosses over her.

Foreign Language, National Identity

These Tawadian ways of life, seemingly depersonalized in the strangeness of being foreign or in the absence from herself, overturn a "German ideology" founded on the depth and nature of being. In Asian art, artifice dominates: nature is stylized or cultivated for its signs, whereas for the Germans nature is a real place and an object of infinite inspiration, the first origins that one seeks and the landmark for everything, an absolute from birth. Zafer Senocak, the Turkish-born German writer, speaks of this difficulty of locating Germany for those who are not German by birth: "The trip to Germany may not be a trip to a country . . . but rather toward a state of mind and a mental space that remain inaccessible."[29] It is worth noting that for Tawada arriving in Germany does not involve moving in or establishing oneself in a way that presupposes that you make an effort to integrate yourself at any price or hide your true self in order to diminish your differences. The very reasons for this voyage, for this change of scenery, remain mysterious: while many of Tawada's texts, especially her essays of poetry criticism, are examples of *autofiction*, recalling her Japanese roots, recounting and plowing the nature of her transition to Europe, the author never reveals any biographical information that would satisfy the reader's curiosity. One does not learn why Tawada interrupted her life and moved to Europe, why an emptiness opens after Moscow and why the other end of this emptiness—or another place in this emptiness, or no place in particular within it—is Hamburg and not some other literary, poetic port city, like Bordeaux, Lisbon, Port Bou, or Brindisi. Thus the idea of the "non-identity with itself of all language"[30] raises questions about national identity given that Tawada's choice to write in German clearly is a break with the tradition of canonical German and western literature.[31] Along with numerous foreign writers, many of whom have won the Chamisso Prize, awarded to authors who have chosen to write in German as a foreign language, Tawada's work provides fodder for the contemporary debate that has resurged recently around the notion of "*Leitkultur*" (leading culture), a verbal shock to the system that highlights a deep-seated need to suppress, because one finds within the other choice for "to lead" (*führen*) a too obvious reference to the *Führer*. For Tawada, as for Senocak, while by no means renouncing their prior identity, having a foreigner's perspective is not a vehicle for proclaiming one's own identity or difference for itself, or for putting one's roots on display in an elusive quest for identity. Far from ignoring the difficulties of an immigrant-émigré,[32] Tawada instead raises long-standing questions about the positive connotations associated with one's origins and roots. Just as the "I" is not a complete and unambiguous subject, so too are doubts cast on cultural identity itself, or at the very least its affirmation is relegated to a secondary rung.[33] Thus as Vilém Flusser puts it in *The Freedom of the Migrant*, "Posed this way, the question of freedom is no longer one of coming and going but one of remaining foreign, of remaining different from the others."[34]

The oeuvre of authors like this simply resists being pulled by either the hazy horizons of "globalization" or the siren calls of a withdrawal into identity. Their dual birth, their rebirth in a foreign land, is also a kind of simultaneous birth—the foreign land is able to transform itself with them, indeed thanks to them, though without evaporating into some illusory global village. Their journey to speaking and writing allows them to understand just how ambiguous the *Heimat* (homeland) is:

In the 1990s I increasingly heard the word *Heimat*. Migrants were often pitied for their so-called *Heimatlosigkeit* [uprootedness], even though the idea of uprootedness expresses more the yearning of the Germans for their *Heimat* than it describes the situation of people from some other background living in Germany. For foreigners the melancholy associated with the word *Heimatlosigkeit* remains difficult to comprehend. An acquaintance of mine, a writer who had to flee her country for political reasons, told me once that migration meant a cultural enrichment for her. Her uneasiness never derived from the flight from her birthplace in itself, but rather from politics, which, among other reasons, forced her to this decision. Oddly enough there are many people in Germany who draw pleasure from hearing that one loses something in the process of migration.

Notes

1. Emmanuel Levinas, "Une religion d'adultes," in *Difficile Liberté: Essais sur le judaïsme*, 3rd ed. (Paris: Le Livre de Poche, 1997), 40. Unless noted otherwise, translations from French sources are by the translator.

2. Yoko Tawada, *Opium für Ovid* (Tübingen, Germany: Konkursbuchverlag, 2000), 104-105.

3. Friedrich Hölderlin, *Mein Eigentum*, vol. 1, *Werke und Briefe*, ed. Friedrich Beißner and Jochen Schmidt (Frankfurt-am-Main, Germany: Insel, 1969), 50.

4. Peter Huchel, *Begegnung*, in *Gesammelte Werke*, Bk. 1. (Frankfurt-am-Main, Germany: Surhkamp, 1984), 235-36.

5. Hilde Domin, *Gesammelte Essays: Heimat in der Sprache* (Frankfurt-am-Main, Germany: Fischer, 1993), 14.

6. For example, Turkish-born writers such as Zafer Şenocak and Emine Sevgi Özdamar, Romanians such as Herta Müller, or Galsan Tschinag, a Tuvan tribesman who went to school in his native Mongolia before studying in Leipzig.

7. Yoko Tawada, "Nachbemerkung," in *Wo Europa anfängt* (Tübingen, Germany: Konkursbuchverlag, 1991), 88. This text, found only in the first edition, is cited by Gelzer, 73.

8. Jacques Derrida, *Monolinguisme de l'autre*, (Paris: Galilée, 1996), 69-70. This translation differs from that found in *Monolingualism of the Other or, The Prosthesis of Origin*, trans. Patrick Mensah (Stanford, Calif.: Stanford University Press, 1998): "I have but one language—yet that language is not mine."

9. The tongue as organ, *Zunge*, is a recurring theme in Tawada's writings, as a metaphor, whether explicit or not, for the language that one speaks, *Sprache*, as well as in the dream-like story *Die Zweischalige* and at the beginning of the novel *Das Bad*.

10. Yoko Tawada, "Canned Foreign," in *Where Europe Begins*, trans. Susan Bernofsky and Yumi Selden (New York: New Directions, 2002). Translation differs.

11. Yoko Tawada, *Verwandlungen* (Tübingen, Germany: Konkursbuchverlag, 1998), 8.

12. Tawada, *Verwandlungen*, 25.

13. Yoko Tawada, "Der Schriftkörper und der beschriftete Körper," in *Zuerst bin ich immer Leser: Prosa schreibe ich heute*, ed. by Ute-Christine Kruppe and Ulrike Jansen, (Frankfort on Main, Germany: Suhrkamp, 2000), 71.

14. Tawada, "Schriftkörper," 72.

15. Tawada, *Europa*, 68.

16. Roland Barthes, *Empire of Signs*, trans. by Richard Howard (New York: Hill and Wang, 1982) 6.

17. Thanks to Rose-Marie Makino-Fayolle for her useful guidance on these matters. See also on this point Yoko Tawada, "Literary Discovery through Translation," *Japanese Book News* 32 (Winter 2000), 22, where she notes that the slowness of reading and of writing has had an influence on the fragmented way in which she understands and writes German.

18. For instance, Yoko Tawada, "Das Tor des Übersetzers oder Celan liest Japanisch," in *Talisman* (Tübingen, Germany: Konkursbuchverlag Claudia Gehrke, 1996), 121-34.

19. Marc-Alain Ouaknine, *Lire aux éclats: Eloge de la caresse*, new ed. (Paris: Seuil, 1994), 150.

20. Yoko Tawada, "Eigentlich darf man es niemandem sagen, aber Europa gibt es nicht," in *Talisman* (Tübingen, Germany: Konkursbuchverlag Claudia Gehrke, 1996), 48.

21. Tawada, "Eigentlich," 48.

22. Tawada, *Das Fremde aus der Dose* (Graz, Austria: Droschl, 1992), 40.

23. Tawada, *Opium für Ovid*, 116 and 124.

24. Tawada notes that everything from the outset was a sign, that the world is a text, which, if not legible, is at least something to be deciphered: "When did everything actually begin? We cannot say when the original text was written. Each text arises as the second one, as a by-product. And so it seems as if man had never begun to write but rather had always written." "Schriftkörper," 72.

25. See also the chapter devoted to the fashion designer Semele in *Opium für Ovid*.

26. See also Louis Dumont, writing about a speech by Thomas Mann, writes, "The individual here is turned in on himself, yet at the same time he knows himself and wants himself to be German; his interiority rests upon his membership and makes of it a part of itself." (64, and on Thomas Mann 76-77.)

27. This detachment and emptiness expresses itself, for example, in a scene from *Opium für Ovid*: "I was sitting on a cloud, my Arms drawn in the form of the number eight, and I let my body hang uselessly loose. . . . 'You only talk about unimportant things; there are bigger topics out there,' Niobe told me. I shrank into myself and answered, 'The smaller a subject, the better it is.' The smallest strands of memory gather together, resist making a connection to a general subject, refuse going to a deepener level, avoid a climax. One way for unintentional concentration to persevere . . ." (Cited in Jullien, 120).

28. "Eine leere Flasche." In *Überseezungen*, 55-57, this version appeared in *NZZ Folio* of the *Neue Zürcher Zeitung* of 9 septembre 1998 under the title *Der Rest ist Reden*.

29. Zafer Senocak, "Ein Türke geht nicht in die Oper," in *Atlas des tropischen Deutschland* (Berlin: Babel Verlag, 1993), 23.

30. Derrida, *Monolingualism of the Other; or, The Prosthesis of Origin*, trans. Patrick Mensah (Stanford, Calif.: Stanford University Press, 1998), 65; org. *Le Monolinguisme de l'autre*, 123.

31. One of the figures of *Opium für Ovid*, Coronis, is a writer from Romania who is asked by the director of a cultural center to write about those writers who were influential on her. When the director mentions Nabokov, Proust and Musil, Coronis responds that she wants neither "grandfathers" nor descendants (91). In the text "Seven Stories of Seven Mothers" (in *Talisman*, 102), the work challenges literary influences and "paternities," the law or model dictated by the "paternal tower," a secular form of the "*uralter Turm*," the metaphorical "ancestral tower" that represents God in a poem by Rilke (Rainer Maria Rilke, *Die Gedichte* (Frankfurt-am-Main, Germany: Insel, 1986), 199). Against this architectural and genealogical verticality, Tawada opposes the idea of life as a "horizontal fall" (*horizontaler Absturz*) (*Opium*, 203), a reference to a phrase from Jean Cocteau's *Opium*.

32. For example, the very precarious existence of the young Vietnamese woman making her way in Germany and in Paris in one of Tawada's most recent novels, *Das nackte auge* (Tübingen, Germany: Konkursbuchverlag, 2004).

33. See also on this point, Jostes and Trabant.

34. Cited in Vilém Flusser, *Von der Freiheit des Migranten: Einsprüche gegen den Nationalismus* (Berlin: Philo, 2000), 108.

Chapter Eleven
Sign Language: Reading Culture and Identity in Tawada Yōko's "The Gotthard Railway"
Suzuko Mousel Knott

Tawada Yōko has chosen to live and work in Hamburg, Germany since 1982, publishing in both her native Japanese and in German. A well-established and lauded writer of contemporary German and Japanese literature, Tawada Yōko's works have become the subject of both German and Japanese literary scholarship over the past twenty years. Working with concepts of translation, mediation and the exploration of language barriers, Tawada's works confront the reader with an enigmatic language that mediates foreign cultures and places explored by the narrative of her texts. Situated outside Japan, Tawada Yōko's own identity as writer has been ambiguously assigned by scholars and critics. In Germany her works are often categorized as *"Migrantenliteratur."* The genre *Migranten-literatur* necessarily conflates other authors of diverse cultural and linguistic backgrounds such as Tawada Yōko (Japan), Jeanette Lander (USA), and Emine Sevgi Özdamar (Turkey), who have migrated to Germany under very different circumstances. *Migrantenliteratur* speaks to the physical location of the author and the author's linguistic and cultural negotiations as a foreigner where they live; however, the term does not fully capture Tawada's unique approach to language, the attempted writing-from-outside, that characterizes her works. As Tawada explains in an interview with Monika Totten:

> The mother tongue is a translation from non-verbal or pre-verbal thoughts, too. Language is not natural for us, but rather artificial and magical . . . Foreign languages draw our attention to the fact that language per se, even one's mother tongue, is a translation.[1]

Consciously writing from outside the L1 or L2 condition (the native or "first" and the acquired or "second" language), Tawada has established her own system of writing.[2] Echoing Lacanian notions of language, Tawada's views on primary and secondary language are brought to bear on her texts. Inverting, subverting, and exploding signs, Tawada Yōko makes apparent the artificial quality of language and the culture it mediates. Through close readings of Tawada

Yōko's short stories "Im Bauch des Gotthards" and "The Gotthard Railway," I
will demonstrate the techniques employed by the author to write from outside
the discrete linguistic systems of German and Japanese, and thereby in postmodern fashion destabilize the traditional notions of national and cultural identity.

Two very different versions of "The Gotthard Railway" were published in
1996. Both the German "Im Bauch des Gotthards" and the Japanese "Gottoharudo Tetsudo" were written by Tawada Yōko and have been termed *Partner-
texte* by Miho Matsunaga.[3] The term *Partnertext* reflects the shared thematic
structure of the stories, but clearly defines them as individual works written in
two separate languages. "Im Bauch des Gotthards" appeared in *Talisman* (1996).
The Japanese version, "Gottoharudo Tetsudo," also appeared in 1996 and is referred to here in English translation as "The Gotthard Railway." Although both
versions share the same general premise (a protagonist travels to St. Gotthard),
the two works remain independent linguistic phenomena and are two distinctly
different texts.

Published in both Japanese and German, "The Gotthard Railway" stands as
an intriguing example of the author's ability to recognize and exploit a creative
potential from within the interstices of cultural and verbal exchange. Informed
by semiotic theorists such as Roland Barthes and Jean-François Lyotard, "The
Gotthard Railway" employs complex "language games," where the boundary
between signifier and signified is collapsed and the meta-narrative of culture
undermined, in the sense that Lyotard has explored. Tawada gathers the rem-
nants and creates little narratives that rupture the "progressivist" or teleological
history attributed to the locus "Gotthard." Adroitly mirroring the linguistic negotiations experienced by a foreigner in an unfamiliar land, and often assuming the
playful persona of an ethnologist abroad, Tawada narratives mimic the dominant
European intellectual discourses that inform her writing.[4]

Japan meets Switzerland in "The Gotthard Railway:" both cultural and national identities are tested, challenged and ultimately cast from their moorings.
Notions of gender, nationality and cultural identity are inverted, turned inside
out, and ultimately reduced to meaningless, phonological units. Language has a
leveling effect in the works of Tawada Yōko. Stripping symbols of national,
cultural and gendered identity, Tawada divests the sign of its referent in the
"imagined community" in Anderson's sense. Tawada's protagonist does not
"'think' the nation," or hold a pre-determined, phantom image of the culture she
encounters. Neither does Tawada Yōko view herself as a member of an imaginary, homologous community called "nation." Instead, Tawada envisions herself
existing in what is referred to as a "net" of language. Tawada relates:

> I imagine the author to become, by means of the language, a knot in a big net.
> This net consists of sentences and paragraphs which already have been uttered
> or could be uttered by other people. When I write, I am not a fisher fishing with
> a net but rather a knot in this net.[5]

Language is privileged over the construction of a national identity. Tawada does not view herself a member of an imagined "German" community, but rather envisions herself in the nexus of language.

Written from the linguistic net, "The Gotthard Railway" demonstrates the author's ceaseless, creative exploration of language. The German text "Im Bauch des Gotthards" falls in the category of *Reisebericht*, or travel essay.[6] The Japanese text "Gottoharudo Tetsudo" bears novella-like qualities, where the narrative gives greater access to the protagonist, providing more of the abstracted ideas and observations made by the traveler. Commenting on Tawada's approach to text translation, Miho Matsunaga comments:

> Tawada currently translates her own texts almost exclusively from German into Japanese. In another interview she said, that yet another translation would be possible, that she could translate a German to Japanese translation into German again, and that thereby an endless chain of translations would be possible.[7]

Matsunaga establishes the creative potential Tawada finds both between and outside the L1 and L2 condition: "Not only does translation occur in Tawada's bilingual writing, but also poetic reformulation and transformation."[8] Closer readings of "The Gotthard Railway" in both languages substantiates Matsunaga's claim and reveals not merely a Japanese language version of an original German text, but rather a richer, extrapolated Japanese continuation of the original themes established in the German text.

What follows is a thematic analysis of "The Gotthard Railway" and an analysis of the deconstructed linguistic signs in both.

Gotthard

The first-person narrator of "The Gotthard Railway" relates, "When I was asked if I'd like to ride through the Gotthard, I didn't yet know a single man who was called Gotthard."[9] Mistaking the mountain for a man, the narrative at once assumes a naïveté that disarms the reader with subtle humor. At the same time, it serves to dislodge the reader's notion of what or who Gotthard might be. Tawada's Swiss mountain is animated and given facial features in both versions:

> The hairs in his beard are hard like steel wire, his lips are the color of blood and shiver incessantly. He doesn't speak. His eyes are full of fear and anger, they are like glass beads, that will soon be shattered.[10]

A severe, imposing man, Gotthard implies the Christian iconography of a "hard god" (echoing the literal meaning of his name). The image Tawada creates is vulnerable, hard like glass but breakable. This imagined man stands in place of the mountain in the narrator's mind; however, the mountain itself is imagined.

According to contemporary atlases, there is no Gotthard mountain.[11] There is, however, the Gotthardmassiv, which is a mountain formation spanning the borders of the Graubünden, Tessin, Wallis and Uri cantons of Switzerland. Historically traversed by the Sankt Gotthard-Pass and later by the Gotthard Railway, the Gotthardmassiv is named for the Milanese archbishop St. Galdinus. A vital early trade route, the establishment of the Sankt Gotthard-Pass is attributed to the Langobards ca. 569 AD and served as one of the most important connections between northern and southern Europe. The founding of the Swiss Confederacy in 1291 is attributed to the success of the Sankt Gotthard-Pass and increased trade and traffic brought to the region that is now Switzerland. The Gotthardstraße was built through the pass from 1819-1830, and in 1872 work on the Gotthard rail tunnel began. The tunnel was completed in 1882 at the cost of 177 lives. The Gotthardmassiv serves as the European watershed to the Mediterranean and North Seas and it is also the point from which the source rivers of the Rhine and Rhone flow.

The significance of the Gotthardmassiv to the region is clear: the geological formation is historically linked to the founding of the Swiss nation, physically linked to both the river and ninetheenth-century German national symbol the Rhine,[12] and serves as the geographical divide for the largest bodies of water north and south of the continent. Situating her short stories at the Gotthardmassiv, Tawada appropriates the sign Gotthard into her own system of representation. In "Im Bauch des Gotthards" and "The Gotthard Railway," Gotthard stands as a concretized symbol of Swiss, German and European identity, which when explored by a foreign woman represents the threatening gaze of the subaltern on the dominant culture.[13]

Considering the many significant valences Gotthard fills in the history and geography of Switzerland, it is not surprising that the mountain is given a privileged seat in the consciousness of Swiss nationalists. Looking at a map of Europe, the narrator comments upon the central geographical location of Gotthard:

> I bought a map of Europe. When I opened it up I saw Gotthard in all his majesty lying right across the center. I didn't know he was right in the middle of Europe. But you can never rely on maps for that sort of information. Japanese maps all put Japan in the center, as any other country seems entitled to do for itself if it feels like it.[14]

The passage reveals the ethnocentric impulse to privilege one's own cultural and national identity over others. Conflating the central position of Gotthard with Japan, both of which cannot be the center, the narrator calls into question this concept of ethnocentrism and thereby destabilizes both Swiss and Japanese centrality. Questioning the centrist meta-narrative mapped by both cultures, Tawada engages in the ethnocriticism of both.[15] According to Thomas Wägenbaur, "In the practice of ethnocriticism cultural values and metaphors lose their structural coherence and enter the constructive process of intercultural translation."[16] He applies the concept of ethnocriticism to Tawada's *Der Fremde aus der Dose*, however the process is also applicable to both "Im Bauch des Gotthards" and "The Gotthard Railway." As Tawada's protagonist examines the central privileged position of Gotthard from a perspective outside the Swiss culture, the "structural coherence" of associations (Gotthard=Switzerland=center of Europe) is broken apart and translated through the protagonist's intercultural filter to create a new de-centralized image of Gotthard.

The narrative draws a concrete relationship between the most overt symbols of Japanese and Swiss nationality. In "Im Bauch des Gotthards," the narrative describes the Swiss coat of arms:

> The national seal showed an intersection, which helped me orient myself: the right street led to Austria, the left to France, above sits Germany and underneath lies Italy. The picture of Europe, that always threatened to dissolve in my head, quickly solidified itself again whenever I saw this flag.[17]

The image of Europe the narrator holds in her mind is solidified and retained only after seeing the national symbol. The protagonist continues to look at the symbol, and the borders of the Swiss cross dissolve. Likewise in the "The Gotthard Railway," upon seeing the Swiss flag on the engine of a train, the Swiss and the Japanese flags merge into one:

> As I stared at the Swiss flag, my vision gradually blurred, and the design began to change. The blood that was supposed to stay frozen outside the cross started to run, seeping slowly into the center. The cross drank it in, and turned into a fat red ball. As it lost its blood, the background grew pale, then finally pure white. Before I knew it, I was looking at the Japanese flag. Until that moment, I'd never noticed how closely the two flags resembled each other: the cross of Christ and the sun of Amaterasu; different shapes, but both islands of a sort, surrounded by the surfaces they lie upon.[18]

The "surfaces they lie upon," the fields of red and white which frame the symbols in the Japanese text, are the traditions that support and legitimate national identity: the red blood of the Judeo-Christian Messiah, and the dawning sun goddess Amaterasu. The coupling of male and female imagery in the flags, Christ and Amaterasu, speak to the literal creation of nations and national identity. Although the Swiss and Japanese flags also collapse into one sign in "Im Bauch des Gotthards," Christ and Amaterasu do not appear in the German text.[19]

Having bought a book about Gotthard in the beginning of her travels, the narrator refers to a text by Felix Moeschlin to better understand the mountain and its significance.[20] The book, a history of the Gotthard tunnel, is saturated with Swiss nationalism and isolationism, at times calling for the total rejection of outside national influences. Both "Im Bauch des Gotthards" and "The Gotthard Railway" include the following:

> Switzerland is a free nation. We do not need the Railroad King. And this one is more unsavory even than the bureaucrats, or the knights of Austria, or the army from Burgundy, and more of a menace than any high-toned aristocrats, or Napoleon's marauders, or a band of old warlords clashing their Prussian swords together. We must drive them back, these serpents that slither their way into the bosom of Helvetia![21]

Naming all of its neighbors and the historical threats they have posed to the sovereignty of Switzerland, this passage reveals an ongoing attempt to locate and hold fast to a uniquely Swiss identity, separate and isolated from the influence of other nations.

Both the German and the Japanese texts continue with another passage from Moeschlin's text, in which he describes an on-going struggle of man against nature:

> Silence may be beautiful, tranquility may be holy for gentle, calm people. We, however, love the noise and the bursting of explosions, for we are wild, restless people. Others may enjoy planting corn and cutting grape vines, but we must work with stone. And when it is the hardest and most difficult, then we love it the most, for then we can prove that we are even harder than stone![22]

Moeschlin describes the Swiss as a people who love to prove their power over nature, by demonstrating that they are harder than the rock they fight. The people of Switzerland, according to the narrator's vision of the blood and cross of Christ as national symbol, practice dominion over the earth in the Judeo-Christian tradition.

Rather than reading the novel from start to finish, the narrator engages in a post-modern reading of the text: "Opening Moeschlin's novel at random, I scanned the pages."[23] The act of reading a history of the Gotthard tunnel in post-modern fashion challenges the nationalist content of the novel. Moeschlin's text assumes a progressive reading from start to finish in order to impart meaning. By blatantly ignoring the progressive structure of the text, the narrator is free to misread or even re-read Moeschlin, resulting in the dissolution of its intended meaning. Re-reading or mis-reading the history of the Gotthard Railway could be linked to a misreading or re-reading of Switzerland, insofar as Gotthard stands at the center of and stands in for the country.

As Benedict Anderson has posited in *Imagined Communities*, the historical conception of a nation or community hinged upon the subscription to three central ideas: a written language that provides "privileged access to ontological truth," monarch rule by some "cosmological (divine) dispensation," and a conflated belief in the "origins of the world and of men."[24] In both "Im Bauch des Gotthards" and "The Gotthard Railway," Tawada deconstructs national symbols which reflect Anderson's pre-conditions to "thinking the nation." As a foreigner reading the history of Gotthard, the birth-place of European and Swiss identity, the protagonist undermines the idea of privileged access. Furthermore, the narrative calls into question the very nature of Gotthard (man or mountain). In the Japanese text, Anderson's theory is tested further, where the Swiss and Japanese flags, the visual representations of the state, are immediately linked to the dominant cosmologies of their respective cultures. Lastly, Moeschlin's assertion of man's dominion over nature speaks to the common origin of man and the world in the Judeo-Christian tradition.

Traveling to Gotthard

Passing through the Gotthardmassiv, a traveler would begin at Andermatt and emerge in the Italian city Airolo. Historically, to reach Italy from Switzerland, one had to traverse either the Sankt Gotthard or Brenner Pass. The protagonist in both "Im Bauch des Gotthards" and "The Gotthard Railway" follows a path traveled by many. The narrative of both stories states, "To be considered an intellectual in northern Germany, you must yearn for the Italian sunshine."[25] This comment alludes to the tradition of *Dichter und Denker* traveling to and writing about Italy. Two competing writers of the *Dichter und Denker* tradition are specifically mentioned in Tawada's texts: Johann Wolfgang von Goethe and Friedrich Schiller. The protagonist of both "Im Bauch des Gotthards" and "The Gotthard Railway" positions herself in the place of Goethe and Schiller, mimicking the *Reisebericht* and re-interpreting the meaning of Schiller's *Wilhelm Tell*. Like her first trip into Europe on the Trans-Siberian Railroad, Tawada's Gotthard narratives deconstruct Germanic models of travel and reconstruct a foreign "other" version.[26]

Goethe traveled to Italy in 1786-1788. The Gotthardmassiv is mentioned obliquely in Goethe's *Italiensche Reise* in an entry dated Sept. 7, 1786. Goethe writes:

> The cliffs, which surround me, are all of limestone, of the oldest sort, which does not contain any fossils. These limestone mountains stand in immense, uninterrupted chains from Dalmatia to the St. Gotthard and beyond.[27]

A letter from Switzerland, dated Nov. 13th, 1779 reveals, however, that Goethe was a guest of the hospice at the summit of the Sankt Gotthard-Pass. The hospice was built in 1629 and was run by Capuchins. Describing his ascent to St. Gotthard, Goethe writes:

> We at last reached the summit of the mountain, of which you can form some idea by fancying a bald skull surrounded with a crown. Here one finds himself on a perfect flat surrounded with peaks. Far and near the eye meets with nothing but bare and mostly snow-covered peaks and ranges.[28]

Goethe's description of the summit evokes a regal, masculine image. Like Tawada Yōko's image of the "hard god," Goethe's description animates and personifies the mountain.

Friedrich Schiller also refers to the Gotthardmassiv in his drama *Wilhelm Tell*, adapted from the Swiss legend of Wilhem Tell. The oldest form of the saga (Tellenlied) dates back to the fourteenth Century. Elsbeth Merz writes:

> The oldest version of the saga is the Tellenlied, a historical song from the 14th Century that tells the story of the apple shooting. It is comprised of nine verses, which were later added to the beginning of the song "On the Origin of the Confederation." Melchior Ruß's chronicle, begun in 1482, also refers to the Tellenlied. The chronicle adds the feudal lords' violent acts to the story's conclusion. Tell is supposed to be bound and taken to Switzerland because of this. He escapes by means of a daring jump, which allows him to shoot the lord.[29]

As Merz reveals, the Tellenlied becomes bound to the history of the Swiss Confederacy, and the figure of Wilhelm Tell becomes a touchstone to Swiss independence and nationhood. The protagonist of "Im Bauch des Gotthard" passes the Schiller-Stein at Lake Urner, commenting that she had heard of the story with the apple. The narrative summarizes:

> He has something to do with a story with an apple, but not with the famous story, in which a woman eats an apple with her husband, which caused human sexual desire. In this story the apple isn't eaten, but destroyed: a hunter was forced to shoot it off his son's head. Either the apple, sexual desire, or a life had to be sacrificed.[30]

The protagonist in the German text does not develop the idea of the apple beyond the biblical and Schiller references. In the Japanese text, however, the narrative further examines the apple, relating differences in idiomatic forms and a more developed discussion of lost sexual pleasure. As the narrator penetrates deep into the Gotthardmassiv, the Japanese text shifts to a discussion of penetration and the corporeal. The shift from the exterior to the interior is indicative of the two genres "The Gotthard Railway" represents. The German *Reisebericht*, or travel essay, remains trained on the exterior experiences and more superficial impressions of the landscape on the traveler, while the Japanese version develops the interior thoughts and feelings of the protagonist. Furthermore, this shift is also indicative of the author's more intense investigation of words and their meaning, as she translates those elements from one language to another. In the German text, the protagonist simply passes through the Gotthard tunnel, thinking about the apple. In the Japanese text, the apple discussed in three German sentences becomes the touchstone to a more developed discussion (four pages) of the protagonist's sexual desire. Gotthard becomes a point of penetration: a liminal space for the exploration of female desire.

Traveling Through Gotthard

As evidenced by the title of the short story "Im Bauch des Gotthards," the reader is immediately confronted with a play on words. A literal English translation of the title would read: "In the Stomach of Gotthard." Gotthard is grammatically marked masculine in German, and the idea of penetrating a male body is mapped out in the title. This story takes place in the stomach of something male and linguistically Germanic. In the Japanese version, Tawada parses the German name "Gotthard" for the Japanese reader. Tawada's narrator explains "'Gott' means 'god' and 'hard' is, well, hard." The mountain is a solid mass, and yet at the same time the narrator adds: "The Swiss talk of the railway 'passing through Gotthard.' Through a man's body, in other words. The mountain penetrated by this long tunnel."[31] The mountain possesses qualities that should exclude one another: it is hard, but somehow still penetrable. Tawada then likens Gotthard to a womb in both versions, as the narrator comments: "Everyone was once trapped in the belly of a woman we call Mother, and yet we go to our graves without knowing what a father's body is like inside."[32] Penetrating into the womb of Gotthard symbolizes the exploration of as yet uncharted, impossible territory, the inside of the "father."

It is in the interior of Gotthard that the German and Japanese texts diverge sharply. In "The Gotthard Railway" the narrative expands, delving deeper into the physical interior of the mountain. Here there is a detailed account of the train ride into the mountain, attended by a train engineer and pseudo-tour guide named "Mr. Berg."[33] The protagonist extrapolates from Mr. Berg to memories of a German boyfriend named Reiner and Dr. Faust. The narrative then shifts to memories of verbal exchanges with Reiner in a German northern coastal town, where she fantasizes about penetrating Reiner.[34]

Gotthard's stomach is not the only male stomach the narrator wishes to enter. In "The Gotthard Railway," the narrator dreams of entering Reiner's belly:

> The night before Reiner's liver operation, I had a dream. His moist, red-black belly, exposed to view, was filled with penises—like a selection of neatly packaged salamis. "With this many stored away, you've nothing to worry about," a nurse said reassuringly. The surgeon grimly stuck a Japanese doll in among those serried penises, which were all about the same size as it. Jet-black hair. Glazed-looking eyes. I was worried he might leave it there when he sewed Reiner up. But, not knowing the medical term for "a Japanese doll," I couldn't protest.[35]

In this passage, the narrator reveals anxiety related to her own representation: as "a Japanese doll." An outsider to German culture, the protagonist is aware of a stereotyped image of the Japanese woman: "Jet-black hair. Glazed-looking eyes." As Sabine Fischer writes, the substitution of a doll for the foreign "other" speaks to the power of the dominant culture to render the "other" harmless.[36] That a female doll, representing the "other," is tucked into a masculine environment (serried penises) is also significant. As Edward Said has demonstrated, the Occidental mind imagines an emasculated or feminized Orient. It is therefore not surprising that Tawada translates a discussion of the "other" and a dominant culture into gendered terms, locating her discussion on the physical male and female bodies.

Penetrating and entering the male belly serves as a form of "knowing" the other. The protagonist fantasizes about being eaten: "I'd sometimes wonder what it would be like to slide down an animal's gullet."[37] Eating is as an act of integration, a mingling of cannibalism and communion. Wanting to be eaten, the narrator seeks to be integrated into Reiner and simultaneously gain access again to the "father's body." Placed into the belly by a surgeon, however, the subject who enters is divested of its agency. The protagonist's desire to enter Reiner is explicit: "I want to get inside your belly;"[38] however, not as a misrepresentation of herself. The narrator's vision of herself as "a Japanese doll" is motivated by a cultural gap of understanding, for she is told: "Japanese faces look alike to them."[39]

As a demonstration of her desire, the protagonist attempts to penetrate Reiner. He reflexively rejects her:

I stuck a finger into Reiner's ear. And then his mouth. The joints on my finger got sticky, covered with lukewarm saliva. "If I push it all the way down to your esophagus, I bet that'd hurt." My finger slipped in deeper. Reiner coughed violently. Our "Buddha in the throat" is what they call an "Adam's apple."[40]

The narrator underscores the failed attempt to communicate and penetrate, by directly linking this image with the linguistic idioms "Buddha in the throat" and "Adam's apple." Idiomatic expressions prove difficult to translate, for a literal translation often renders the phrase ridiculous. Like idioms that do not translate a one to one semantic meaning, neither the narrator nor Reiner achieves a mutual understanding of her desire.

In a further attempt to communicate this desire for integration to Mr. Berg, the protagonist is again confronted with misunderstanding. While in the Gotthard tunnel, the protagonist experiences intense pleasure, which she seeks to share with her guide: "When we entered the single-track tunnel, I itched with pleasure from my shoulder to my elbows, inside and out. The tunnel was a gullet, and I was its food. The thrill of sliding down a throat. Do the things we eat feel it, too?"[41] The narrator realizes Berg may not share the same appreciation for the sensation of being eaten, however she chooses to communicate these feelings to him anyway. The failure to understand is two-sided: "I knew Berg trusted me, because he told me so many things that didn't make sense to me."[42] Reacting to his initiative, the narrator tells Mr. Berg: "This feels like going down someone's throat. It's terrific."[43] The narrator fails to make her point, and Mr. Berg fails to understand: "He obviously didn't understand, just as I'd expected. I was only trying to tell him how pleased I was."[44] The failure to communicate pleasure at the point of penetration demonstrates more than a cultural misunderstanding. As Mr. Berg is male and the narrator female, this constitutes a form of sexualized misunderstanding.

Reading the Signs

As the protagonist encounters the Gotthardmassiv, inside and out, Italian and German signs are read and deconstructed. The narrative of "Im Bauch des Gotthards" and "The Gotthard Railway" reflects the linguistic reduction of Italian and German words to their phonological parts:

> Göschenen—a name that itself was made of stone. A name harsh on the ear. One that no human sensibility had shaped according to its taste, whether good or bad. Just stone become a word. GÖ: hard rocks grinding together. SCHE: gravel sliding down the slope to become NEN: the moist clay at the bottom of the valley.[45]

Reading the German sign Göschenen, the narrator assigns semantic meaning to a word which has no semantic meaning in German apart from the referent town of Göschenen. The signs are literally linguistically reduced to their meaningless phonetic components, reinterpreted as fragmented phones, and assigned new semantic meaning to replace the lexeme *Göschenen*. In similar fashion, the narrator deconstructs the Italian sign "Airolo" in the Japanese text and assigns new meaning to it: "Airolo, designed to open a bright, cheery hole in you every time you said the word. All together now, 'Airolo!'"[46] The narrator detaches the referent, the town of Airolo, and assigns a performative linguistic function to the lexeme: to open holes. The referents Göschenen and Airolo remain physically located at the Sankt Gotthard-Pass, however Tawada has dislodged the signs from their moorings and created signs with new referents: rocks, gravel, clay, and in the Japanese text, hole making.

Not only are the cities and their names dislocated, but the location of self and the identity are confused as well. The German text does not specifically indicate the nationality of the protagonist, although it becomes evident that the protagonist is a foreigner. The Japanese text specifically problematizes the identity of the narrator. The protagonist is invited to tour Gotthard, but reveals: "The only trouble is that I am not the Japanese writer he'd been planning to ask for an article about the tunnel. Nor was it a case of mistaken identity. It was more like deliberate fraud, actually."[47] The narrator willfully refuses to assign or reveal her own identity. The narrator carries no traditional markers of identity: she has no name, no physical characteristics and reveals "I don't have a profession."[48] In contrast, other characters and places are named. This affords the narrator anonymity, to pass through Gotthard and Switzerland unnoticed: "I was alone there. No one else knew where I was."[49] Although the ability to slip behind identities grants the narrator access to Gotthard and allows her to re-interpret its cultural meaning; if she cannot communicate her experiences meaningfully with anyone, they and the narrator exist in a void. The narrator, in fact, exists outside of community. Re-interpreting the signs which confront her in the Sankt Gotthard-Pass, the narrator not only re-assigns their meaning, but in doing so "re-thinks" the foreign community she meets.

Choosing Andermatt

The narrator of "The Gotthard Railway" remains unnamed and un-fixed. By committing identity fraud, the narrator offers no truths of herself, nor for that matter of the world around her. The signs Tawada offers in her system of language can neither be read as truth nor as representing any normalized referent, but rather bespeak the attempt to create new forms of representation. As Thomas Wägenbaur notes: "Tawada de- and reconstructs the metaphors of the given German culture and thus subverts the stable *Metaphors We Live By*."[50] Beyond metaphor to the very building blocks of language, phonemes, Tawada deconstructs European, Swiss, and Italian in "Im Bauch des Gotthards" and "The Gotthard Railway."

Tawada's partner texts represent an almost literal reading of Jameson's writings on postmodernism.[51] The beginning of the short story marks the liberation of the sign Gotthard from its referent. No longer merely a mountain, Gotthard is termed god, saint, man, Switzerland. The narrator then penetrates "the interior of the sign itself," penetrating Gotthard as she enters the tunnel. This

play, and in the Japanese text sexualized play, represents a new form of communication: "pure or literal signifiers freed from the ballast . . . [that] generates a
new kind of textuality." Where literal communication breaks down, the narrator's nonsensical exchanges actually represent "the mirage of some ultimate
language."[52] This becomes evident at the end of both "Im Bauch des Gotthards"
and "The Gotthard Railway," where the narrator refuses to pass completely
through the Sankt Gotthard-Pass. Turning her back on southern Airolo, the narrator chooses the Andermatt.

In "Im Bauch des Gotthards," and "The Gotthard Railway," the narrator
enters a removed space. Traveling through the Sankt Gotthard-Pass into the Gotthard tunnel in the Gotthardmassiv, the protagonist travels in the liminal space
of borders.[53] Forming the geographical borders of the Graubünden, Tessin,
Wallis, and Uri cantons, the linguistic borders of German and Italian and the
division between north and south Europe, the Gotthardmassiv is borderland par
excellence. Abandoning Gotthard as a point where difference collides, Andermatt represents an alternative to the confrontation of different languages and
culture. The new mountain, the new sign, is covered in fresh snowfall, which
"gave the mountain an air of wisdom." The narrator views the mountain in isolation: "A huge, empty plain lay surrounded on all four sides by sheer slopes. The
shower of light continued to fall on its pristine surface. I was alone there. No
one else knew where I was."[54] This new space, Andermatt, is clean, but only a
mirage. The narrator finds there is no "pristine surface," for even in isolation,
the language exists:

> But then the snowfall stopped, and with it my daydream vanished. For right in
> the middle of this expanse of white, I saw a sign that stopped me dead in my
> tracks. NO WALKING HERE. It was incredible! . . . I was sure to find other
> signs as I went along. Like, NO USING TYPEWRITERS HERE. Or, SEN-
> TENCES WITHOUT SUBJECTS ARE FORBIDDEN. It was just officialdom
> making sure people didn't think they could do as they liked out here in the
> snow.[55]

Without freedom from the sign, there is no freedom for the narrator. Although she plays with signs of national, cultural and gender identity, though she
penetrates and subverts the signs of the meta-narratives, the protagonist cannot
escape the sign. To do so would mean to exit language and enter a void: "The
snow sucked everything into it, even light. There was nothing above it, nothing
below. And confronting it, I too went blank."[56] Only by re-affirming the concrete sign does the narrator return from the brink of self-extinction: "I disappeared completely, like a picture on a screen, leaving nothing behind. It was
only by chanting that stone word—Göschenen—that I could hope to find some
trace of my lost self, and find my way home."[57]

The narrator retains the ability to play with signs, to re-interpret and rewrite the sign, and this affords her a limited freedom from the meta-narratives
the signs create. She comments: "Reiner doesn't like it when I say things his
friends can't understand. Because if they find me incomprehensible, it means
I'm out of reach for him as well."[58] Likewise, by playing upon the stereotyped

representation of Japanese women as dolls who all look alike, the narrator is able to pass into an assumed identity which affords her the freedom to pass through Gotthard. Therefore although the narrator (and in this same light Tawada) can achieve no ultimate liberation from the sign and its meta-narratives, through the creation of her "little narratives" and "language play," she achieves a measure of free space in her own sign language.

Notes

1. Monika Totten, "Writing in Two Languages: A Conversation with Yoko Tawada." *Harvard Review* 17 (1999), 95-96.

2. Karin Schestokat suggests that "Tawada attempts . . . among other things, to explore her own language and the meaning of individual Japanese and German words through the linguistic investigation of objects, as well as through interpretations of German literature."

3. Miho Matsunaga, "'Schreiben als Übersetzung.' Die Dimension der Übersetzung in den Werken von Yoko Tawada," *Zeitschrift für Germanistik* 12, no. 3 (2002), 540.

4. Claudia Breger reads Tawada Yōko's texts as mimicry (Homi Bhabha) of works by such theorists as Walter Benjamin and Roland Barthes.

5. Totten, "Writing," 95.

6. See the discussion by Miho Matsunaga, 532-546. She terms the *Gottohardo Tetsudo* a *japanische Erzählung* (Matsunaga, "Schreiben, " 540).

7. Matsunaga, "Schreiben," 541.

8. Matsunaga, "Schreiben," 541. This conclusion is based on Tawada's comments and read in conjunction with Derrida's *Babylonische Türme.*

9 Yoko Tawada, "Im Bauch des Gotthards," in *Talisman.* (Tübingen, Germany: Konkursbuch, 1996), 93.

10. Tawada, "Bauch," 9.

11. The current ADAC Atlas 2005/2006 lists no Gotthard mountain or summit, only the pass (ADAC, 2004: 245). Other mountains in the area are indicated, including the Muttenhörner, Punto Lucendro, and the Andermatt.

12. The subject of many a *Volkslied* and the setting of Heinrich Heine's famous poem "Die Lorelei," the Rhine is widely viewed as a symbol of German nationalism.

13. As put forth in Homi Bhabha's *The Location of Culture* (1994). Claudia Breger also follows this theoretical line when discussing Tawada's *Wo Europa anfängt* in her article "Mimikry als Grenzverwirrung" (1999).

14. Yoko Tawada, "The Gotthard Railway," in *The Bridegroom Was a Dog*, trans. Margaret Mitsutani (New York: Kodansha International, 1998), 135.

15. Ethnocriticism here is to be understood as critiquing from the outside.

16. Thomas Wägenbaur, "Semiotic Ethnocriticism: Tawada's *Das Fremde aus der Dose,*" in *Semiotics Around the World: Synthesis and Diversity*, ed. Irmengard Rauch and Gerald Carr (Berlin: Mouton de Gruyter, 1997), 344.

17. Tawada, "Bauch," 95.

18. Tawada, "Railway," 139.

19. "Until then I hadn't noticed that both flags shared a common feature: they both made an island (either a round island or an island in a cross shape), that isolated them from their surroundings and secretly placed themselves in the middle" (Tawada, Railway, 96).

20. Felix Moeschlin (1882-1969) published *Wir durchbohren den Gotthard* in two volumes in 1947 and 1949, respectively. His works are associated with the "geistigen

Landesverteidigung" (spiritual/philosophical defense), which describes a large number of movements asserting Swiss national pride and raison d'être directed against both German and Italian fascism before and during WWII.

21. Tawada, "Railway," 156.

22. Tawada, "Bauch," 97.

23. Tawada, "Railway," 156.

24. Benedict Anderson, *Imagined Communities: Reflections on the Origin and Spread of Nationalism* (New York: Verso, 1993), 36.

25. Tawada, "Railway," 133.

26. Claudia Breger posits that Tawada incorporates elements of Walter Benjamin's "Moskau" in *Wo Europa anfängt*.

27. Johann Wolfgang von Goethe, *Letters from Switzerland, Letters from Italy*. Translated by A.J.W. Morrison, et al. Edited by Nathan Haskell Dole. (Boston: Wyman-Fogg, 1902), 14.

28. Goethe, 1902: 79.

29. Elsbeth Merz, *Tell im Drama vor und nach Schiller* (Liechtenstein: Kraus Reprint, 1970), 14.

30. Tawada, "Bauch," 96.

31. Tawada, "Railway," 131.

32. Tawada, "Railway," 131.

33. Mr. Berg is a pun, "Berg" meaning mountain in German.

34. Likely Hamburg, the capital of Schleswig-Holstein, located on the Baltic Sea.

35. Tawada, "Railway," 163.

36. Sabine Fischer, referring to the shaman in the museum in "Rothenburg ob der Tauber: ein deutsches Rätsel." "Durch die japanische Brille gesehen: die fiktive Ethnologie der Yoko Tawada." In *Gegenwartsliteratur: Ein Germanistisches Jahrbuch*, vol. 2., edited by Paul Michael Lützeler and Stefan Schindler. Tübingen, Germany: Stauffenberg, 2003, 60.

37. Tawada, "Railway," 143.

38. Tawada, "Railway," 158.

39. Tawada, "Railway," 146.

40. Tawada, "Railway," 143.

41. Tawada, "Railway," 141.

42. Tawada, "Railway," 141.

43. Tawada, "Railway," 142.

44. Tawada, "Railway," 142.

45. Tawada, "Railway," 163.

46. Tawada, "Railway," 154.

47. Tawada, "Railway," 132.

48. Tawada, "Railway," 133.

49. Tawada, "Railway," 160.

50. Wägenbaur, "Ethnocriticism," 344.

51. As defined by Frederic Jameson in "Periodizing the 60s," in *Modern Literary Theory: A Reader*, edited by Philip Rice and Patricia Waugh (New York: Arnold, 1998), 292-322.

52. Jameson, "Periodizing," 313.

53. Claudia Breger also analyzes the liminal space embodied by the border and traveled by Tawada's protagonist in *Wo Europa anfängt* in "Mimikry als Grenzverwirrung."

54. Tawada, "Railway," 160.

55. Tawada, "Railway," 161.

56. Tawada, "Railway," 163.

57. Tawada, "Railway," 164.
58. Tawada, "Railway," 133.

Bibliography

ADAC *Straßen und Städte Atlas 2005/2006*. Bad Soden/Taunus: CartoTravel Verlag, 2004.

Anderson, Benedict. *Imagined Communities: Reflections on the Origin and Spread of Nationalism*. New York: Verso, 1993.

Bhabha, Homi. *The Location of Culture*. New York: Routledge, 1994.

Breger, Claudia. "Mimikry als Grenzverwirrung. Parodistische Posen bei Yoko Tawada." In *Über Grenzen: Limitation und Transgression in Literatur und Ästhetik*, edited by Claudia Benthien and Irmela Marei Krüger-Fürhoff. Stuttgart, Germany: Metzler, 1999, 176-206.

Fischer, Sabine. "Durch die japanische Brille gesehen: die fiktive Ethnologie der Yoko Tawada." In *Gegenwartsliteratur: Ein Germanistisches Jahrbuch*, vol. 2., edited by Paul Michael Lützeler and Stefan Schindler. Tübingen: Stauffenberg, 2003, 59-80.

———. "'Verschwinden ist schön': Zu Yoko Tawadas Kurzroman *Das Bad*." In *Denn du tanzt auf einem Seil: Positionen deutschsprachiger MigrantInnenliteratur*, edited by Moray McGowan, Tübingen, Germany: Stauffenberg, 1997, 101-111.

Goethe, Johann Wolfgang von. *Italienische Reise*. 4th ed. Edited by Erich Trunz. Hamburg, Germany: Christian Wegner, 1959.

———. *Letters from Switzerland, Letters from Italy*. Translated by A.J.W. Morrison, et al. Edited by Nathan Haskell Dole. Boston: Wyman-Fogg, 1902.

Jameson, Frederic. "Periodizing the 60s." In *Modern Literary Theory: A Reader*, edited by Philip Rice and Patricia Waugh. New York: Arnold, 1998, 292-322.

Kilgour, Maggie. *From Communion to Cannibalism: An Anatomy of Metaphors of Incorporation*. Princeton, N.J.: Princeton University Press, 1990.

———. "The Function of Cannibalism at the Present Time." In *Cannibalism and the Colonial World*, edited by Francis Barker, Peter Hulme, and Margaret Iversen. Cambridge: Cambridge University Press, 1998, 238-259.

Laudenberg, Beate. "Aspekte der deutschsprachigen Migrantenliteratur, dargestellt an Yoko Tawadas Roman *Ein Gast*." In *Literatur im interkulturellen Dialog*, edited by Hans-Cristoph Nayhauss, Manfred Durzak, and Beate Laudenberg. Bern, Switzerland: Peter Lang, 2000, 130-143.

Lyotard, Jean-François. *The Postmodern Condition: A Report on Knowledge*. Minneapolis: University of Minnesota Press, 1999.

Matsunaga, Miho. "'Schreiben als Übersetzung.' Die Dimension der Übersetzung in den Werken von Yoko Tawada." *Zeitschrift für Germanistik* 12, no. 3 (2002): 532-546.

Merz, Elsbeth. *Tell im Drama vor und nach Schiller*. Liechtenstein: Kraus Reprint, 1970.

Said, Edward. *Orientalism*. New York: Random House, 1994.

Schestokat, Karin. "Bemerkungen zur Hybridität und zum Sprachgebrauch in Ausgewählten Texten von May Ayim und Yoko Tawadas." *Glossen: Eine Internationale Zweisprachige Publikation zu Literatur, Film, und Kunst in den Deutschsprachgen Ländern nach 1945*, no. 8 (1999).
http://www.dickinson.edu/glossen/heft8/schestokat.html.

Schiller, Friedrich. *Wilhelm Tell*. Stuttgart: Reklam, 1999.

Tawada, Yōko. "Im Bauch des Gotthards." In *Talisman*. Tübingen, Germany: Konkursbuch, 1996, 93-99.

Chapter Twelve
Tawada Yōko's Quest for Exophony: Japan and Germany

Reiko Tachibana

Transnational writers have rapidly increased in number in the Japanese literary world, since the early 1990s. Among those who have gained prominence are Mizumura Minae (b. ca 1952), who returned from the United States after a twenty-year absence and writes in Japanese; Tawada Yōko (b. 1960), who has lived in Germany since 1982 and writes in both Japanese and German; and Hideo Levy (b. 1950), a Polish-Jewish American who has lived in Japan since the 1980s and writes in Japanese. They can be called writers of "exophony" (those who step out of their mother tongue), to borrow Tawada's neologism and the title of her 2003 book, *Exophony: Journey to Stepping Out of the Mother Tongue (Bogo no soto e deru tabi).*[1]

For Tawada, "exophony" refers to the productivity of writers whose creative curiosity leads them to compose a symphony of fresh tunes using a new instrument—in this case a language other than their "mother" tongue (*bogo*).[2] Some exophonic writers use languages other than their own due to forced relocations, such as exile, immigration, colonization, flight from the homeland, etc., while others (including Tawada) have chosen to use the acquired languages for more personal reasons. The language chosen by such writers is deconstructed and re-constructed in adventurous experiments as they embrace exophony rather than seeking to achieve "euphony," a smooth and assimilated flow in harmonious tones. In a broader sense, to practice exophonic literature implies what Deleuze and Guattari describe as "to be a foreigner, but in one's own language, not only when speaking a language other than one's own. To be bilingual, multilingual, but in one and the same language, without even a dialect or patois."[3] In the cases of Tawada and Mizumura, they both attempt to be "foreigners" in their mother tongue, Japanese. Tawada states that a foreigner inside her simultaneously reads her writing,[4] while Mizumura's anticipated audience is either for-

153

eigners who can read Japanese, or Japanese people who can read their mother tongue as if they were foreigners.

Tawada's attempt to produce exophony both in her mother tongue (Japanese) and her acquired tongue (German), and to dismantle what she calls the "ultranationalistic" (*kokusuishugitekina*) concept of a "beautiful" Japanese language,[5] focuses attention on the Japanese language per se. The language, of course, did not exist a priori. When was modern Japanese, known as *nihongo*, created as the national language (*kokugo*)? This question takes us back to the Meiji era (1868-1912), when, confronted by the West, Japanese culture tried to absorb, emulate, and also resist "western-ness," particularly that exemplified by Prussian Germany. This question of language also takes us to the prominent Meji writer Mori Ōgai (1862-1922), whose literary imagination stemmed from his experience in Germany, as Tawada's later would do. I will briefly review the formation of the modern Japanese language as *kokugo* (the national language) in relation to the West, especially Prussia, and then comparatively examine Ōgai's semi-autobiographical stories and Tawada's narratives. Through this historical and comparative analysis, I intend to articulate Tawada's resistance to the nationalistic ideology that has been wrapped around the language (*kokugo*) since the Meiji era, and thus to show how she problematizes Japan's modernity and ethnocentricism.

Following the nearly 300-year regime of isolation under the Tokugawa Shogunate (1604-1868), when Japan leaders decided to accept western influences and interchanges as a result of the Meiji Restoration of 1868, Japan's linguistic situation was complicated. Directly ruled by the head of the *han* or domains, people used languages and local dialects in a distribution that reflected the prevailing social hierarchy, as each class had its own characteristic way of speaking. The official written language, Classical Chinese, was used mainly by the privileged class, consisting of the samurai and intellectuals. As this was a language used elsewhere as well, it did not function as a specifically national language for Japan or as a language that created unity within Japan, as was desired. In order to respond to threatening western powers, Japan needed not only to hastily catch up with the technologically and culturally advanced nation-states of the West (Europe and the U.S.), but also to construct what Benedict Anderson has called an "imagined community" of the nation,[6] based on the assumption that the people of a nation share one language, culture, and history. That is, the Meiji government needed to create an "imagined" vernacular language to unite the imagined nation. Many political leaders and intellectuals were sent to the West to learn about western civilization, while foreign experts were invited to assist in developing Japan's political and educational systems. In the meantime, the creation of one standardized language—spoken and written—for the entire population, along with the dissemination of the concept of a national language (*kokugo*), were major tasks undertaken to hasten the building of the new modern nation-state.

Prussian Germany, in particular, was the region and culture that Meiji Japan looked to as it sought to create a modern nation: by the end of the 1890s, Prussia's influence on Japan had become pervasive, and Japan was called "the Prussia of the East."[7] A young professor of linguistics at Tokyo Imperial University, Ueda Kazutoshi (1867-1937) played a key role in the formation of the Japanese language and the concept of *kokugo*.[8] At the age of 23, Ueda was sent to Europe (mainly Germany) for nearly four years—1890–1894. In Germany Ueda witnessed the exploitation of a tie between language and nation. Defeating its historical rival France, the Second Reich was born under Kaiser Wilhelm I and Chancellor Bismarck in 1871, only three years after the Meiji Restoration. Unlike Japan, Germany had developed its own common language (*hoch Deutsch*) by the early ninetheenth century,[9] and the new national unity further promoted the study of German language and culture, rather than classical Greek and Latin. Ueda observed Germany during the reign of Kaiser Wilhelm II, who reinforced an ideology of "German-ness" and the German spirit through a program of "patriotic" education designed to "foster good soldiers for the army."[10] With a knowledge of this intimate bond between language and nation, and the significance of education in the national language, Ueda returned to Japan in 1894 and began to establish a standard Japanese language and the concept of a national language (*kokugo*).

Ueda's famous 1894 lecture entitled "Kokugo to kokka to" (*Kokugo* and the Nation-state) marked the official debut of the term *kokugo* before a Japanese audience. He declared that

> if we talk about the national language of Japan (*nihon no kokugo*), the Japanese language (*nihongo*) can be said [to be] the spiritual blood of the Japanese people. Japan's *kokutai* is mainly supported by that blood. . . . the language is not only the *kokutai*'s sign (*hyoshiki*), but also a sort of educator, like a kindhearted mother.[11]

Ueda clearly infuses the notion of *kokugo* with the ideology of *kokutai*, the national polity or the political and aesthetical "essence of Japanese nationalism."[12] While earlier or more neutral terms such as *nihongo* fell out of favor, the term *kokugo* soon became the cornerstone of a program for national education in the Japanese language.

The intimate relationship between *kokugo* and *kokutai* persisted even after Japan's defeat in World War II. Today, terms of simple dichotomy persist: there is *kokugo* education for the Japanese and *nihongo* for foreign learners. As Lee Youngsuk explains, *kokugo* is not considered (merely) one of (many) languages in the world, but is the very language that fosters "Japanese-ness" and shapes the minds/souls of Japanese people.[13]

Tawada problematizes this notion of language in which *kokugo* is draped with *kokutai* ideology. She also both associates herself with and differentiates herself from the well-known Meiji writer Mori Ōgai. In 1884, six years before Ueda, Ōgai was sent to Germany (at the age of twenty two which is, coincidentally, the same age at which Tawada went to Germany) to study European methods of military hygiene. Unlike Ōgai, who had close ties with Japan's central power structure and expected to return to his homeland to serve the government, Tawada explains, nobody expects or cares whether she goes back.[14] Acquiring a passion for European literature during his four-year stay in Germany, Ōgai started writing fiction in Japanese and introduced European literature to Japanese audiences by translating numerous texts into Japanese, including works by Hofmannsthal, Nietzsche, Kleist, Goethe, and Shakespeare. Fluent in classical Chinese, Dutch, and German, and in this respect a forerunner of the current phenomenon of the multilingual and multicultural author, Ōgai pursued a successful career in two diametrically opposed social worlds of the Meiji and Taisho (1912-1926) eras upon his return to Japan—as the director of the Medical Corps in the Imperial army, and as a distinguished writer.

Despite wide differences in time, style, and perspective, Tawada and Ōgai are united in some aspects of their response to living in Germany and in having a keen interest in bringing together various languages (including German and Japanese). Tawada has written critically and cogently about Ōgai. She points out Ōgai's ambivalence in his writing and life and mentions his 1909 semiautobiographical short story entitled "Dai hakken" (Huge Discovery), in which the first-person narrator, *boku* (the first-person pronoun "I," suggesting Ōgai himself) talks about his experience studying abroad in Germany at the Meji government's expense, and boasts about a huge discovery that he has made. Upon his arrival in Berlin, he goes to pay his respects to the Japanese minister. He immediately senses the despising eyes of the people in the Consulate, including the minister, who see him, a fellow countryman, through the filter of the West. The minister, according to the narrator, is quite a large man for a Japanese, with a wide forehead and a pepper-and-salt beard on a rather dark face: "Since I've heard he has a German wife, I imagined he must be sophisticated (*haikara na hito*), but in reality he rather looks unrefined." In discovering that the narrator has been ordered to study hygiene (*eiseigaku*), the minister says, "What? Hygienics? Nonsense! People who walk with straws tied between big and second toes[15] and who pick their noses in public can't be hygienic!"[16] The protagonist then attempts to discover whether Europeans do or do not also pick their noses. Although he never witnesses this action during his three-year stay in Germany, or during his visits to other European countries such as France and England, after years of persistent research in Japan, he finally discovers a description of nose-picking in a novel from Denmark and reacts to this passage with an outburst of joy. It is a huge discovery for him that Europeans (i.e., whites) also indulge in this activity!

Ōgai's story portrays through the narrator's experience the Orientalist view that Germans hold of Asians as the narrator becomes the object of "exotic" exhibition. He is asked by a university professor to demonstrate how to use chopsticks in front of the students.[17] He is also laughed at by people in the dining hall when he enters and bows to them as an expression of greeting in the Japanese style. He later finds that Germans too learn how to bow when practicing ballroom dance in junior high school, so he was mocked not for the act of bowing itself, but because his bow was "strange" (in the German view) in displaying a "barbaric" manner and occurring on a wrong occasion. Ōgai's story thus describes, in humorous, cynical, and detached tones, not only the Orientalist perspective of the westerner, but also his fellow Meiji people's rejection of their own culture as backward based on their binary paradigms of the West (perceived as advanced/civilized) and the East (perceived as barbaric/uncivilized).

The reader's "huge discovery," however, does not come until the very end of the story:

> Dear Minister of the Imperial Japan in Berlin, Viscount S.A.[18] Your Excellency, I would humbly report to you. Europeans also pick their noses! * * * * *
> After writing this, I happen to read Leonid Andrejew's novel... in which the farmer... picks his nose in the court. It seems that *Rokusuke* too pick their noses.[19]

The contrast here between the narrator's (overly polite) address to the minister, and his use of a derogatory term, *Rokusuke*, for Russians might be a reflection of the era, as the story was written a few years after Japan's victory over Russia in the Russo-Japanese War (1904-1905)—the first victory over the West. The narrator's detachment throughout most of the story seems to be replaced here with a more subjective tone, for he exults as if he had indeed made a huge discovery or achieved a significant victory. His two faces—distinguished writer, and devoted medical director in the Imperial Army—coincide here. That is, as a military man, his belief in Japan's Imperial power moves him to bare his feelings of superiority.

Ōgai's debut work "Maihime" (The Dancing Girl, 1890)[20] closely parallels his experience in Germany two years earlier, and appeared nearly twenty years before the publication of "Huge Discovery." "Maihime" begins when the first-person narrator, Ōta Toyotarō, is on a ship on his way back to Japan after five years' stay in Berlin to study political science. After a nearly twenty-day voyage, the ship lies at anchor in Saigon, where all the passengers, except Toyotarō, have disembarked to stay overnight in hotels. His feelings of alienation, apathy, and remorse (we do not know, yet, why), and images of transience are emphasized in entries in his travel diary, where he makes comparisons between the two worlds. Five years earlier, when he was on his way to the West, in other words to Germany, as one of the few who were "chosen" by the Japanese government to make this journey, his travel diary was filled with "thousands of words" detailing his hopes, while now the notebooks that he has brought "intending to use for a diary remained untouched," and he feels that he has become "a very different person from when [he] set out."[21] The reader is then informed that the narrator is nevertheless going to write his story, and indeed his troubling experiences in Berlin are gradually revealed, especially his abandonment of a German girl named Elis who pregnant with his child, went insane when she discovered that he intended to betray her by returning home to Japan without her.

Toyotarō's affair with Elis begins after he has stayed in Berlin for three years (and after nearly a third of the story is completed), during which period he has led an ascetic life, concentrating solely on his studies. One evening as he walks home, he happens upon a young German girl who is sobbing on the steps of the old church. She is sixteen or seventeen years of age, with "light golden hair . . . blue and clear" eyes.[22] Her innocent beauty with its "irresistible" charm catches his attention. Toyotarō then discovers that she is a dancer, and that to pay the expenses of her father's funeral, her mother wants her to become the mistress of the manager of the theater where she works. The "rich" gentleman from the East, Toyotarō, redeems the poor girl from the West, Elis, by handing her his expensive watch.

Ōgai established a reversed dichotomy of West and East in the relationship that then develops between Toyotarō and Elis. As an educated man from the East, Toyotarō speaks western languages (German and French) fluently, while as an uneducated woman of the West, Elis speaks even her mother tongue German poorly and with an undesirable accent. He, who reads Schopenhauer and Schiller, becomes her teacher in German language and literature. In their "teacher-pupil relationship," [23] Toyotarō represents the West (educated/advanced), and Elis, the East (uneducated/backward).

Yet we should not forget that this relationship is feasible only in their private and marginalized world. Due to the rumor that Toyotarō has had an affair with a cheap girl and neglected his studies, his stipend is cut off. At the same time, he learns of his mother's sudden death in Japan. Having lost his father many years ago when he was a child, Toyotarō now becomes an orphan with no guardian and no financial support. In this desperate situation, he starts an intimate relationship with Elis and allows himself to be persuaded to move into the "romantic" world of the Other to live with Elis and her mother. Thanks to his only Japanese friend, Aizawa, he finds a job as a foreign reporter for a Japanese newspaper.

The anthropologist Yamaguchi Masao explains Toyotarō's crossing over the two worlds as the shift between what George H. Mead calls the two phases of the self, "I" and "me." According to Mead, the "me," dialectic in nature, is a "habitual individual. It is always there," [24] while the "I," a response to the individual "me," is the principle of action and of impulse, and in its action it changes the social structure. [25] As Yamaguchi suggests, Toyotarō's movement from the center of power to the periphery, and then his return to the elite world of Japan, can be explained as the shift from "I" to "me" and then back to "I." A similar opposition is evident in the way in which Ōgai describes contrasting spaces through images of light and dark. On the evening of his first encounter with Elis, Toyotarō walks from the "sea of lights" of the authoritarian space of the Tiergarten and Unter den Linden, and enters the "gloomy passage" of Old Berlin, with its "three-hundred-year-old church . . . washing hanging out . . . on the roofs, and a bar where an old Jew with long whiskers was standing." [26] The brilliant and colorful picture of Prussian soldiers and fashionable German women in the center of the city, noted earlier, is replaced here by the maze-like alleys of a peripheral world, where Toyotarō will live with Elis and where he soon feels trapped, and from which he wants to be "rescued." In other words, Elis, female and German, is the "trickster" who lures Toyotarō into the "me" world, while his friend Aizawa, male and Japanese, is the one who pulls him back into the "I."

We could say that "Maihime" is about the protagonist's relationship with Japan, or the authority of Japan, and that it demonstrates Ōgai's conviction that this tie cannot be broken. Embodying the viewpoints of the author and of readers of the Meiji era, Toyotarō believes that as an elite Meiji man, he is expected to serve as a modern "machine" for the Meiji government upon his return from abroad. His irresponsible action in abandoning the pregnant Elis, who has decided she is willing to live in what Germans regard as a barbarian country of the East in order to return with him to Japan and be his wife, is represented as justified for the sake of the nation-state. In order to alleviate Toyotarō's responsibility for this transgression, Ōgai cunningly spares him from confronting it directly, for it is while Toyotarō lies ill that Aizawa discloses to Elis her lover's decision to go back to Japan without her. Toyotarō, not having to directly explain himself to Elis, just "observes" her madness and contemplates the affair sometimes with remorse and sadness. The story thus ends with his ambivalent feelings toward Aizawa: "Friends like Aizawa Kenkichi are rare indeed, and yet to this very day there remains a part of me that curses him."[27]

As mentioned above, Toyotarō's expression of "remorse" at the beginning and the "curse" with which he thinks of his friend at the end highlight his (and Ōgai's) emotional conflicts as he oscillates between two worlds, the peripheral world of Elis ("me") and authoritarian world of Meiji ("I"). Kobori Keiichirō indicates that as with Faust and Gretchen in Goethe's *Faust*, Elis becomes the victim of Toyotarō's experimentation with freedom in modern life.[28] It is not a coincidence that their relationship begins with money, when Toyotarō gives his watch to Elis, and also ends with money, when before his departure Toyotarō leaves money for her and "her" baby. Toyotarō's strong class-consciousness as a member of the Japanese elite, and thus what he sees as the impossibility of continuing to be cut off from the center of hegemonic power, leads him to abandon the poor, uneducated, and low-class Elis. In short, the story implies Toyotarō's (and the Meiji elite's) inability to function without being connected with authority, wealth, and power.

Moreover, Toyotarō's actions seem to reflect Ōgai's own choices and beliefs. He too abandoned a German girlfriend in Berlin. She followed him all the way to Japan, but returned to Germany after being so persuaded by his family and friends. The imagined narrative conclusion of Ōgai's "Maihime" was created after he had witnessed his family's implacable resistance, much more obdurate than he had anticipated, against the German woman who loved him. For Ōgai, as the eldest son of a very dominating patriarchal family, there seemed to be no other feasible conclusion, even though he knew that marriages between men of the Meiji elite and women from the West were actually not impossible, as shown by the example of the minister Aoki's German wife in his own story "Huge Discovery."[29] Ōgai, however, committed himself to the world of "I," the Imperial army, although memories of the world of "me" were imbedded in his literary works.

More than a century after Ōgai's experience in Berlin, Tawada Yōko, living in Hamburg, began to write fiction both in German and Japanese. Knowing that she might be compared to Ōgai, she has repeatedly said that she is not like him—stating that, in contrast to Ōgai, she is not obliged (and expected) to return to her country and she has no tie to the hegemonic powers in Japan. That is, she is free to go in and out of her native land, while stepping inside/outside of Japanese and German contexts. Like Ōgai's stories, however, Tawada's narratives often portray their protagonists' experiences in Germany as a foreign land.

Tawada's short story "Perusona" ("Persona," 1992),[30] written in Japanese, uses third-person narration to describe the experience of a Japanese woman named Michiko. At the opening of the story she and her younger brother Kazuo have been living in Hamburg for a year (although the name of the city is not mentioned, the names of its streets, train stations, etc., are identified). They have both come to Germany as scholarship students (a much less elite status, compared to that of Toyotarō in "Maihime"); Michiko is working on a thesis on "exophonic" women writers from Turkey who live in Germany and write in German, while Kazuo is studying more "authentic" medieval German literature.

Focusing on the image of the Other as it is perceived through sight and vision, and drawing upon concepts such as masks and the ways in which Asian faces are seen, Tawada's story starts with an episode in a mental institution, where a female patient falsely accuses a Korean male nurse named Seonryon of sexual misconduct. According to Michiko's German friend Katrina, who works in the hospital library, nobody at first gives credence to the patient's claim, but people gradually come to believe that while Seonryon appears gentle, he hides his cruelty beneath his mask-like face. The consequences of this accusation cost him his job. The image of the supposedly mask-like face of East Asians is reinforced by Michiko's German (ex-) boyfriend Thomas, who comments to her: "I don't know what you really think. I can't read your face, so I can't tell when you tell a lie. Your face has no expressions."[31]

The scene in the mental institution scene is followed by another episode set in a mental hospital that again emphasizes sight and vision, though this time through the medium of film. In the mental hospital where Katharina continues to work, she and Michiko watch an educational film on "natural selection" that was made during World War II. The scene in the film in which mothers are combing the shiny blond hair of their light-skinned, plump young children, with the caption, "good genes are flourishing, but . . . "[32] quickly shifts to an image of the mental patients' room where they are tightly bound to their beds. The Germans' discrimination against minorities is connected to Japan by Katharina's question to Michiko, asking whether the Japanese also killed mentally ill patients during the war.

Tawada's story is thus not a simple description of a dichotomized world (victim/victimizer and East/West) or a revised dichotomy as in Ōgai's "Maihime"; rather, it problematizes the biases found in the ethnocentric minds of all groups, including Japan-centric views. For instance, Michiko's brother Kazuo shows little reaction to Seonryon's situation and the film about the recent past. On the contrary, he tries to distance himself from others. His attitude represents that of the Japanese communities (mostly businessmen and their families) who reside in Europe but live in the closed world of "Japan, Inc.," and thus refuse to "articulate its relationship to the non-West, especially Asia, both in the past and the present."[33] Like the minister in Ōgai's "Dai hakken," the dichotomy of an East-West contrast has not changed, except that technologically advanced Japan now regards herself as a privileged "non-White" member of the West and behaves accordingly.

Michiko too becomes an "alien," even from her own people and her own body. First, her appearance prevents her from fitting into the Japanese community, for her face, bare of make-up, is scornfully regarded as Vietnamese-like. Second, she finds that language, including her mother tongue, is powerless: "When I want to tell the truth, my Japanese becomes awkward. Japanese is my mother tongue and it is the language that has created my persona, though."[34] Michiko's feelings of disorientation and desperation, "hageshiku karitaterareru yōna okashina kankaku" (a strange sensation fiercely driven from the inside of her body), which stem both from the impossibility of communicating with people even in her own language and from her awareness that people who gaze upon her see an "emotionless, incomprehensible" face, impel her to walk restlessly and incessantly around the town.

In that desperate condition of seeking alternative locations in the city, which recalls Toyotarō's move to Elis's home in the world of the Other, Michiko crosses over to a district where many refugees from East Europe and Africa live, and which she has avoided entering until now. Soon surrounded by refugees, all men, she is again the object of their gaze. Asked if she is Vietnamese, Korean, Philippine, or Thai, she answers, reluctantly "No, I'm Japanese." One of the refugees' immediate responses is, "Oh, a Toyota," which equates her with an emotionless machine. (Toyotarō, the Meiji elite's, fear of becoming a "machine," and his final acquiescence to that role, are here realized.) Before leaving the district, she hurries to the door of the refugee house known as "floating Europe," since it is literally floating on the river, where she meets a young refugee from Eastern Europe with whom she probably has sex (there are allusions to sexual conduct here but their act, if it occurs, remains unseen by the reader).

As Toyotarō wanders the streets of Berlin to discover Elis's world, Michiko's internal restless urges make her hurry in a circular motion as if she were running from the violence of people's gazes. The reader follows Michiko, rushing from her apartment, east toward the Great Mt. Street (Großeberg), to Reeperban Station, to Great Freedom Street (Große Freiheit), and then south to the Elbe River and the refugee district. She then returns (or intends to return) to her apartment to "become" a Japanese by applying make-up and then goes further west to enter the Japanese community, where the representatives of "Japan, Inc." live with their families. This location of the Japanese community toward the west implies its "quasi"-identity with the West and with hegemonic power, while the house of the refugees, called "floating Europe," reinforces their floating situation, uncertain and powerless.

As in Toyotarō's shift between the two dimensions of the self, we can associate Michiko's actions with the dialectic interaction of "I" and "me," or the Symbolic and the Semiotic, to use Kristeva's terms. Michiko's entry into the "forbidden" district of the refugees represents her process from the world of the Symbolic to the Semiotic, from the "family and society" structure tied to the social order and rules, to the energies that connect and orient the body to the mother (womb).[35] Toyotarō experiences a crossing of the two worlds and then a

return as he moves from "I" to "me" to "I" again, while the "instinctual energies" and impulses of her body (womb) cause Michiko to wander incessantly in
both worlds.

As connoted by Michiko's circular movements, the end of the story links
back to the beginning and to the ostensibly mask-like emotionless faces of
Asians. To doubly reinforce the image, Tawada displays Michiko wearing a Noh
mask in the typical Orientalist image of old Japan. Taking down a Noh mask
that hangs on the wall of a Japanese family's home, Michiko puts it on, sneaks
out of the house, and walks around town. Wearing the mask on her face, which
others already regard as mask-like, ironically allows her to regain her persona.
She has the sensation that "her body suddenly has grown much bigger . . . and
everything she was not able to put into words before is clearly revealed, given
expression in the mask." Her body, whose irresistible restlessness has previously
caused her to walk around restlessly, now becomes a body in "possession of
powerful words," as she feels that she is becoming transformed (from a small
Toyota) into "a new powerful self." People on the street, however, take her action of wearing the mask as a practical joke or "madness," and either ignore or
ridicule her. Seen through "the small holes" that are the eyes of the mask, their
reactions look to Michiko like "a scene from a video."[36] She is now a powerful
gazer who watches the fragment of a "video-like" world through the holes and
believes that her body is no longer alien to her. Yet we are not sure if her strong
sense of regaining herself might not be just a "fake," as in a video, for Michiko
wanders around, in vain, trying to find a Chinese restaurant where she is supposed to meet Kazuo and his mentor from Japan. The ending of the story, with
the observation that "when Michiko appears most Japanese-like, people [on the
street] did not notice she was Japanese,"[37] implies (at least) her separation from
the image of East-Asians as identified with a mask-like face.

A year before the appearance of "Perusona," Tawada had published her first
work in Japan, "Kakato o nakushite" (1991, "Missing Heels," 1998),[38] a story
which presents, allegorically and metaphorically, the six-day "marriage" of a
nameless first-person narrator in a nameless town in a foreign land. Crossing an
invisible border, she arrives as a mail-order bride in the town where, stigmatized
as an inferior person from a barbarian country, she experiences the impact of a
hegemonic culture rather than merely a different culture. As in Ōgai's story, the
East–West dichotomy is visible in this story.

Where "Perusona" focuses on the eyes and on vision, and especially on seeing in relation to Asian mask-like faces, "Missing Heels" concentrates on another part of the body, the heels, and the idea of people walking abnormally as if
they had no heels, as the title implies. Just as in "Perusona" Michiko stumbles
through the city streets in a mad rush, "Missing Heels" emphasizes the protagonist's sense of stumbling and floating not only in her physical movements, but
also in her words and long "stumbling" sentences. The story begins with the
protagonist's remarking that in the alien town where she has arrived, everything—the platform, floor, and ceiling of the train station, the streets, her other
surroundings—seems slanted, and that everyone is stumbling and moving with
an odd posture as they walk: "Staring up, the roof looked cockeyed, but when I

looked down again I realized that the floor seemed slanted because everyone was stumbling forward as they walked, never glancing down, their eyes trained on some far-off spot."[39] In the reaction of her body to this strange environment, she feels that she too is "stumbling," but she believes the town itself is built on an incline.

The title of the story, "Missing Heels" or "Kakato o nakushite," is a metaphor for those who, living in foreign lands, are said to lose their heels:[40] they do not walk firmly and naturally on the ground but instead seem to be "floating" or rootlessly alienated within the societies in which they try to settle (like the "floating" refugee house in "Perusona" and Toyotarō's temporary residence in a marginal world in "Maihime"). This image of what it means to be the Other coincidentally overlaps with the earlier image of foreigners, mainly the Dutch, that was prevalent in premodern Japan, when people believed that these foreigners wore European-style shoes, rather than the Japanese-style *zori* or *geta*, in order to hide their missing heels. This Occidental picture also recalls the Japanese minister's comments in Ōgai's "Huge Discovery" that Japanese people were barbarian enough to wear *zori* instead of civilized western shoes. As with the minister's reception of the narrator in "Huge Discovery," in "Missing Heels" the townspeople react to the poor mail-order bride from a barbarian country in a contemptuous, suspicious manner. For instance, when she goes to school to learn the town's customs, a female teacher, smelling of sleeping pills and accusing her of being a spy for the school authorities, tells her that "a woman like you is not only a social problem but a political problem as well,"[41] and that "education or the lack of it is a problem of the class, not of the individual,"[42] while another female teacher says, "poor people have no will of their own."[43]

Furthermore, in the hospital, the male doctor informs her that she needs to have an operation to reconstruct her "lacking" heels so that she can adjust to walking in the same (refined) manner as the townspeople. Her rejection of the doctor's order, and her positive identification with what others see as her imperfect feet or her bodily "lack," demonstrate not only her challenge to the townspeople's denigration of the poor and of foreigners who "have no will of their own," but also her resistance to integrating into society as the Other and completely denying her own culture.

The narrator's decision to confront her husband, who leaves breakfast and money on the table for her every morning, whose footsteps and gazes she sometimes hears and senses, but who never shows up except in dreams during their brief marriage, leads to her "huge discovery." When she has a locksmith break open the door of the room where her husband has hidden himself, she discovers, in the middle of the room, not a man but a dead squid! Tawada here makes a playful pun on *ika*—the Japanese word both for squid and defamiliarization—and creates the effect of *ika* or defamiliarization to shock the reader and "increase the difficulty and length of [the reader's] perception," to use the Formalist Schklovsky's term.[44] In other words, Tawada produces an "enigma" within the narrative in order to "render [the] incomprehensibility visible, and thus the reader becomes a collaborator in creating the text."[45]

At the end of the story, facing the dead-squid husband, the "widowed" protagonist explains that in breaking into his room, she just wanted to get her "notebooks back"[46]—these are blank notebooks that she had brought in her suitcase, so that she could write her new story. Like the blank diary in Ōgai's "Maihime," her notebooks have remained blank in this strange land where her subjectivity is not allowed to speak and choose for itself. Through her protagonist's act of refusal to have her feet remodeled, Tawada suggests the possibility of living without heels, and the Freudian connotation of "lack" is problematized. The dead squid can also be considered the mirror image of the protagonist herself, to borrow Lacan's term. Ōgai presents an elite male protagonist, who cannot stand the discomfort of living in a marginal world as if he were a person with "missing heels," and thus he sees no choice but to return to his country, destroying his pregnant German girlfriend's plans to be his wife and thus her sanity (Toyotarō is indeed a "dead squid" for her). In very different circumstances, Tawada too presents a protagonist who chooses to throw away her "marriage" but here this action denotes regaining her self and her use of language, for her recovered notebook will be soon filled with stumbling words in her new life. We could say that this outcome represents not wishful thinking, but the selective assurance of Tawada's narrative.[47]

As demonstrated above, Tawada's incessant efforts to create a literature of exophony resist the notion of a euphonic language, especially that of her native tongue. Her conviction that she is unlike Mori Ōgai has invited a reexamination of Ōgai and his times, including Japan's entrance into modernity as the "Prussia of the East," along with the concomitant institutionalization of the nationally defined Japanese language in *kokugo* education and the dispatch of Ōgai and others to Germany in order to acquire and import Western knowledge and behavior. This comparison of Ōgai and Tawada has enabled us to more fully uncover the significance of Tawada's exophonic writing. Inclusive in nature, the literature of exophony can engage the reader who needs to step outside/inside of their mother tongue and acquired languages in order to become what Deleuze and Guattari call a foreigner in our own language. This may be expanded further to the notion of becoming a foreigner in our own culture, nation, and history.

Notes

1. Tawada first heard the term "exophony" at the symposium held in November, 2002, in Dakar, Senegal, organized by the Goethe Institute. Exophonian writers referred to the writers (like Tawada) who write their works in languages other than their mother/native tongues, no matter what their reasons (their own choices or for historical reasons as seen in Colonial Literature and Creole Literature). In short, the term is, in a strict sense, not Tawada's neologism.

2. The definition of mother tongue is not simple, especially in an era of globalization. Instead of mother tongue, the term first language (dai ichi gengo) is sometimes used. I however agree with Sakai Naoki who suggests that the determination of the mother tongue "comes from [the] absence of the need to know its grammar; the mother tongue precedes the thematization of its existence in terms of its grammatical features; in principle, it is that on the ground of which any linguistic articulation is made possible, so that

its existence cannot be linguistically thematized" Sakai, Naoki. *Translation & Subjectivity: On "Japan" and Cultural Nationalism* (Minneapolis : University of Minnesota Press, 1997), 21.

3. Gilles and Felix Guattari Deleuze, *A Thousand Plateaus: Capitalism and Schizophrenia*, trans. Brian Massumi (Minneapolis: University of Minnesota Press, 1987), 104-105.

4. Levy, Hideo and Tawada Yōko. "Bokokugo kara toku hanarete." Interview, *Bungakukai*, no. 5 (May 1994): 147.

5. Yōko Tawada, *Katakoto no uwagoto* (Tokyo: Seidosha, 1999), 37.

6. Benedict Anderson, *Imagined Communities: Reflections on the Origin and Spread of Nationalism* (New York: Verso, 1983), 27.

7. Anderson, *Communities*, 31.

8. It is worth mentioning that one of the prominent writers in postwar Japan, Enchi Fumiko (1905-86), is the daughter of Ueda Kazutoshi.

9. Long before the appearance of the term *Staatssprache* (the language of the nation state) in 1867 in Germany, France had declared French the language of the nation (*langue nationale*) during the French Revolution. Meiji era reformers thus also studied French education as the process of establishing of kokugo education.

10. Christopher M. Clark, *Kaiser Wilhelm II* (New York: Longman, 2000), 60.

11. Youngsuk Lee, "'Kokugo' to gengoteki kokyosei," in *Gengo teikokushugi to wa nanika*, ed. Miura Nobutaka and Kasuya Keisuke (Tokyo: Fujiwara Shoten, 2000), 341.

12. Milton W. Meyer, *Japan: A Concise History*, 3rd Ed. (Lanham, Md.: Rowman & Littlefield Publishers, Inc., 1993), 125.

13. Lee, "Gengoteki," 338-339. This mentality also leads to the indifferent use of the term *bokokugo* (mother tongue of the nation) and *bogo* (mother tongue) as the translation of mother tongue. In her 1999 book, *Katakoto no uwagoto*, Tawada also used the term *bokokugo*: She hopes to see "more writers, whose *bokokugo* is not Japanese, write their novels in Japanese" (Tawada, *Katakoto*, 37). In her 2003 book, *Exophony*, she consciously used *bogo*, instead.

14. *Levy and Tawada*, Interview, 155.

15. Instead of shoes, Ōgai refers here to wooden sandals (*geta*) or straw sandals (*zori*).

16. Ōgai Mori, "Dai hakken," in *Ōgai zenshū* Vol. 2. (Tokyo: Iwanami, 1936), 162. In his diary entitled "Doitsu nikki," (Diary in Germany) Ōgai wrote about his actual meeting with the minister Aoki Shuzo (1844-1914), who, like Ōgai, was a medical doctor and sent to Germany in 1868, almost two decades earlier than Ōgai, and then became the ministry of Japan in Europe such as Austria, Holland, and Germany. He indeed had a German wife. In the meeting Aoki told Ōgai "it is good to learn hygiene, but it may be difficult to execute hygiene upon your return to Japan. People walking with *geta* . . . don't need hygiene. Study (abroad) means not only to read books, but also to learn ideology, lifestyles, morals of Europeans" (Oct. 13, 1984: quoted in Ikeno, 213). Unlike the minister in the fiction, who ridicules Toyotarō, Aoki's advice leads Ōgai to study European literature, culture, and lifestyle, in addition to his "obliged" field of hygiene.

17. Ōgai, "Hakken," 164.

18. Ōgai uses here the initial of the minister, Aoki Shuzo, in the western order (given name first and family name last).

19. Ōgai, "Hakken," 172-173. Italics added.

20. Ōgai's "Dai hakken" was written in the *genbun itchi* style, whereas "Maihime," like Akutagawa's story, was written in the classical style of *gabuntai*. The written style matches the title, "Maihime" (literally, dancing princess), but the title blurs, according to Maeda, the significance of the low-class dancing girl, Elis.

21. Ōgai, "Maihime," 151.

22. Ōgai, "Maihime," 155.

23. Ōgai, "Maihime," 157.

24. Yamaguchi 131.

25. Yamaguchi 131-132.

26. Ōgai, "Maihime," 134. Saito Minako's excellent critical work entitled "Ninshin shōsetsu" (Pregnant Novels/Fiction) investigates "Maihime" as the first and "father" of the pregnant novel in modern Japanese literature. Ōgai's story is retrospectively told by the first-person male narrator with high social status and intelligence who makes his young powerless girl friend pregnant, avoids decision (169), yet is somehow "saved" at the end. According to Saito, the girlfriend's (unexpected) pregnancy is "spice" for the story. Saito imagines that if Elis were not pregnant, she would not have lost her sanity when she discovered Toyotarō's betrayal.

27. Ōgai, "Maihime," 166.

28. Kobori Keiichirō, "Maihime-ron," in Mori Ōgai 'Maihime' sakuhinron shū, edited by Hasegawa Izumi. (Tokyo: Kuresu shuppan, 2000), 228.

29. Among Ōgai researchers, "Maihime" is often read as shishōsetsu (I-novel) and thus the question of who the model for Elis would be has been significant. The woman has not been conclusively identified, but it is known that following Ōgai, the German woman arrived in Yokohama on September 12, 1888 (Ōgai arrived there on September 8) and left from there for Germany on October 17 in the same year. According to his family's wishes, Ōgai then married a daughter of the vice admiral Akamatsu in February 1889, and divorced her a month after the birth of their son, Oto, in October 1890. Ōgai's "Maihime" was published during his short marriage in January 1890.

30. Further analysis of "Perusona," see Reiko Tachibana's "Beyond East and West: Tawada Yoko and Levy Hideo," PAJLS 3 (2002): 23-36.

31. Yōko Tawada, "Perusona," in Inumukoiri (Tokyo: Kodansha, 1998), 66.

32. Tawada, "Perusona," 45.

33. Perry Anderson, "The Prussia of the East?" in Japan in the World, edited by Masao Miyoshi and H.D. Harootunian. (Durham, N.C.: Duke University Press, 1993), 5.

34. Tawada, "Perusona," 53.

35. Julia Kristeva, Revolution in Poetic Language, trans. Margaret Waller (New York: Columbia University Press, 1984), 27.

36. Tawada, "Perusona," 73-74.

37 Tawada, "Perusona," 76.

38. Further analysis of "Missing Heels," see Reiko Tachibana's "Monadic Writers of Japan: Tawada Yoko and Mizumura Minae," PAJLS 2 (Summer 2001): 400-19.

39. Yoko Tawada, "Missing Heels," in The Bridegroom Was a Dog, trans. Margaret Mitsutani. (New York: Kodansha International, 1998), 66.

40. "Chi ni ashi no tsukanai" in Ueno Chizuko's phrasing. Ueno Chizuko, Uwa no Sora (Tokyo: Asahi Shinbunsha, 1996), 134.

41. Tawada, "Heels," 83.

42. Tawada, "Heels," 90.

43. Tawada, "Heels," 104.

44. Victor Shklovsky, "Art as Technique," in Russian Formalist Criticism, Four Essays. Trans. and Intro. Lee T. Lemon and Marian J. Reis (Lincoln: University of Nebraska Press, 1965), 12.

45. Yoko Tawada, "Writing in Two Languages: A Conversation with Yoko Tawada," interview by Monika Totten, Harvard Review 17 (Fall 1999): 96-97.

46. Tawada, "Heels," 128.

47. In the interview with Monika Totten, Tawada states the "advantage" of women's experiences in foreign lands: "Women are kind of locked up, mute in their own society. But when a woman leaves her society, and her culture and language, then she gains more freedom and more force and freedom of expression. Whereas a lord of language like Thomas Mann, who held a position of power in his culture, would not gain anything by leaving. That is my theory" (Tawada, "Writing," 99). By comparing the experiences of Tawada and Ōgai through their works, we might want to agree with Tawada.

Bibliography

Akutagawa Ryunosuke. "Butokai" |The Ball|. In *Akutagawa Ryunosuke shū* |Collected Works of Akutagawa|. Nihon kindai bungaku taikei vol. 88. Tokyo: Kadokawa, 1970. 181-88.

Anderson, Benedict. *Imagined Communities: Reflections on the Origin and Spread of Nationalism*. New York: Verso, 1983.

Anderson, Perry. "The Prussia of the East?" In *Japan in the World*, edited by Masao Miyoshi and H.D. Harootunian. Durham, N.C.: Duke University Press, 1993.

Clark, Christopher M. *Kaiser Wilhelm II*. New York: Longman, 2000.

Deleuze, Gilles, and Felix Guattari. *A Thousand Plateaus: Capitalism and Schizophrenia*. Translated by Brian Massumi. Minneapolis: University of Minnesota Press, 1987.

Hijiya-Kirshnereit, Iremela. "Post-World War II Literature: The Intellectual Climate in Japan, 1945-1985." In *Legacies and Abmiguities: Postwar Fiction and Culture in West Germany and Japan*, edited by Ernestine Schlant and J. Thomas Rimer. Baltimore: Johns Hopkins University Press, 1991. 99-119.

Ikeno, Makoto. *Mori Ōgai no seishun bungaku*. Matsue: San'in bungei kyokai, 1999.

Karatani, Kojin. *Origins of Modern Japanese Literature*. Translated by Brett De Bary. Durham, N.C.: Duke University Press, 1993.

Kristeva, Julia. *Julia Kristeva Interviews*. Edited by Ross Mitchell Guberman. New York: Columbia University Press, 1996.

——. *Revolution in Poetic Language*. Translated by Margaret Waller. New York: Columbia University Press, 1984.

Kobori, Keiichirō. "Maihime-ron." In *Mori Ōgai 'Maihime' sakuhinron shū*, edited by Izumi Hasegawa. Tokyo: Kuresu shuppan, 2000. 172-284.

Lee, Youngsuk. "'Kokugo' to gengoteki kokyosei." In *Gengo teikokushugi to wa nanika*, edited by Miura Nobutaka and Kasuya Keisuke. Tokyo: Fujiwara Shoten, 2000. 337-50.

——. *"Kokugo" to iu shiso*. Tokyo: Iwanami, 1996.

Leitch, B. Vincent, ed. *The Norton Anthology of Thoery and Criticism*. New York: W.W. Norton & Company, 2001.

Levy, Hideo, and Tawada Yōko. "Bokokugo kara toku hanarete." Interview. *Bungakukai* (May 1994): 138-157.

Maeda, Ai. *Toshikukan no naka no bungaku*. Tokyo: Chikuma, 1992.

Mason, R.H.P. and J.G. Caiger. *A History of Japan*. Rev. ed. Rutland, Vermont: Charles E. Tuttle Company, 1997.

Mead, George H. *Mind, Self, and Society: From the Standpoint of a Social Behaviorist*. Chicago: Unviersity of Chicago Press, 1934.

Meyer, Milton W. *Japan: A Concise History*, 3rd Ed. Lanham, Md.: Rowman & Littlefield Publishers, Inc., 1993.

168   Reiko Tachibana

Miyoshi, Masao, and H.D. Harootunian, eds. *Japan in the World*. Durham, N.C.: Duke University Press, 1993.
———. *Postmodernism and Japan*. Durham, N.C.: Duke University Press, 1989.
Mizumura, Minae. *Shishōsetsu: from Left to Right*. Tokyo: Shinchōsha, 1995.
Mori, Ōgai. "Dai hakken" (Huge Discovery). In *Ōgai zenshū*. Vol. 2. Tokyo: Iwanami, 1936, 155-173.
———. "Maihime" (The Dancing Girl). Translated by Richard Bowring. *Monumenta Nipponica* 30, 2 (Summer 1975): 151-166.
Morley, David, and Kevin Robins. *Spaces of Identity: Global Media, Electronic Landscapes and Cultural Boundaries*. New York: Routledge, 1995.
Rimer, Thomas. J., ed. *Mori Ōgai*. Twayne's World Authors series 355. Boston: Twayne Publishers, 1975.
Said, Edward W. *Orientalism*. New York: Vintage Books, 1979.
Saito, Minako. *Ninshin Shōsetsu* (Pregnant Novel). Tokyo: Chikuma shōbo, 1994.
Sakai, Naoki. *Translation & Subjectivity: On "Japan" and Cultural Nationalism*. Minneapolis: University of Minnesota Press, 1997.
Seyhan, Azade. *Writing Outside the Nation*. Princeton, N.J.: Princeton University Press, 2000.
Shklovsky, Victor. "Art as Technique." In *Russian Formalist Criticism, Four Essays*. Translation and Introduction by Lee T. Lemon and Marian J. Reis. Lincoln: University of Nebraska Press, 1965. 3-24.
Suzuki, Tomi. *Narrating the Self: Fictions of Japanese Modernity*. Stanford, California: Stanford University Press, 1996.
Tanaka, Katsuhiko. *Kotoba to kokka*. Tokyo: Iwanami, 1981.
Tawada, Yōko. *Ekusophonii: bogo no soto e deru tabi*. Tokyo: Iwanami Shoten, 2003.
———. "Kakato o nakushite." *Gunzō* (June 1991): 6-35.
———. *Katakoto no uwagoto*. Tokyo: Seidosha, 1999.
———. "Missing Heels." In *The Bridegroom Was a Dog*. Translated by Margaret Mitsutani. New York: Kodansha International, 1998. 63-128.
———. *Nur da wo du bist da ist nichts/anata no irutokoro dake nani mo nai*. Tübingen, Germany: Verlag Claudia Gehrke, 1997.
———. "Perusona." In *Inumukoiri*. Tokyo: Kodansha, 1998. 9-76.
———. "Writing in Two Languages: A Conversation with Yoko Tawada." By Monika Totten. *Harvard Review* 17 (Fall 1999): 93-100.
Ueno, Chizuko. *Uwa no sora*. Tokyo: Asahi Shinbunsha, 1996.
Yamaguchi, Masao. "Maihime no kigogaku: taidan Yamaguchi Masao and Maeda Ai." In *Nihon no Sakka: Mori Ōgai*. Edited by Ikezawa Natsuki, et al. Tokyo: Shogakukan, 1992. 124-141.

Index

About the Contributors

Hiltrud Arens is associate professor of German Literature at the University of Montana. Her most recent book-length publication is *'Kulturelle Hybridität'* in *der deutschen Minoritätenliteratur der achtziger Jahre* (Stauffenburg Verlag: Tübingen, Second revised edition, forthcoming). She has written and presented widely on contemporary transnational writers in Germany, such as Libuse Moníková, George Tabori, Rafik Schami, Zafer Senocak, and Yoko Tawada, as well as on German women writers in the 19th century.

Bernard Banoun is professor of German Literature at the Université François-Rabelais, Tours, France. He has translated many of Tawada's works from German into French. He has published widely on German and French literature, on translation, and on music, especially of Richard Strauss and Bertolt Brecht.

Bettina Brandt is assistant professor at Montclair State University, New Jersey. She has published on Romanticism (Rahel Varnhagen) Surrealism (Meret Oppenheim, Dorothea Tanning), contemporary literature (Elfriede Jelinek, Yoko Tawada, Barbara Honigmann, Emine Özdamar, Marguerite Duras), German comedy, and translation studies. She is currently completing a book manuscript entitled *Cutting Out: The Literature of Migration and the Aesthetics of the Avant-garde in Germany after 1989.*

Suzuko Mousel Knott is completing her Ph.D. in German literature at Washington University in St. Louis. Her dissertation focuses on the work of Tawada Yōko. She was a Fulbright scholar at the University of Kiel in 2005.

Christina Kraenzle is assistant professor of German Literature at York University, Canada. She has completed a book project entitled *Mobility, Space and Subjectivity: Yoko Tawada and German-language Transnational Literature.* She has presented and written widely on women writers in Germany, and on the production of trans-national literatures.

Margaret Mitsutani teaches at Kyoritsu Women's University in Tokyo. She is widely respected as a translator, especially of Tawada Yōko, Hayashi Kyōko and Nobel Prize Laureate Ōe Kenzaburō.

Marjorie Perloff is a poetry critic and professor emerita of English and comparative literature at Stanford University and a past president of the Modern Language Association of America. A prolific writer, she is best known for her work on contemporary American poetry, and, in particular poetry associated with the avant-garde.

Doug Slaymaker is Associate Professor of Japanese and the director of the Japan Studies Program at the University of Kentucky. He is the author of *The Body in Postwar Fiction: Japanese Fiction after the War* (Routledge, 2004). Current projects concern the production of art across national boundaries, and follows Japanese intellectuals and artists to France during the twentieth century.

Keijirō Suga is professor of English, French, and cultural studies at Meiji University, Tokyo. A prolific essayist and translator, he is the author of six books on literature; recent volumes include *Omniphone* (Tokyo: Iwanami, 2005) and *honolulu, braS/Zil* (Tokyo: Inscript, 2006).

Reiko Tachibana is associate professor of Comparative Literature and Japanese at the Penn State University. Her book publications include *Narrative as Counter-Memory: A Half-Century of Postwar Writing in Germany and Japan* (New York: State University of New York Press, 1998) and articles on Gunter Grass and Ōe Kenzaburō, and Mishima Yukio and Heinrich Böll. She is working on a book on translational women writers.

Yasemin Yildiz is assistant professor of German at the University of Illinois at Urbana-Champaign. She has published essays on Holocaust testimonies, minority discourse in contemporary Germany, and on the globalization of the German language. She is currently completing a book manuscript on literary multilingualism.

K Ltd.

0001B/43/P